THE CHARMER

The True Story of Robert Reldan — Rapist, Murderer, and Millionaire — and the Women who Fell Victim to his Allure

THE CHARMER

The True Story of Robert Reldan — Rapist, Murderer, and Millionaire — and the Women who Fell Victim to his Allure

RICHARD MUTI
CHARLES BUCKLEY

™CHARMER

Copyright © 2012 Richard Muti and Charles Buckley

TitleTown Publishing, LLC
P.O. Box 12093 Green Bay, WI 54307-12093
920.737.8051 | titletownpublishing.com

Edited By: Katie Vecchio
Cover Design By: Erika L. Block
Interior Layout and Design By: Erika L. Block

PUBLISHER'S CATALOGING-IN-PUBLICATION DATA:

Muti, Richard.
The charmer : the true story of Robert Reldan -- rapist, murderer, and millionaire -- and the women who fell victim to his allure / Richard Muti, Charles Buckley. -- Green Bay, WI : TitleTown Publishing, c2011.

p. ; cm.
ISBN: 978-0-9852478-7-4

1. Reldan, Robert (Robert Ronald), 1940-
2. Serial murderers--New Jersey--Biography.
3. Rapists--United States--Biography.
4. Serial murder investigation--New Jersey.
5. Trials (Murder)--New Jersey.
6. Heynes, Susan, d. 1975.
7. Reeve, Susan, 1953-1975.
8. Inheritance and succession--New Jersey.
9. Limitation of actions--New Jersey.
10. Reeve, Arthur, 1927-
11. Reeve, Barbara.
I. Buckley, Charles (Charles R.), 1933- II. Title.

HV6533.N5 B88 2011
364.152/3209749--dc23   1112

Printed in the USA
first edition ♻ printed on recycled paper
10 9 8 7 6 5 4 3 2 1

This book is dedicated to the police officers, investigators, F.B.I. agents, prosecutors, and medical examiner personnel who persevered in their pursuit of Robert Reldan, until they took this dangerous criminal off the street for good.

CONTENTS

Preface
Bob sports that collegiate look.

It is not a monster's face that looks up at the reader, there on page 31 of the Fort Lee, New Jersey, high school yearbook, class of 1958; rather, the young man appears as carefree as any 17-year-old should be. Yet, at the time this photo was taken, Robert Reldan already had a troubling juvenile record, including the assault and robbery of a woman in New York City, and he had done time in a reformatory. His classmates surely knew his history, yet whoever wrote Reldan's yearbook entry was kind.

"Bob sports that collegiate look," the blurb below his picture reads, a reference to what a later generation would call "preppy." He is an amateur pilot, it says, and intends a stint in the Air Force. The only glimpse into future reality is a remark about Reldan's "acid sense of humor." Although young Robert had athletic ability, especially in basketball, school activities are sparse. Understandable, when the youth's extracurricular interests lay elsewhere.

It is a handsome face with an engaging smile—a smile that promises a charming personality and inspires trust. A smile that would, over the next 20 years, cause unsuspecting women to drop their guard and place themselves under the power of one of New Jersey's most ruthless criminals.

Robert Ronald Reldan was born in Brooklyn, New York, on June 2, 1940, the first child of William and Marie Reldan. Three years later, a daughter, Susan, was born into what was, by all appearances, a hard-working, middle-class American family. The Reldans operated the Sweet Sue Coffee Shop, a bustling establishment one block from New York City's Fifth Avenue and its fashionable department stores. Marie doted on Robert, her only son, but the relative who would figure most prominently in Robert's life was his Aunt Lillian, Marie's sister.

Lillian Vulgaris was an aspiring actress, but, like most newcomers to that profession, she needed to support herself with less glamorous work until her big break came along. Brother-in-law William Reldan was happy to give her a job waiting tables in his coffee shop. While not beautiful, Lillian did possess an attractiveness and warmth that made her popular with patrons of the Sweet Sue, among them an older man—"Colonel" Ferris Booth.

Ferris Booth's father was a financier and early investor in IBM and Hotpoint Appliances. He made millions on those and other shrewd investments and would leave a fortune to his son. Lillian Vulgaris's big break came sooner than expected—not on Broadway, but when she caught the eye of Ferris Booth. The two were married and enjoyed a loving relationship for 10 years. When Booth died suddenly of a stroke in 1956, 40-year-old Lillian inherited $50 million. By the time she, herself, died 51 years later, Lillian Vulgaris Booth, a shrewd investor in her own right, would quadruple her wealth, even while donating millions to hospitals and churches, a retirement home for aging actors, and other charities. Having no children of her own, she lavished attention and financial favors during her lifetime on nieces and nephews. Her particular favorite was Robert Reldan, whom she called "Bobby."

In 1951, when Robert was 11, the Reldan family moved from New York to Fort Lee in Bergen County, on the New Jersey side of the George Washington Bridge. With their proximity to New York City and location atop the Hudson River palisades, Fort Lee and its neighboring communities to the south would soon see a population explosion, as high-rise apartment buildings affording spectacular views of the metropolis across the river began to proliferate.

Robert Reldan had everything going for him early in life—innate intelligence, good looks, and a loving and supportive family, including his wealthy aunt, who not only idolized him but was generous with her money. Yet, something was driving him toward a darker world, one beyond the ken of most teenagers.

Chapter 1

He had the look of someone who could kill without remorse.

Fourteen-year-old Anna Maria Hernandez awoke to the sound of her dog barking. Glancing at the bedroom clock, she saw it was 3:20 AM, but she wasn't alarmed. Her dog barked at the slightest provocation, and it wasn't unusual for her sleep to be disturbed. She got out of bed and went to the window to see if something outside might have aroused the animal. Seeing nothing, she quieted the dog and returned to bed. Moments later, she heard a sound coming from the kitchen. Thinking it might be the dinner dishes settling in their drain, she arose again to have a look.

Anna Maria lived in the Fort Lee home of an older married sister, Tomasa Suarez, but both her sister and brother-in-law were in Spain on business. So, on this early Sunday morning, February 25, 1962, the high school freshman was being looked after in the Suarez home by another sister, Leonor Munoz.

In the hallway near the kitchen, Anna Maria saw why the dog had been barking. There, inside her home, were two male intruders, their faces covered by pieces of cloth. The frightened girl began screaming, calling out to Leonor in Spanish. One of the men had a gun and the other an iron rod, perhaps a crowbar. They grabbed her by the arms, telling her to shut up and asking if anyone else was in the house. The girl said her sister and nephew were there, and the men went to a bedroom to get them, dragging Anna Maria along.

Leonor's immediate reaction—she had her three-year-old son with her—was to lock the bedroom door. One of the men told Anna Maria they would kill her if the sister didn't let them in. He instructed the girl to tell that to her sister. Finally, with her child in arm, Leonor opened the door. The men pushed Anna Maria into the room, following her in.

One man had a handkerchief over his head, partially obscuring his face. The other had what looked like a bathroom towel over his head, with a narrow opening so he could see. The man with the handkerchief covering said, "Your brother-in-law is in Spain, right?" indicating knowledge of the household circumstances and lack of a male presence to challenge them. Both young women nodded, confirming that Francisco Suarez was away. The men demanded to know where "the money" was, but Leonor and Anna Maria denied knowing of cash in the house.

The man with the towel over his head took Anna Maria back to her room and began searching it, while the other remained behind with Leonor. The towel kept slipping from the man's head, allowing the girl to see his face. More than a year later, Anna Maria would identify Robert Reldan in a jailhouse lineup as the man with the towel over his head, the man who robbed the Suarez residence and sexually assaulted her that night.

The terror-stricken women watched helplessly as the intruders ransacked the place, looking for jewelry and money. At one point, Reldan was alone with Anna Maria in her bedroom. He tied her hands behind her back and her legs together at the ankles, then stuffed a sock in her mouth and put a blouse over her head, presumably to block her view of his face.

Anna Maria would later testify that the blouse was sheer and she could see him through the material. Reldan lifted the girl's pajama top to her neck and pulled her pajama bottoms down to her ankles. He then began touching and kissing her body. As the girl writhed in his grasp, Reldan struck her several times in the head with the iron rod, not enough to knock her out but enough to cause bruises. Finally, the accomplice came into the room and, seeing what Reldan was doing, said, "Leave her alone." The accomplice, clearly the leader, repeated his demand that Reldan stop sexually assaulting the girl, and Reldan complied. The two men left the house shortly thereafter, and the frightened women ran to a friend's home a few blocks away. Police were called, but no arrests were made at the time. The accomplice was never identified.

Sensing his absence from New Jersey might lessen the chance he'd be identified as one of the perpetrators of the Fort Lee home invasion, Reldan drifted for the next nine months, spending time in Connecticut and Missouri, where he enrolled, briefly, in a small college. His travels were financed by his family, including Aunt Lillian, whose generosity toward her Bobby apparently knew no bounds. In November 1962, Reldan turned up in southern Florida, and it didn't take long for the 22-year-old to run afoul of the law in that jurisdiction.

On November 30, Reldan was arrested in Miami Beach on a charge, ironically enough, of impersonating a police officer. A records check showed no criminal record. His previous escapades had all been dealt with through the juvenile justice system, or hadn't been detected yet, as with the recent Fort Lee burglary and assault. As far as any inquiring police agency could determine, especially one 1,400 miles from Reldan's home turf, the pleasant, cooperative young man in custody was a first-time offender.

Dade County authorities allowed Reldan to plea bargain the impersonating-an-officer charge just five days after his arrest, and the result was a 90-day suspended jail sentence. A month later, he was once again in Dade County Court for one of his favorite criminal activities—breaking and entering, or burglary. With just the impersonating charge on his record, as far as local police knew, he was able to achieve yet another plea deal that avoided incarceration. He pleaded guilty and got two years probation. Still no hard prison time, but Reldan was beginning to accumulate adult convictions.

Returning to New Jersey in the spring of 1963, Reldan continued his chosen path. He was arrested by Closter police on July 27, 1963 for carrying a concealed weapon—a handgun—in a motor vehicle. His long-suffering but loyal parents posted bail, and he was again released, pending grand jury consideration of the case.

Within a month, police in North Arlington, New Jersey, arrested Reldan on a charge of breaking and entering a residence, but this time the B&E included an assault with a tire iron on the woman living there. He was again granted bail until a grand jury could consider the two pending cases, but, prior to his release, Fort Lee detectives took Anna Maria Hernandez to the Bergen County jail, where she identified Robert Reldan as her assailant.

While the Closter weapon complaint and North Arlington burglary and assault were still pending further action by prosecutors, a Bergen County grand jury indicted Reldan, charging him with breaking and entering the Suarez home on February 25, 1962, stealing money and jewelry, and committing an assault with intent to rape against Anna Maria Hernandez. Reldan was arraigned on the indictment, and the matter was set down for a jury trial before County Court Judge Joseph Marini.

Robert Reldan's first adult criminal trial began on December 2, 1963, with Frank P. Lucianna, a prominent Bergen County attorney, hired to defend him.* Representation like that does not come cheap, and Reldan, who had no job or money of his own, was clearly the beneficiary of his aunt Lillian Booth's generosity, once again.

The State presented just three witnesses—Leonor Munoz, Tomasa Suarez, and Anna Maria Hernandez. Both Leonor and Anna Maria testified that Reldan, the man seated in court at the defense table, was one of the intruders in their home during the early morning hours of February 25, 1962—the one, Anna Maria said, who had sexually assaulted her. She'd picked Reldan out of a jail lineup in August 1963, but admitted under Lucianna's cross-examination that she was shown a picture of the defendant by police before the lineup took place. There was no physical evidence or other corroboration to back up the testimony of the women.

Robert Reldan's first criminal trial resulted in a hung jury when the panel could not reach a unanimous verdict, either guilty or not guilty. The upshot of a hung jury is always a victory for the defense, because it

---

*Lucianna, a World War II veteran and marathon runner, would still be practicing before the criminal bar in Bergen County, and still winning cases, almost 50 years later.

forces the prosecution to choose among three equally distasteful options: try the case again, using additional criminal justice resources and the same imperfect evidence; offer up a more enticing plea bargain to the defendant; or dismiss the case outright as not being worth the time and expense.

In reading the trial transcript, one can see the skill of attorney Frank Lucianna having a bearing on the outcome, but he had help. Although a jury is supposed to base its finding on the evidence alone, the freshly scrubbed good looks of Robert Ronald Reldan, the alert, confident 23-year-old in the dock, clearly had an effect on the 12 men and women sitting in judgment. For a criminal defendant to get one hung jury was rare. This was the first of *three* hung juries Reldan would achieve over a long criminal career.

* * *

During this same period in 1963, New York City detectives were investigating a series of six assaults and robberies that occurred between June 4 and July 23—one in the Bronx and five in apartment buildings on Manhattan's Upper West Side. This was the general location of Reldan's first known juvenile offense back in 1957, when he was a high school junior. And the *modus operandi*, or MO, was strikingly similar.

In each of these Upper West Side crimes, a neatly dressed man— about six-feet tall, muscular, and in his early twenties—followed a lone woman into her apartment building's otherwise unoccupied elevator and politely allowed the woman to select her floor first. After making his selection for a lower floor and allowing the elevator to begin its ascent, the young man seized each victim by the throat and, while holding her that way to render her immobile, grabbed her pocketbook and any accessible jewelry. When the elevator arrived at the man's chosen floor, he stepped out, waited for the door to close—taking the stunned victim to her higher floor—and then fled the scene.

As might be expected, all five women assaulted and robbed in this manner were traumatized by the events. One victim remarked to investigating officers, "He [the attacker] had the look of someone who could kill without remorse."

Although efforts in the investigation initially concentrated on New York City, police were mindful of the crime locale's proximity to the George Washington Bridge escape route to Jersey. Good detective work eventually brought Robert Reldan to the attention of investigators. They used resources of the Bergen County Sheriff's Office to obtain a recent photo of Reldan, taken when he was arrested for the Closter weapons charge and the North Arlington assault and B&E, and assembled a photo array.

Detectives put Reldan's photo in with others having like characteristics and showed the lineup to victims of the elevator robberies, one at a time. All five women unhesitatingly picked out Reldan's photo and identified him as their assailant, as did the lone Bronx victim, a vending machine worker robbed at gunpoint of his night's collection proceeds.

On January 3, 1964, detectives arrested Reldan and charged him with the six New York robberies. When he was taken into custody, Reldan showed no remorse and tried to justify his actions by citing a need for money. It was a bogus claim, in that Reldan's parents and Aunt Lillian still amply supported him. He had traveled the country and lived well for the two years he'd been out of prison, with no lasting job and no other means of support.

If money wasn't Reldan's motivation, perhaps a deeper force was driving him. With their ironclad case, NYC authorities didn't waste time pondering Reldan's psyche. But if someone had paid closer attention at this stage of the young man's criminal career, particularly to psychiatric reports warning of Reldan's "strong repressed hostility towards women," one has to wonder how the future might have changed. These New York assaults may have been the first indications that Robert Reldan could no longer contain his aggressive instincts against women.

Despite violent attacks on five women and the strong evidence against him, Reldan managed a lenient plea bargain in New York's Supreme Court, the trial-level court in that state. He was allowed to plead guilty to one elevator robbery (the other four were dismissed) and the Bronx robbery, and he was sentenced to two, five-year terms of incarceration at the Great Meadows reformatory, which housed other youthful offenders in addition to juveniles. Incredibly, the two five-year sentences were ordered to be served concurrently, not consecutively.*

While serving his New York time, Reldan was brought back to Bergen County to answer for the Closter gun charge and North Arlington B&E, which also involved assault with a tire iron on a woman in the house he burglarized. Attorney Frank Lucianna arranged another plea bargain, in which Reldan pleaded guilty to the gun charge and burglary, but the assault on the housewife was dismissed. For good measure, the burglary involving the Suarez residence in Fort Lee and the sexual assault against Anna Maria Hernandez—the case that had resulted in the hung jury and that was still pending retrial—were also dismissed as part of the deal.

---

*Concurrent sentencing, a device used by prosecutors to encourage plea bargains, allows an offender to get a two-for-one—sometimes a three-for-one, or more—deal for his criminal activity. It permits the sentences to run together instead of consecutively, where they would have to be served one after another, one separate sentence for each separate crime.

The judge imposed indeterminate sentences at Bordentown reformatory in New Jersey for each charge, but allowed those sentences to run concurrently with each other *and* with the New York sentence Reldan was then serving. The youth was returned to Great Meadows to complete his prison term.

Robert Reldan had committed a string of nine serious crimes as an adult—seven involving violence against women—and received, in effect, one five-year prison sentence. And it wasn't a forgone conclusion that he would be required to serve that full term. Early release is exactly what played out. Paroled on September 15, 1966, Reldan had served just over half his sentence. He was able to obtain this release from prison even though an early parole evaluation in New York concluded, "It might be essential to consider this case carefully . . . . In our opinion he will be a poor risk [for parole]. He has considerable potential toward criminal acts, particularly assaults . . . ."

Plea bargains are a fact of life in every state's criminal justice system. Simply put, there are not enough resources to bring every case to trial. Without the "let's make a deal" functioning of the justice system, courts would grind to a halt with a backlog of cases waiting to be tried. In the case of this particular plea deal in the summer of 1964, prosecutors in New York and New Jersey exercised poor judgment by allowing six offenses involving violence against women to be dismissed as part of the bargain—four of the elevator assaults in New York City, the tire-iron assault against the North Arlington woman during the burglary of her home, and the sexual assault against Anna Maria Hernandez. With the dismissal of those significant crimes, it was as though they never happened. Future judges passing sentence on Reldan would never be able to take those offenses into consideration. And future parole boards evaluating Reldan's fitness to rejoin society would not have those violent episodes as part of the man's conviction record, nor as the warning flags they should have represented.

Upon his release from prison in September 1966, Reldan returned to live with his parents in Closter while he looked for work. Maintaining gainful employment was a parole requirement, and Reldan was able to get a job as a clerk in a convenience food store near home. William and Marie Reldan continued to support Robert with free room and board and extra money whenever he needed it. They were encouraged when he appeared to stay out of trouble for five straight months—quite an accomplishment in the parents' eyes, considering his history. In late February 1967, they took him on a family vacation to Florida, where budding career criminal Robert Reldan met a girl and fell in love.

Chapter 2

Be quiet, I'm almost finished.

Bernice Caplan had a lot to be thankful for that April 27, 1967. She was happily married, with an 18-year-old son about to graduate high school and a 14-year-old daughter just beginning that time of life when mothers and daughters establish lasting bonds. Everyone was in good health, and there were no pressing problems. *Life is good, praise God*, she thought.

It was a beautiful spring day, the kind that invites anticipation of the warmth May and June would soon bring. Bernice was returning to her Teaneck, New Jersey, home after dropping off Passover cookies to her mother in nearby Hackensack. She arrived at about 3:10 PM, the trip taking less than 15 minutes. Bernice parked in the driveway of the single-family residence and entered through a side kitchen door. After putting a kettle on for her afternoon cup of coffee, she immediately set about gathering the dirty clothing a family of four accumulates, with an eye toward doing a wash load before dinner.

Shortly after 3:00 PM that same day, Robert Reldan left the North Forest Drive home in Teaneck where he had been visiting with Renee Ross and her mother. He had been dating Renee about five months and spent most of that particular day running errands with her. It was a hard time for Renee—she and her young daughter had recently moved in with her mother while her divorce was pending.

Reldan had a second love interest he was cultivating—Beverly Moles, a 21-year-old he met the previous October. He had only been paroled a month and was working in a food store. She came in to buy groceries one day, and they hit it off right away. Beverly was a bank teller in Fort Lee and lived with her parents in Closter, Reldan's hometown.

In fact, Reldan was juggling three romances at the time, two local and one long-distance. His third and newest girlfriend was Judy Rosenberg, an attractive 27-year-old he met on a recent Florida vacation with his parents. Judy was staying at the same hotel with her four-year-old son, Eddie. Her husband, Alan Rosenberg, was back in Chicago, under indictment and not able to leave Illinois—a circumstance Judy didn't mind. She was happy to escape his abusive control. When she met the handsome and athletic-looking Bob Reldan at poolside near the end of her vacation, she was immediately interested. They chatted and flirted that first afternoon, and Judy would later admit she fell in love with Bob almost from the first moment she saw him.

Not long after Judy Rosenberg and the Reldans returned to their respective homes—Judy to the lingering cold of Chicago in early March and Bob and his parents to Closter—Bob got a call from Judy. Her husband Alan had been murdered, his body found in the trunk of his car, riddled with seven gunshot wounds. Judy—frightened to death because of her husband's ties to organized crime—begged Bob to come to Chicago and stay with her and Eddie for a few days.

Reldan's unexplained absence from work to see Judy in Chicago had cost him his job. His boss was a good guy and probably would have given him the time off, but Reldan wasn't supposed to leave New Jersey under the terms of his parole and didn't want to go on record with his boss as having done so. The vacation with his parents had been approved by his parole officer, but an unsupervised trip to comfort a woman whose husband had just been bumped off, mobster-style, would not have been approved. So, he hadn't bothered to ask permission.

As he drove home from Renee's house, Reldan felt a mounting depression over his poor financial state. His Aunt Lillian's $1,000 Christmas gift had already been expended, and Reldan was subsisting on unemployment insurance and $50 a month from a worker's compensation claim. His aunt had also given him a new Volkswagen convertible when he was released from prison, and, while appreciative for that means of transportation, he often sulked at the thought of her immense wealth and the meager amount she seemed willing to part with for him. Each of her gifts only bred more resentment in him, and now, with no job and no ready cash, he was more depressed than ever.

Reldan's impending return to Florida was also on his mind. William Reldan was opening a restaurant there and had asked for his son's help in setting things up, an unpleasant prospect in the younger Reldan's mind. He and his father hadn't gotten along since high school, but he felt he owed his father enough to give it a try. As Reldan stopped at a T-intersection, waiting to turn north on Windsor Road, his most direct route back to Closter, he would have been in position to see Bernice Caplan pass by—the timing was right and the paths both individuals would have traveled to get to their respective destinations were right.

Why Reldan selected Bernice Caplan as his prey is a matter of conjecture, but his future behavior in this regard supports the theory that it was simply a random choice. She happened to be in the wrong place at the wrong time. Reldan followed the woman north on Windsor Road in Teaneck that afternoon and saw her turn onto Briarcliffe Road, where she lived. There was no other reason for him to be on that quiet residential street. Robert Reldan saw that Bernice Caplan was alone and vulnerable; he followed her and watched as she walked from her car to the house.

Reldan drove around for a time, mulling over what he was about to do; then, he parked in front of the woman's home, a scheme to gain entry already formed in his mind. From the back seat of the car, he grabbed a suit he had picked up at the dry cleaner's earlier that day. It was still wrapped in plastic. Draping it over his arm, Reldan approached the front door and rang the bell.

Hearing the doorbell, Bernice set down her coffee cup and wondered who might be calling on her. It was too early for the kids to be coming home from their after-school activities, and they would have entered the side door, anyway. She went from the kitchen to the front door and, peering through a small window, saw a well-groomed, pleasant-looking young man, dressed in a light-colored windbreaker and checked pants and holding what appeared to be dry cleaning. He was about six-feet tall and had a muscular, athletic build.

Bernice opened the door slightly. Before she could say anything, the man spoke.

"Brantley?" he said.

Somewhat confused but certainly not alarmed or on guard, Bernice just stood there for a moment, not responding.

"Brantley?" the man repeated, with an expectant smile.

Bernice smiled back and, recovering her composure, said, "No, I'm sorry, you must have the wrong house. This is the Caplan residence, but there are no Brantleys in this neighborhood, as far as I know." It was then Bernice noticed a green convertible with a white top parked at the curb in front of her house. She would later describe the car as "new, very clean, very shiny."

Now it was the young man who put on a confused air. He asked Bernice if he could use her phone to call his employer and get the correct address for the delivery.

Bernice was reluctant to let a stranger into her home, but lulled by his clean-cut look and polite manner, she decided to go with her positive instincts. Stepping aside, she pointed toward the den, where the phone was, and told him to go ahead and make his call.

Reldan put down the suit he was carrying, went to the den, and pretended to make a call. The phone company would later report the call was discontinued in a second or two. After a few moments, Reldan came out of the den and told Bernice his boss wasn't in and he couldn't get the information he needed. Bernice checked a local directory to see if she could assist in finding the right address. She asked if the name was "Brandt." No, Reldan said, it was "Brantley," spelling out the name. Bernice found no such listing in Teaneck.

Reldan then walked toward the front door, with Caplan following. Before they reached the entryway, he spun around and grabbed the startled woman. He turned her so her back was to him and, in what seemed like a practiced and familiar move, roughly placed his left arm around her neck, locking the woman's throat in the crook of his arm.

"Don't scream or I'll kill you," he said. He then demanded money.

Stunned and terrified, Bernice Caplan struggled, using both hands to try to break the vise-like grip around her throat, but Reldan was too strong. His hold got tighter and her breathing more restricted. Still demanding money, Reldan pushed the woman toward the back of the house, stopping near a wall between the den and bathroom. Bernice cried out that her pocketbook was in the kitchen, and he could have all the money she had. She would later tell investigators her attacker no longer seemed interested in money.

Shoving Bernice Caplan's face against the wall, Reldan slid his left arm down and grabbed her throat with his left hand, increasing pressure on the still struggling woman. Bernice could feel Reldan reach under her dress with his right hand and pull down her girdle and panties. She then felt his penis thrusting between her legs and against her vagina. Later, at trial, both she and a medical expert would testify that vaginal penetration had occurred, a necessary element to prove a rape had been committed.

During the sexual assault, Caplan repeatedly begged her assailant to stop, crying, "Why are you doing this?"

Reldan replied, "I'm crazy, don't you know."

When Caplan warned that her son would soon be home from school, perhaps hoping that information would get the madman to stop what he was doing to her, Reldan said, "If that boy walks through the door, I'll kill him. I have a gun in my pocket."

Continuing his sexual assault, Reldan told her, "Be quiet, I'm almost finished." He never released his chokehold on her throat during the rape. The more she tried to scream or break free, the stronger his grip became. Caplan would later tell police, "His fingers seemed to be searching for something in my throat." The chokehold tightened as her attacker neared his climax.

Reldan ejaculated on his victim's buttocks and then directed her to go into the bathroom and "clean up." He told her not to try to escape through the bathroom window, or he would kill her. Locking herself in the bathroom, Bernice waited in fear until she thought her assailant had fled. She opened the bathroom door, but to her horror, the man was still inside the front door. He turned and coldly stared at her for what seemed like an eternity but was more likely seconds. Bernice knew she would never forget that look or the man's face. After he opened the front door and left, she ran to the den and called police.

As the rape was taking place, before Reldan made good his escape from the scene, a 14-year-old neighborhood boy was walking past the Caplan residence on his way home from school. The youngster, a self-proclaimed sports car enthusiast with a special interest in Volkswagens, took notice of the green convertible parked in front of 330 Briarcliffe Road. Later, at trial, the teenager described the vehicle as "a nice, shiny car." He also reported that there were two distinctive decals on the back of the vehicle and later used that fact to positively identify police photos of Reldan's car as the vehicle he saw that day, April 27, 1967.

Teaneck police began calling Volkswagen dealers in Bergen County and checking motor vehicle records to identify owners of late model green convertibles fitting the description they had received. They turned up the name of Robert R. Reldan, a Closter resident. By contacting detectives in that town, investigators learned about Reldan's extensive criminal background, especially as it related to assaults on women. They also found out he was on parole from New York State, something that would enable them to force his appearance at police headquarters. Believing they had their man but wanting a positive identification before making an arrest, Teaneck detectives asked their Closter colleagues to call Reldan and have him come to their headquarters that evening—April 29—for questioning on some unspecified criminal matter. As a parolee, Reldan had no choice but to comply.

The detectives transported Bernice Caplan to the Closter police station, where Reldan was being kept in an enclosed room, visible only through one-way glass. Upon spotting Reldan, Caplan immediately and emotionally identified him as her attacker. She also saw Reldan's car in the police parking lot and spontaneously identified it as the vehicle she saw parked in front of her home before the assault.

Reldan was arrested on the spot and taken to the Bergen County jail, pending a court appearance on the charge of rape. Despite frantic attempts by his family to get him released on bail, Reldan remained locked up, primarily because New York State authorities filed a "detainer" against him as a parole violator.*

On June 2, 1967, Robert Reldan's twenty-seventh birthday, a Bergen County grand jury returned an indictment charging him with raping Bernice Caplan. He was arraigned on that charge—a formal procedure in which a defendant enters a not-guilty plea—on June 9, and the matter was listed for trial the following month.

---

*Getting arrested on a new criminal charge while out of prison on parole is always a violation; a "detainer" meant the parolee had to be held in custody by any police agency until the parole violation was resolved.

Thomas M. Maher, an accomplished member of the criminal defense bar in Bergen County, represented Reldan. It was just the second time Reldan would be facing a jury, the first time being the Fort Lee home invasion and sexual molestation case four years earlier, a trial he *won* by getting a hung jury. Assistant Prosecutor Thomas J. Ryan presented the State's case, which began on July 13, 1967, before County Court Judge John Shields, sitting in Hackensack.

The State's proofs consisted largely of the testimony of Bernice Caplan and Keith Strickland, the boy who observed Reldan's car in front of the Caplan residence. It included Mrs. Caplan's identification of Robert Reldan as her attacker, a fact she was absolutely certain of. The physician who examined Mrs. Caplan after the rape also testified as to vaginal penetration.

This was an era before the science of DNA identification, and lab work was not as conclusive as it is today. Nevertheless, a state police lab technician testified that semen was detected on the dress Bernice Caplan had been wearing when the attack occurred and that semen was also detected on tissue paper discovered in the pocket of Reldan's tan windbreaker. Also, human hair found on Reldan's jacket was of the same color and texture as Caplan's hair. That was as precise as forensic science would allow in 1967.

Reldan's attorney could offer no testimony to rebut the State's medical and lab evidence, but did call Reldan's two girlfriends—Renee Ross and Beverly Moles—to the witness stand to provide an alibi for him. Renee testified that Reldan left her house at 3:10 PM on the day of the rape. (Her mother, also a witness, put the time closer to 3:05.) Beverly Moles said that, at about 3:30 PM, as she was leaving work for the day, Reldan showed up unexpectedly at the bank parking lot in Fort Lee where she worked though they had no plans to meet that afternoon.

By Monday, July 17, witness testimony was completed and all evidence presented. The lawyers delivered their summations, each carefully laying out for the jury what he considered strong points of his case and weak points of his opponent's case. It all hinged on whose testimony jurors would give the greater weight to: Bernice Caplan's tearful but unequivocal identification of Robert Reldan as her attacker, or the alibi provided by Reldan's two girlfriends. If the alibi witnesses were to be believed and Reldan was in their company at the times they specified, then he could not have committed the Caplan rape. There just wasn't time, considering the 15 minutes or so it normally took to get from Teaneck to Fort Lee.

As in every criminal trial, the burden of proof was on the prosecution, and that burden had to be met beyond a reasonable doubt, a legal concept that defies precise definition and is often confusing. All that was left was for the judge to give his *charge* to the jury.*

Robert Reldan's jury took the Caplan rape case from the judge at 2:05 PM on Monday, July 17, 1967. After deliberating less than two hours, they were back in court telling the judge they were deadlocked. Judge Shields gave them the standard "jury deadlock" charge and sent them back to their deliberations, but it was no good. They were back less than an hour later, insisting they could not reach a verdict.

Reldan had *won* again—the jury was hung, and a mistrial declared by the judge. The handsome young man with the "collegiate look," despite a positive, in-court identification by his victim, somehow avoided a conviction—at least temporarily. One or more jurors disregarded Bernice

---

*Charging the jury is the most boring part of any criminal trial. It is a mandatory exercise lasting one to three hours, depending on the complexity of the case. The judge reads page after page of legal jargon from a charging notebook, each passage crafted to comply with tangled rules of law created by appellate court decisions and ambiguously worded criminal statutes. The entire body of case law—both state and federal—is in play, and no judge wants to have his or her trial result overturned on appeal by a higher court because of something left out of the charge. So, judges try not to leave anything out.

Courtroom personnel see a lot of nodding heads and glassy-eyed stares in the jury box toward the end of the charge. Everyone—jurors, lawyers, court personnel, and even defendants—breathes a sigh of relief when the judge intones the final set piece of the charge: "You may take the case, members of the jury, and render such verdict as in your conscience and reason and candid judgment seems to be just and proper."

The jury then files out and enters the jury room, there to begin deliberations. Criminal cases in New Jersey require a unanimous verdict. All 12 jurors must agree on either the guilt of the defendant or the finding that guilt has not been proven beyond a reasonable doubt. There is no "innocent" verdict—just "guilty" or "not guilty"—although a presumption of innocence cloaks every defendant from the start.

Some pundit long ago—Churchill, perhaps—said about democracy that it was a form of government fraught with error and inefficiencies, but that man had never devised a better form of government. One could say the same thing about the jury trial in our criminal justice system.

Juries make mistakes, lots of them. Sometimes—infrequently, one would hope—the truly innocent are convicted. Appellate courts try to control judge- or prosecutor-induced mistakes, but those courts are not permitted to invade the province of the jury and its right to decide guilt or guilt-not-proven, except when they see a most blatant and egregious miscarriage of justice. And, sometimes, a guilty defendant walks.

Embedded in our jurisprudence is the notion that it is better for a thousand guilty defendants to go free than to convict one innocent person. Perhaps, but when those guilty defendants go free, all one thousand of them, it is most likely they will return to their lives of crime, emboldened by having beat the system. The recidivism rate is high. And, when that happens, how many additional innocent victims are harmed in the bargain, victims who might have been spared had a different jury verdict been rendered?

Caplan's identification and chose to believe that the clean-cut preppy seated confidently next to his attorney, with his supportive family in the row behind him, could not have committed so evil a crime. And he didn't even have to take the witness stand, where he would have been subject to cross-examination by the prosecutor and where his prior convictions could have been used to impeach his credibility.

On September 25, 1967, Reldan's re-trial for the Caplan rape began before Judge Arthur J. O'Dea. On the first morning, Reldan requested permission to fire his experienced defense attorney, giving "drastic changes in circumstances" as the reason. Reldan refused to specify what those circumstances were, and Judge O'Dea properly denied his request. This was a gambit Reldan would use again in his criminal career in an attempt to delay trial proceedings against him. Delay always works in favor of a criminal defendant and against the State. Memories fade, witnesses disappear, evidence sometimes gets misplaced, and defendants reap the benefit.

The second trial also lasted three days, but First Assistant Prosecutor Fred Galda—a tough, take-no-prisoners litigator who would later have a long and distinguished career as a judge—prosecuted the case. With a different prosecutor, a different judge, and a different set of jurors in the box, justice was served. The jury convicted Reldan of all charges, and he was remanded to the Bergen County jail to await sentencing.

Convicted of a sex crime, Reldan was required by law as part of the presentence report to be evaluated by the State Diagnostic and Treatment Center in Rahway, New Jersey, to determine if he was a sexual predator. Three doctors examined him on October 18, 1967. They concluded that Robert Reldan "showed a compulsive pattern of sexual behavior" and noted that Reldan strived to be "ingratiating and manipulative," using terminology from psychology and psychiatry in an effort to impress his examiners.

The caseworker interviewed Reldan's parents and put together the presentence report. The family of an innocent crime victim deserves the sympathy and support of everyone connected with the criminal justice system, but one also can feel, at times, a legitimate regard for the criminal's parents, whose offspring has taken a path at odds with the way they had brought him up. It is difficult to feel any sympathy for William and Marie Reldan's continuing denial of reality. Their blind loyalty to their son, taking his side in every criminal endeavor he ever engaged in, actually facilitated Robert Reldan's lifetime of crime . . . and resulted in a tragic aftermath of brutalized female victims. The presentence report said that Reldan's parents "maintain[ed] their son's innocence in regard to the charge of rape." They were hoping the court would not incarcerate their son and had arranged to have him admitted to a private treatment facility in Canada, if he could be kept out of prison. "They understand that the boy has a mental problem," the report continued, "and they are very distraught over this whole matter." But the report went on to state that the parents "cannot picture their son committing this offense, as he has many girlfriends and, further, that he did not need money."

The report recommended Reldan be sentenced in accordance with the New Jersey Sexual Predators Act, which specified "indeterminate" terms of incarceration at the State Diagnostic and Treatment Center, with a specified maximum. Following this recommendation, Judge O'Dea sentenced Reldan to an indeterminate term at the Rahway facility, not to exceed 30 years.

After sentencing, Reldan's first stop was the diagnostic section of the prison, where he remained for four months while the evaluation process continued. Classified as a "special sex offender," he was transferred to the treatment section of the facility, there to begin psychological counseling and therapy to eliminate or, at least, bring under control his "repetitive, compulsive pattern of sexual behavior."

From the outset, Robert Reldan became a model prisoner/patient in the sex offender treatment program. He impressed the staff with his intelligence and eagerness to be cooperative and to learn. His attitude of superiority initially put off his fellow inmates, but they, too, were soon won over. Reldan eventually gained everyone's acceptance, it seemed. Even normally skeptical staff members were hard put to resist membership in the "Bobby Reldan Fan Club."

No one, however, was more taken with or charmed by Robert Reldan than William Prendergast, the assistant superintendent of the Rahway treatment unit. In time, the relationship between Prendergast and Reldan became so close that staff were concerned the unit's supervisor was neglecting other inmates to act almost exclusively as this one prisoner's full-time therapist.

In less than three years, Prendergast would become Robert Reldan's ticket to freedom and he would lead Reldan, inadvertently, to his next female victim.

Chapter 3

(Ten Years Earlier)
The young man has no sense of values.

Robert Reldan's first reported involvement with the criminal justice system occurred on January 11, 1957, when he was a junior at Fort Lee High School. He accosted Mary Graham Bonner in the entrance hallway of her Riverside Drive apartment building on New York's Upper West Side, near the G.W. Bridge and its easy escape route home to New Jersey. Reldan grabbed the middle-aged woman by the throat and tore loose her pocketbook, before fleeing the scene. When New York City police arrested Reldan, the pocketbook contained just six dollars in cash.

On March 27, 1957, Reldan appeared before Judge Joseph Schurman in Manhattan's General Sessions Court. He acknowledged his guilt and offered no explanation for his actions, stating that he hadn't needed the money. He was classified as a "youthful offender," or juvenile delinquent. Because this was his first known offense, Reldan avoided reformatory time and was placed on indefinite probation, despite the physical violence in his robbing of Ms. Bonner. He had used a chokehold on her. It would become his signature means of gaining control over his female victims, but it would be his good looks and friendly manner that allowed him to get close.

Young Reldan's probation was transferred to Bergen County authorities, normal procedure given his residence there. All that was required of him was to report once monthly to the county probation department and stay out of further trouble with the law. Reldan's grateful parents escorted their seemingly repentant son back across the river to Fort Lee. Within seven months, Robert Reldan would again test the criminal justice system.

Police in the Sussex County community of Byram Township, a bucolic village tucked into the northwest corner of New Jersey,* arrested

---

*New Jersey, the most densely populated state, is often viewed in terms of its NJ Turnpike/ I-95 corridor between New York City and Philadelphia, especially sights and smells along the northern stretch of that highway. Secaucus, in Hudson County, was famous in the 1940s and 50s for its pig farms, New York metropolitan area garbage being a staple on the porcine menu. The odoriferous effects of that land use would greet turnpike travelers decades after the pig farms disappeared. The standard reply to anyone's assertion of New Jersey residency was, "What exit?" But in Sussex and much of the state's northwestern region, far from congested areas to the east, cows and other farm animals still outnumber people.

Reldan and charged him with three residential burglaries, occurring on October 9, 10, and 12, 1957. They ran Reldan's name and identifiers through State Bureau of Identification records and learned that the young man was on probation in Bergen County. A decision was made to transfer his case to that jurisdiction. On December 19, 1957, Judge Martin Kole, in the county seat of Hackensack, found Robert Reldan to be a juvenile delinquent with respect to the Byram Township charges and sentenced him to an indeterminate term at Annandale Reformatory. But the judge then suspended the sentence and, instead of requiring incarceration, put Reldan on indefinite probation once again.

New Jersey courts require a presentence report for both juvenile and adult offenders before any penalty is imposed. Reldan's report for the Byram offenses had a revealing entry Judge Kole duly noted. The report said Robert Reldan was "disturbed and had strong aggressive tendencies with underlying hostilities." With that finding in mind, the judge required as a condition of Reldan's probation that he undergo a psychiatric examination at Menlo Park State Psychiatric Hospital and submit to any treatment plan the doctors recommended. Reldan and his parents agreed, and the young man, now a high school senior, was released pending his scheduled appointment at Menlo Park.

While Reldan awaited his psychiatric examination, Fort Lee police arrested him and charged him with stealing automobiles in that town and selling parts he had stripped from them. He was released to the custody of his parents.

On January 13 and 17, 1958, prior to disposition of the Fort Lee auto-theft charges, Menlo Park psychiatrists examined Robert Reldan. Then, before they issued their report, Reldan again appeared before Judge Kole to answer for the Fort Lee matter. New York authorities had been contacted and given the opportunity to revoke his probation for the Riverside Drive assault and robbery, but they declined and, instead, allowed Bergen County to continue handling the matter of Robert Reldan. On February 20, Judge Kole once again found Reldan to be a juvenile delinquent. This time the judge revoked his probation and sentenced him to an indeterminate term at Annandale Reformatory.

Judge Kole allowed the case to remain open for further action once he received the report from Menlo Park psychiatrists and, indeed, when that report was forwarded to him, the judge ordered Reldan brought back from Annandale to his Hackensack courtroom.

Menlo Park doctors concluded that Robert Reldan exhibited a "narcissistic character disorder symptomatic of neurotic conflict" and "a strong repressed hostility toward women." The 17-year-old was "in a massive rebellion against his own passive feminine impulses," they said, compensated for by "pseudo-masculine, Don Juan-type behavior." They also noted, "There is a marked hostility directed at the mother and a strong yearning for closeness with the father."

Despite this disturbing evaluation, Judge Kole on April 17, 1958, suspended Reldan's indeterminate sentence to Annandale and placed him, once again, on probation. After having committed at least six criminal offenses before the age of 18 and after having been found to be a danger to society in general and women in particular, Robert Reldan was back on the street. He had served less than two months at Annandale.

It is not unusual for young offenders to be given multiple opportunities to avoid prison or reformatory time. The reasonable assumption is that putting first- or second-time offenders in with more criminally hardened juveniles would only increase the likelihood of their recidivism. Whenever possible, especially where caring parents seem to provide a stable home life, these newbies in the system are routinely given probation, not incarceration. Indeterminate terms of incarceration for youthful offenders are also the rule in New Jersey. Such offenders are receptive to counseling, so the theory goes, and, when no longer a threat, they should be released rather than detained further in the poisonous atmosphere of a prison or reformatory.

Judge Kole did impose a condition of this new probation: Reldan would be required to undergo the psychiatric care Menlo Park doctors had recommended. He commenced treatment on April 30, 1958, with Dr. S. I. Heller in New York City, but after just one session with the youth, Dr. Heller was uncertain he wanted to take him on as a patient. The doctor told Reldan's caseworker that the young man "has no sense of values." He would continue treating him on a trial basis for one month, he said, reserving the right to terminate the doctor-patient relationship if things did not go well.

In early June, Dr. Heller sent a letter to Bergen County Probation advising that Robert Reldan had unilaterally terminated his treatment. Authorities took no action to revoke Reldan's probation, even though psychiatric care was a requirement for him to avoid reformatory time. Probation departments throughout the nation are uniformly understaffed, under-funded, and overworked. It's not surprising, then, that Bergen County Probation simply overlooked that a seriously disturbed young man was back in the community and getting no treatment for his problems, thereby placing society at risk once again.

Fort Lee High School graduated Reldan in June 1958, when he ranked ninety-first in a class of 128 students. School officials were aware of Robert's capabilities—he was considered above average to "bright," intellectually—and attributed his performance to an indifferent attitude, poor attendance, and disciplinary problems. Soon after graduation, the

Reldans moved to Closter, one of the small towns in Bergen County's northern valley region. Although it would grow into the most populous of New Jersey's 21 counties, Bergen was primarily a collection of hamlets— 70 municipalities in all—with Hackensack, Englewood, Garfield, and Teaneck being the most populous. Much of the northern part of the county was still undeveloped farmland in 1958, unlike the suburban sprawl that exists today. No doubt, William and Marie Reldan hoped the change to quieter surroundings would have a positive influence on Robert's behavior. Their disappointment in that regard would continue.

Robert had no sense of purpose or direction after high school graduation. He began a series of low-end jobs, most of which ended when he simply failed to show up for work. He was under no financial pressure, however, as his parents and Aunt Lillian continued to be generous with their support. William Reldan was just as generous with his criticism, often contrasting the young man's poor performance, both in school and in life, with his sister Susan's exceptional school record. Despite these unfavorable comparisons, it appears Robert maintained a close, loving relationship with his sister—at least on the surface. It is ironic (but probably no more than coincidence) that his two murder victims, years later, were both named Susan.

William Reldan's constant carping soon caused Robert to have a negative reaction to anything his father said. There were frequent arguments between the two. Marie Reldan, on the other hand, was never critical of her son and gave him everything he asked for. Robert knew he could get over on her whenever he wished, and that probably contributed to his lack of respect for her. Both parents ceased to have any influence over Robert's life, even though he continued to live with them and accept their financial support. In his later adolescence and early adulthood, Robert became completely indifferent to his parents' attempts at guidance and supervision, as his evolving criminal escapades would show.

Now 18 years old, Robert could no longer expect the lenient treatment he'd experienced as a juvenile in the criminal justice system, or at least that was the way the system was supposed to work. For Robert Reldan, that would not be the case. He got another bite of the juvenile justice apple when police arrested him on July 17, 1958, in his new hometown of Closter. They charged him with stealing five automobiles. It was determined that these offenses all occurred before June 2, Reldan's eighteenth birthday, so he was handled as a juvenile and remanded to jail to await a hearing on the charges. His hearing was purposely delayed so he could once again be evaluated.

On August 1, Reldan was transported to the state hospital at Greystone Park in Morris Plains, New Jersey. He remained there under observation until December 24, 1958, when he was released to his parents' custody, pending a juvenile court hearing scheduled for January. Holiday releases of prisoners are not uncommon, as the "peace on earth, good will toward men" spirit often overcomes rational thinking in the criminal justice system.

On January 15, 1959, Robert Reldan appeared once again before Judge Martin Kole. The Greystone psychiatric evaluation concluded that Reldan had a "sociopathic personality disturbance with anti-social reaction." Judge Kole found that the automobile thefts in Closter constituted a violation of the youth's prior probation and sentenced him, once again, to an indeterminate term at Annandale Reformatory. Despite this troublesome psychiatric diagnosis, Judge Kole again suspended Reldan's prison sentence and put him on indefinite probation—the third such "get-out-of-jail-free" card the young man had redeemed.

Reldan had failed to abide by a prior probationary requirement that he accept psychiatric care, and authorities had ignored that violation. Nevertheless, as a condition of Reldan's new indefinite probationary term, Judge Kole again ordered that Reldan undergo psychiatric treatment by a court-appointed doctor. The court ordered Reldan to be treated by Dr. M. Silberman, a Park Avenue, New York, psychiatrist. Moreover, Reldan was ordered to reside with his aunt, Lillian Booth, in New York City under the supervision of her male companion, Misha Dabich. Aunt Lillian's hand in this rescue of her beloved Bobby was evident.

New York State had once again declined to revoke Reldan's probation for his 1957 assault and robbery charge in that state. The New Jersey court, aware Reldan had turned 18 in June, 1958, most likely believed that this would be his last appearance in juvenile court. That was a wrong assumption. Reldan would get still another pass on being handled as an adult offender.

In February, 1959, Reldan stole a car from a Midtown New York parking garage. City police arrested and charged him, but the Manhattan District Attorney's Office was not about to invest the resources necessary to move Reldan through its criminal justice system as an adult, which would have involved presenting the case to a grand jury and obtaining an indictment. Then, for an 18-year-old with no job or visible means of support, the court most likely would have had to supply a legal aid attorney at public expense. After pretrial motions and plea bargaining ate up more time, a trial—with no guarantee of conviction—would have been the next step, absent a guilty plea. Even if a conviction at trial ensued, Reldan would still be a first-time *adult* offender, meaning he would probably get probation for the non-violent offense of car theft.

Once again, officials handled Reldan as a juvenile, but, in truth, it was probably the most advantageous way to resolve the case. The DA referred the car theft charge back to General Sessions Court, which could treat it as a violation of Reldan's New York probation for the assault and robbery offense he committed two years earlier. On March 24, 1959, a judge sentenced Reldan as a juvenile probation violator to three years at Great Meadows Reformatory in Elmira, New York.

As Reldan began serving the New York sentence, Judge Kole, back in Hackensack, dismissed all pending New Jersey probationary terms and all conditions of probation, including psychiatric counseling. Reldan did 22 months at Great Meadows. When he was released on parole in January 1962—despite an extensive juvenile record—Reldan could truthfully state that he had never been convicted of a crime. Because offenses committed as a juvenile are considered *delinquencies* and not crimes, Reldan would face his first offense as an adult with a clean record—assuming, that is, that he was caught and successfully prosecuted for that first adult offense.

But, as the Anna Marie Hernandez case would prove, nothing could be assumed with Robert Reldan.

Chapter 4

I find it hard to believe Bobby could have committed this crime.

William Prendergast's November 1968 report to the Special Classification Review Board (SCRB) regarding Robert Reldan stated that he had personally given the patient/inmate 100 hours of general therapy and 70 hours of "intensive" therapy. In his capacity as assistant superintendent of the Rahway Diagnostic and Treatment Center for convicted sex offenders, Prendergast was required to issue semi-annual reports on each inmate in the Treatment Center. The purpose was to detail the inmate's progress and recommend any continued treatment or parole consideration. The SCRB would then make its own periodic evaluation of each individual and forward that to the NJ State Parole Board for review and final determination.

Prendergast said that these sessions with Reldan generated "terrific improvement and the development of a trusting relationship." After just eight months of treatment, Reldan gained great "insight," he said. "Prognosis for a future positive parole recommendation is considered excellent," Prendergast concluded.

His subsequent report, six months later, was even more positive in its praise of Robert Reldan. He recounted 242 hours of therapy that he had personally conducted with Reldan, whom he called the most "intense" individual the Rahway facility had ever treated. "Insight flowed from him like water," Prendergast gushed. The young man was "able to ventilate his feelings for the first time in his life and to bring to light many repressions, hurts, and rejections that affected his overall social maladjustment."

After Reldan's original admittance to the *diagnostic* side of the facility, doctors there had concluded the convicted rapist "showed a repetitive, compulsive pattern of aggressive sexual behavior." Prendergast was not a psychiatrist. Though he held just an MA degree in psychology, he supervised the treatment side of the Center and now turned the diagnostic finding on its head. "The Caplan rape," Prendergast said, "was the result of pure displaced hostility toward [Reldan's] mother and not sexual in content or purpose." The May 1969 SCRB report ends with the chief therapist "strongly" recommending Robert Reldan for parole.

Parole was not granted at that time, and, in November 1969, William Prendergast issued his third report on Reldan, who apparently remained Prendergast's personal project. In his most effusive account yet, the therapist cited more than 350 hours of direct treatment he had given Reldan, noting the patient's tremendous "zeal and initiative." No one had shown such insight into his problems since the opening of the Rahway sex offender treatment facility, according to Prendergast, who again recommended parole. There was "a highly favorable prognosis with respect to Reldan's return to society," he said.

In support of his parole recommendation, Prendergast provided the SCRB with his own analysis of Reldan's extensive criminal history, conceived after he reviewed the man's rap sheets and discussed each entry with Reldan, himself.

"SBI reports [rap sheets] can be quite deceiving," Prendergast allowed. "Without close observation, [Reldan's] three sheets appear to indicate a rather long and extensive criminal history, with almost 25 different offenses." Prendergast then spun the issue: "However, when they are analyzed, there are only actually seven prior offenses . . . and in reality [the Caplan rape] is only the second crime that involves any type of violence." Acknowledging that rap sheets require an experienced eye for correct interpretation and disclosing that he did not seek corroboration from the Bergen County Prosecutor or any other law enforcement agency, William Prendergast embarked on a concerted effort to downplay Robert Reldan's criminal history and win his release on parole. Not just his criminal history, but the extensive violence directed at women—a propensity every past psychiatric evaluation of Robert Reldan had noted.

Prendergast disregarded Reldan's first known offense against a woman (the chokehold assault and robbery in a Riverside Drive apartment building when Reldan was 16½). He disregarded the five elevator assaults and robberies of women on Manhattan's Upper West Side with the same MO. (One victim commented to police, "He had the look of someone who could kill without remorse.") He disregarded the sexual assault of 14-year-old Anna Maria Hernandez. He disregarded the assault with a tire iron on the North Arlington woman during a burglary. And, of course, he disregarded the rape of Bernice Caplan. It was true that Reldan received liberal plea bargains that dismissed most of these offenses, but that did not mean that Reldan had not committed them or that a therapist should have ignored them.

Despite William Prendergast's unwavering intervention on Reldan's behalf, the SCRB, in November 1969, refused to recommend parole. That did not deter the chief therapist from taking up the cause once again in his next report to the review board on May 18, 1970. Citing more than 440 hours of personally delivered therapy, Prendergast showed an even more determined effort to gain Reldan's release from incarceration. In an unbelievable quote from his report, especially in light of the crimes Reldan would eventually commit, Prendergast stated, "He has dug to the core of his problem [and] has gained all of the insight necessary for a successful adjustment to society. All prior negative attitudes of all types are gone. Parole is again strongly recommended with a very high prognosis for successful community adjustment. *It is anticipated that Reldan will probably be one of the most successful people who ever graduated from the Rahway treatment unit.*" (Emphasis added.)

Looking at this series of SCRB reports by Prendergast in support of Reldan, the assistant superintendent's lack of objectivity seems clear. This supposed professional was turning a convicted rapist and serial predator of women into a paragon of psychological *patienthood*, someone from whom "insight flowed . . . like water." Members of the Special Classification Review Board had to be perplexed by such one-sided evaluations of an inmate; nevertheless, they finally accepted Prendergast's recommendation, perhaps out of exasperation, and forwarded it with their own favorable endorsement to the State Parole Board in Trenton.

Throughout Reldan's incarceration on the rape charge, Judy Rosenberg wrote to him regularly and, one must assume, romantically. She was still living in Chicago, but they had to have had an understanding between them because, in 1970, when it seemed likely that Reldan would soon be approved for parole, Judy came east with son Eddie and moved in with William and Marie Reldan in Closter. It was temporary, until she could find a place of her own. She finally settled on an apartment on Church Lane in Valley Cottage, a hamlet in Rockland County, New York, not far from the Jersey line. Rents were cheaper there than in Bergen County. But Judy did not know that a condition of Robert's expected parole would be that he reside in New Jersey.

On October 20, 1970, Robert Reldan got his parole, after serving just over three years of a potential 30-year sentence and doing his time in the relatively comfortable setting of a prison hospital, rather than in a maximum-security lockup.

One has to wonder at William Prendergast's apparent crusade to gain this particular inmate's release and at how the assistant superintendent of the NJ State Diagnostic and Treatment Center—presumably an able, experienced psychologist—could have been so wrong about Robert Reldan. Was it professional egotism, a need to achieve unqualified success with a hard case? Or was he simply hoodwinked—*charmed*—by a cunning young man? As subsequent events would demonstrate, Robert Reldan had pulled off his most successful hoax yet, playing Prendergast as effectively as any Ponzi artist ever played a mark into emptying his bank account.

Less than five months after the NJ State Parole Board ordered his release, Robert Reldan would terrorize a young Metuchen woman, holding a knife to her throat while attempting to rob and/or rape her. She was another random victim of opportunity, one whose path Reldan would cross after a visit to his friend, William Prendergast.

* * *

Robert Reldan had reason to feel depressed as he left JFK Hospital in Edison, New Jersey, the night of March 16, 1971. William Prendergast—aside from Judy Rosenberg, the person Reldan felt closest to after Prendergast had almost single-handedly secured his early release from prison—was now hospitalized for back surgery. During the visit with his friend, Reldan felt powerless, unable to help the man who had done so much for him.

Compounding Reldan's depression was a letter he received that day from authorities supervising his parole. He had been denied permission to marry Judy. The letter said he needed more time to establish himself, whatever that was supposed to mean. Now, Reldan would have to continue the risky proposition of living with Judy at her apartment in Valley Cottage, New York, an arrangement prohibited under terms of his parole. He had permission to visit Judy for day trips, but could not reside out-of-state.

Reldan needed Judy to give up the Valley Cottage apartment and take a place in New Jersey, but rents in Jersey were beyond their means. Living with his parents in Closter was out of the question. Judy wanted them to have their own home, a more stable environment for her son, Eddie. So, Reldan continued to assume the risk that his living arrangements would be discovered. He was becoming irritable and paranoid about the possibility that this violation might land him back to prison. His present financial situation did nothing to lessen the stress.

Another condition of his parole was that he had to maintain gainful employment. He'd been fortunate in getting a sales job at an appliance store in Wood-Ridge, New Jersey, a bothersome commute from Valley Cottage. It wasn't easy for a parolee to get a job, but family connections had helped. At first, he was getting $160 for a five-day workweek, but his employer had recently cut back his hours and, now, he was taking home less than $90 a week.

Aunt Lillian Booth was aware of his situation, but had made no offer of financial assistance. Perhaps she, too, had reached her limit with Reldan. As he feared that she might have been changing her will and cutting him out, his feelings about her intensified—his hatred of her and her wealth . . . and the parsimonious way she doled out small bits to him.

As he was exiting the hospital parking lot, Reldan noticed a single woman drive past. Almost without thinking, he eased into the flow of traffic and followed her, keeping her car in sight for a few miles until she turned into the large Metuchen Manor apartment complex. As with the Caplan home invasion and rape four years earlier, Reldan would never offer an explanation for what attracted him to this particular woman or what motivated him to follow her. Other than the fact that she was a lone woman, nothing had happened to suggest that she might have been an appropriate target. He'd simply glimpsed her briefly as she drove by. But, as with the Teaneck incident, he was overcome by the urge to follow her.

Tracking the woman from a discreet distance, Reldan saw the woman drive around to the back of the apartment complex. He watched her go down a slight decline toward a dimly lit area where a row of parking garages stood. Stopping at the top, Reldan saw the woman pull up to a garage. She got out and raised the door, then got back in her car and drove into the garage.

Now, with a plan in mind, Reldan leapt from his parked car. It was about 8:00 PM when he sprinted through the darkness, down the sloped driveway approximately 50 yards to the still-open garage door. He peered into the garage and saw the woman. The door on the driver's side of the car was partially open and the interior dome light was on. She appeared to be rifling through her handbag, looking for something, perhaps apartment keys. Moving swiftly, Reldan entered the garage and yanked the car door all the way open. He jumped into the driver's side of the car, pushing the woman across the bench seat toward the passenger's side. Holding a long-bladed hunting knife to the woman's throat, Reldan ordered her not to yell or scream.

Thirty-year-old Blanche Mate was frightened out of her wits. Reldan said he wanted money, but when she offered her pocketbook, he shut the car door and turned off the headlights. Blanche sensed that her attacker was not after money, but something else. Despite Reldan's warning and the knife at her throat, she screamed, sliding farther away from her assailant.

Attempting to gain control, Reldan put his left hand over her mouth. He held the knife in his right hand, brandishing it in her face while sliding his left hand down to grab her neck in a chokehold. He threatened to hurt her if she didn't stop screaming.

Blanche flailed about helplessly with her right arm and, fortuitously, found the latch to the passenger's side door. She jerked the latch and pushed the door open. Tumbling to the garage floor, Blanche scrambled to her feet and ran out into the night, screaming.

Porch lights blinked on and apartment doors opened. Blanche ran to one of her neighbors and, as she stood in the doorway, tried—through her panic—to explain what had happened. Crying for police to be summoned, she spotted her attacker, hurriedly walking up the driveway toward the main thoroughfare. Before she lost sight of him, he stopped momentarily, turned, and coldly stared back at her with a look that Blanche would never forget. With the sudden realization that she was very lucky to be alive, she felt a chill slither down her spine.

Metuchen police arrived in a matter of minutes and Blanche Mate, now somewhat composed, gave police an excellent description of her attacker. She said he had a "clean-cut appearance, with dark hair and a medium-to-olive complexion." She remembered he was wearing "light blue pants and a dark blue jacket."

An immediate, intensive search of the area ensued. Officer Charles Moore was contacted by radio while was patrolling in a marked police vehicle. Given the description, he was ordered to conduct a sweep of nearby Colonial Village Shopping Center, where the suspect might have sought anonymity among lots of people.

Arriving at the shopping center in less than a minute, Moore saw someone fitting the description—a man who was walking away from the patrol car in a furtive manner, as if trying to avoid notice. His suspicions aroused, Moore radioed headquarters for back-up and requested confirmation of the suspect's physical description. The man darted into a Carvel Ice Cream store. Double-parking his vehicle, Moore continued to observe the man from outside. Just as the police radio began re-broadcasting the description, Moore saw the suspect turn and walk quickly toward the rear of the store. He discarded something in the area between the two ice cream counters, then walked back to the middle of the store, trying to mingle with the other customers.

Patrolman Moore entered the Carvel store and confronted the man, who appeared nervous. Moore told him to keep his hands out of his pockets, where the officer could see them, and asked him to step outside to answer a few questions. "What's wrong?" the man asked.

As they exited the store together, the officer explained that there had been a knife assault a short distance away and that he fit the description of the assailant. Just then, Metuchen police Captain Charles Reader and Detective Herman Bauman arrived in an unmarked vehicle and stood by, watching. Patrolman Moore bent the suspect over the hood of his patrol car and frisked him for weapons. Fruitless as to weapons, the search was otherwise remarkable in that it produced no personal identification, and the suspect refused to give his name and address, although he did provide an alibi. He said that he had been visiting a friend at JFK Hospital. He provided the name of William Prendergast as his hospitalized friend.

The suspect was then handcuffed. Detective Bauman placed him in the back seat of the unmarked police car and transported him back to the Metuchen Manor apartment complex, where the victim could see him and, perhaps, identify him as her attacker. While seated in the back of the detective's vehicle, the suspect attempted to hide his face from her view, but Blanche Mate immediately confirmed that the man in custody was the one who had attacked her at knifepoint. No more than 25 minutes had elapsed from the time police received the initial call to the time Blanche Mate gave her positive identification.

Meanwhile, Patrolman Moore reentered the Carvel store. He walked to the area where he thought he'd observed the man discard something and, with the store manager as his witness, Moore found a 7½-inch throwing knife in a leather sheath, stuck between two ice cream counters.

Returning to headquarters with the knife, Moore showed it to the suspect, who declined to give a statement. He would not even provide his name and address. Officers formally placed the suspect under arrest as a "John Doe," charging him with assault, and then they placed him in a holding cell.

Meanwhile, officers contacted JFK Hospital, asking whether William Prendergast was a patient; the arrested man had offered that name as his alibi when officers first approached the suspect. The hospital confirmed that Prendergast was a patient, so Moore and Detective Bauman proceeded to the hospital to interview him.

William Prendergast acknowledged that he'd had a visitor earlier that evening, a man he identified as Robert Reldan. He described the clothing Reldan had been wearing as blue pants and a dark blue jacket. Both Prendergast and his hospital roommate said Reldan had left their room before 8:00 PM. When the officers informed Prendergast that Reldan was under arrest for assaulting a woman with a knife and attempting to rob or rape her, Prendergast revealed that he was a supervisor at the Rahway prison treatment unit. He said Reldan had been under his care at that facility and was presently out on parole for a rape conviction. Prendergast, apparently still a card-carrying member of the Bobby Reldan Fan Club, told the officers, "I find it difficult to believe Bobby could have committed this crime."

Returning to police headquarters, the officers confronted Reldan with the information they'd received, and Reldan finally admitted his identity; thereafter, he cooperated fully with the booking process, which proceeded with correct information replacing the previous "John Doe" documentation. Reldan also told officers where he had parked his car at the apartment complex, just before Blanche Mate had driven down to the garage.

The next day, police observed a green Ford Pinto where Reldan had said it would be, and its license plate and registration confirmed Reldan as the owner. Using keys that Reldan provided, the car was entered and searched. Police found an 11½-inch pinch bar and a green plastic bag containing a chisel, two screwdrivers, a pair of black gloves and several roles of duct tape—all of which were items commonly used as burglar tools. Police impounded the car, releasing it a few days later, minus the burglary tools, to Reldan's father.

That same afternoon, Blanche Mate came to police headquarters and Officer Moore showed her the knife, which she identified as the weapon Reldan had used in his attack on her. Blanche also informed police that she had been treated at JFK Hospital that morning. She had multiple contusions to her neck and other parts of her body, injuries sustained from Reldan's chokehold and from scrambling out of her car and falling to the garage floor. She was also being medicated for the mental trauma she experienced.

After spending several days in the county jail, Reldan's parole was formally revoked and, on March 23, 1971, he was returned as an inmate to the Rahway prison treatment facility. Six months later, in September, a Middlesex County grand jury indicted Robert Reldan on several charges related to the assault on Blanche Mate. Represented by a public defender, Reldan appeared in court on October 18, 1971. He entered not guilty pleas to the charges against him.

Reldan's public defender and the Middlesex County Prosecutor's Office engaged in prolonged negotiations, the primary point of contention being whether Reldan would have to serve any additional custodial time beyond that which he was serving for the Bernice Caplan rape conviction. They reached a plea deal. In return for his guilty plea to the indictment for the Blanche Mate crimes, Reldan would receive a five-to-seven-year sentence, served concurrent to and not consecutive to the time he was already serving for the Caplan rape conviction, since his parole had been revoked. Robert Reldan would get still another free ride, serving not one additional day for the Mate knife assault and attempted robbery—or, more likely, attempted rape.

On February 14, 1972, despite reservations he expressed from the bench regarding the concurrent nature of the sentencing, Judge John E. Bachman, sitting in Middlesex County Court in New Brunswick, accepted the plea bargain fashioned by the public defender and a very generous prosecutor's office. The judge imposed the agreed-upon sentence. Though judges have the power to reject a plea bargain, they rarely exercise this power, deferring, instead, to the prosecuting attorney's superior knowledge of the case.

After sentencing, Reldan was initially returned to the Rahway treatment facility, where he had been housed since the time of his parole revocation. Now, however, because he was considered a "graduate" of the sex offenders' treatment unit, and because the new crime involved no provable sexual misconduct, *per se*, Reldan, to his dismay and utter disappointment, was removed from the comparatively cushy environs of the prison treatment center and transferred to the general prison population at Rahway State Prison.

Reldan's time in the general population at Rahway was uneventful, except that, near the end of his stay there, he developed a close personal relationship with prison guard Irene Lippert. Officer Lippert would be instrumental in getting Reldan choice job assignments during his later prison terms. And, at two subsequent trials, she would testify for him, which was unusual, to say the least, for a prison guard, one apparently not immune to the charms of Robert Reldan.

When the lease expired, Judy Rosenberg vacated her apartment in Valley Cottage, New York, and went to live with William and Marie Reldan in Closter, where she awaited Robert's hoped-for early release on parole. She and Reldan's parents visited him frequently in prison, where, once again, Reldan came under the benevolent sway of his staunchest supporter, William Prendergast. In May 1975, Reldan was interviewed on celebrity David Frost's nationally televised talk show, no doubt at the instigation of Prendergast. Reldan used that forum to make a plea for better treatment and understanding of sex offenders.

Judy's faith in her boyfriend's ability to gain still another parole within a relatively short period of time—rather than the maximum 30-year sentence he might have been subject to for the Caplan rape—was vindicated.

On May 30, 1975, just four years after his knife attack on Blanche Mate and eight years after his brutal rape of Bernice Caplan (though he was on parole for part of this time) Robert Reldan walked out of Rahway State Prison. He was a free man, having been granted parole yet again by the NJ State Parole Board, based on a positive recommendation by prison authorities.

On June 17, 1975, Robert Reldan married fiancée Judy Rosenberg in a brief religious ceremony, with Robert's sister, Susan, standing as one of the witnesses. The happy couple took up residence in an apartment on Central Avenue in Tenafly, New Jersey.

Two other *Susans*—Susan Heynes and Susan Reeve—had less than four months to live.

Chapter 5

Proceeding on the assumption she has been either abducted or murdered.

Jonathan Heynes arrived home at 5:55 PM that Monday evening, October 6, 1975. He was late, but he'd phoned Susan at lunch to let her know that the work day was running long. His job at British Leyland Motors kept him busy, shuttling between the Leyland sales compound at Port Newark docks and the headquarters in Leonia, New Jersey. His main task Monday was checking on a silver Jaguar XJS and correcting a few minor problems with it.

Jonathan saw that Susan had taken in the empty dustbins from the street, where the collectors usually left them, and she had put them back in place near the garage. He smiled. She was so meticulous about everything—not just the spotless house she kept, but even small things like collecting the garbage pails, as the Americans called them, almost as soon as the dustmen set them down on their Monday morning rounds. *There's a good wife*, he thought, pulling his TR7 into the driveway.

He and Susan had been in the States just three months and were still getting used to the American version of the English language, as opposed to their native British usage. Was it George Bernard Shaw who described England and America as two countries "separated by a common language"?

The garage door was open. Jonathan saw Susan's yellow Austin next to the blanket-covered antique sports car he planned to restore, when he found the time. To let his wife know he was home, Jonathan sounded the horn, expecting her to come out to greet him as she normally did. But, no, she stayed indoors.

He wondered if she was still emotional after her little upset of that morning, before he left for work. She was dreadfully homesick for England—family and friends, more than anything else—and her inability to land a job in the nursing profession wasn't helping things. And then, of course, there was the baby thing. Susan wanted to start a family—all her friends were either pregnant or on their second child—but he kept putting her off, everything being so unsettled at the moment, what with the job and everything else. After all, they had been in their rented house in Haworth, New Jersey, for only about two months and they were still getting to know their neighbors.

As he got out of his car, Jonathan noticed the afternoon newspaper on the stoop. The garden gate was open, too. *Odd*, he thought. *That's not like Susan*. She always shut the gate after herself and usually grabbed the paper as soon as it arrived, if only to get a head start on the job listings. Jonathan retrieved the paper as he walked to the kitchen door, the entrance closest to the garage. It was locked, but he had his key so he let himself in.

The kitchen was back in order, everything Bristol-fashion, despite their having had house guests—three male friends from England—Sunday night. Jonathan had borrowed an XJ12 from work the previous week and left his TR7 for repairs, and they used the larger vehicle over the weekend to take their English friends to the Grand Prix auto races at Watkins Glen, New York. He had dropped the boys off at their hotel on his way to work, and they were flying back home later that night. At work, he swapped the borrowed car for his own sports car, which had been repaired.

Susan must have spent the morning cleaning up. He noticed nothing out of place. Yesterday's paper was on the kitchen table, opened to the jobs section, along with a felt-tipped pen and notepad. He called to his wife, but got no response.

Feeling the first throes of uneasiness, Jonathan went through the house, room by room. In their bedroom, he saw a tampon on the dressing table, which heightened his anxiety. Susan was private about personal hygiene. It was idiosyncratic with her; she never left something like that out for him to see. He had never even known where she kept her supply of them.

That night, Susan was to go to the Bergenfield Adult School to attend a pottery class, a weekly activity she relished. Jonathan saw her clothing for class neatly laid out on the bed. In the lavatory, he saw piles of folded towels and linens. Apparently, she'd done the laundry, too.

Jonathan went outside and checked the garden. Nothing. He went into the garage and looked in Susan's car. Her car keys were on the driver's seat, and her house keys on the front passenger's seat next to a wrapped parcel addressed to Susan's mother, who was in England. She had mentioned that morning that she was going to post something home, and this, he guessed, was it.

Maybe she had walked down their street, Schraalenburgh Road, to meet him on his way home from work. She had never done that before, but Jonathan was becoming worried. *Too many things are not right*, he thought. *Too many un-Susan-like things*. He got in his car and drove back along his normal route, down Schraalenburgh Road. No Susan.

Back home, Jonathan went straight around to the Slater residence, next door, to see if his neighbors had seen Susan. Yes, Dorothy Slater said, she'd seen and spoken with his wife at about 3:30, in the backyard, where Susan was taking in wash from the clothesline. The two backyards were separated by a low hedge, so the neighbors often saw each other outside.

Susan had seemed her normal, cheerful self, Dorothy noted. Leland Slater accompanied Jonathan home. Perhaps Susan had fainted, he said, and was lying out of sight in one of the rooms.

Together, Jonathan and Slater searched the house. Nothing. Mrs. Slater and Mr. Belcher, another neighbor, arrived at the Heynes home, and all of them looked about the garden and then the basement, moving out of the way everything that might conceal Susan, in the event she'd lost consciousness and fallen. They could find no trace of her.

It was about 6:40 and beginning to get dark. Jonathan, deeply worried, decided it was time to report Susan's disappearance. He phoned Haworth police and gave his name and address. He told the officer on the line that his wife was missing. He asked if there had been an accident or other occurrence that might account for her absence. The dispatcher said his department was not investigating anything of that nature, but promised to send an officer to the Heynes residence as soon as possible.

* * *

Patrolman Victor Pizza slowed his cruiser and pulled into the driveway of 359 Schraalenburgh Road at 6:45 PM. As the officer parked, three men approached and identified themselves: Jonathan Heynes, husband of the missing woman; Leland Slater, a neighbor; and Mr. Belcher, another neighbor. Mrs. Slater joined the group shortly thereafter. It took a moment for Pizza to calm everyone and get a coherent picture of what had transpired.

Mr. Heynes said he'd spoken with his wife by phone a little before 1:00 PM, and she seemed okay at that time. He told her he might be late getting home from work and, indeed, he arrived about 5:55. The husband said his wife's car was in the garage, with her car keys on the driver's seat and her house keys on the front passenger's seat, but she was nowhere to be found. Mrs. Slater told the officer she saw Susan Heynes taking in laundry in the backyard at about 3:30 that afternoon. They chatted briefly, and Susan seemed to be acting normally, in Mrs. Slater's opinion.

In most cases involving a missing woman who remains missing or who later turns up dead, the husband or "significant other" turns out to be the perpetrator of the crime. Everyone in law enforcement knows this established fact, which *always* makes the husband or boyfriend the prime suspect until proven otherwise. Patrol officer Pizza, a trained officer, knew the drill on this. He knew that he needed to be especially observant and careful to preserve any possible evidence, should charges be brought later.

Pizza asked Jonathan Heynes if he had searched the premises, and the husband responded that he had done so, several times. Pizza asked if Heynes would mind them searching again, and Heynes readily agreed. Getting the husband's permission was imperative. Without permission or a search warrant, the husband could block a future prosecutor's presentation of any evidence that implicates him in his wife's disappearance, if such evidence turned up during the search.

Together, they went through every room. Pizza looked into closets and packing trunks, but found nothing. He asked Jonathan what his wife would use if she were going to leave him a note, and Jonathan showed the officer a small white pad that had been on the kitchen table. Pizza carefully examined the top sheet of the notepad. Though it was blank, the officer wanted to see if there were any impressions in the paper to indicate that a note had been written on the preceding page before it had been torn off the pad. He saw no such impressions.

Pizza called the adult school where Susan was to have attended the pottery class that evening. He got through to someone in the pottery classroom, but Susan Heynes was not there.

Pizza noticed the orderliness of the house, with nothing seeming out of place. With the husband, he went back to the garage, and then the officer asked Heynes to open the trunk of his wife's car. There was nothing of interest inside. Thinking that Mrs. Heynes may have had trouble with her car and then decided to walk somewhere, Pizza asked Heynes to try starting the vehicle. It started without much difficulty, turning over once or twice before catching.

Pizza's attention turned to the vehicle next to Mrs. Heynes's Austin. He asked Heynes about the blankets covering the old sports car. They appeared to be undisturbed, Heynes said, exactly the way he had left them the last time he covered the car. The officer observed the close quarters between the two vehicles and concluded a struggle in the garage was unlikely to have happened—there wasn't enough room for a forcible abduction to have occurred without disturbing things. The two men removed the blankets, and Pizza went through the sports car, including the trunk. He found nothing.

The officer asked Heynes if there had been any trouble between him and his wife, and Heynes denied having any problems, though he mentioned the issue of his wife's homesickness. They were married just four months earlier in England and, after a honeymoon in Bermuda, had come to the States for his job. They were very much in love, he said.

Pizza returned to headquarters to relay the information to his shift sergeant, who put out an alarm for Mrs. Susan Heynes as a missing person. She was described as a white female, age 28, 110 pounds, five feet, six inches tall, shoulder length brown hair, blue eyes, fair complexion. She was last seen wearing a white blouse, blue denim skirt, blue shoes, and a cardigan sweater.

The three houseguests whom the couple had entertained on Sunday night were contacted later that evening, before they were to fly home to England. Before being allowed to depart, their chartered aircraft was searched to make sure that the homesick Englishwoman hadn't stowed away. No one fitting her description was on board.

* * *

News of Susan Heynes's disappearance hit the press with the October 9 edition of *The Record* of Bergen County, an afternoon newspaper at that time with fairly wide circulation, mostly in northern New Jersey. "Briton vanishes in Bergen," the headline read. The article reported her continued absence since late in the afternoon on October 6, and described the fact that there was no evidence of criminality, combined with the woman's expressed desire to return to England. The newspaper story carried a plea by Haworth police asking anyone with information to call them.

Because there was no outward sign of foul play at the Heynes residence, Haworth police initially worked under the assumption that Mrs. Heynes left of her own volition, without telling her husband. Jonathan reached out to friends in Canada to see if she might have gone there. No, they said, shocked that Susan would consider leaving without informing anyone. Susan's mother was known to have a heart condition, and no one who knew Susan could ever believe she would voluntarily disappear in this way, placing added stress on her mother.

The October 10 headline in *The Record* was more ominous: "Wife kidnapped, police fear." One newly reported development would help track Susan Heynes's activities on October 6 more closely. According to the paper, the missing woman had visited the offices of two Westwood, New Jersey, dentists between 2:30 and 3:00 that afternoon, seeking work as a nurse or receptionist. So, she had actually left the house in mid-afternoon, a fact not previously known. At least police were able to narrow down the time of the crime—if, indeed, that's what it was—to some time between 3:30 PM, when Mrs. Slater saw her in the yard taking in wash, and 5:55 PM, when Jonathan Heynes returned home. That is all they had to go on. No other substantive leads were forthcoming.

* * *

The Bergen County Prosecutor's Office (BCPO) is involved in the investigation of all major cases reported by the 70-odd police agencies in the county. Under New Jersey law, the County Prosecutor is the chief law enforcement officer, with authority to supersede any local department. This has a practical side that is beneficial in serious crimes such as murder, kidnapping, and arson. The county office has the resources and trained personnel to conduct a thorough and exhaustive investigation, so local departments mostly don't mind the BCPO's intervention. It also takes pressure off them when a crime is especially difficult to solve.

The first order of business in any case involving a missing wife is to question the husband—and to do everything necessary to rule him out, if possible, as the perpetrator. That means that they need to check an alibi, go over the crime scene (if there is one) with the proverbial fine-toothed comb, interview potential witnesses . . . and put pressure on the husband to voluntarily take a polygraph (lie detector) examination.

Since the scientific community hasn't accepted the technology as reliable, no United States court allows polygraph results as evidence in criminal trials, where the standard of proof is higher than in civil litigation. Consequently, unless a criminal defendant, with the advice of counsel, specifically waives his rights regarding polygraph results, they cannot be used in court.

However, even with restrictions on their use in court, polygraphs have a bona fide use as a law enforcement tool, and just about every investigative agency of any size has one or more trained polygraph operators on its staff. Their main purpose? To obtain confessions from guilty parties. So long as the operator follows established procedures, those confessions *are* admissible in court, with care taken *not* to mention how they were obtained.

It is psychological pressure that produces these confessions. The polygraph subject is interviewed before being hooked up to the machine. Then, wires and blood-pressure cuffs and other sinister-looking paraphernalia are attached to the subject's body, and the operator begins examining the already-nervous person, asking questions that call for a *yes* or *no* answer. The operator starts with mundane questions about issues not in dispute. "Do you work at Leyland Motors in Leonia," for example. Or, "Are you a British subject?" Or, "Is Susan Heynes your wife?" Then, the operator gets to the meat of the inquiry, taking care to frame questions in a way that leaves no ambiguity. "Did you participate in the disappearance of your wife, Susan Heynes?" And, "Do you have any knowledge of Susan

Heynes's whereabouts or her disappearance?" And so forth.

A well-trained, experienced polygraph operator will discern any answers that indicate deception, and then use these responses against the test subject in a way that will facilitate a confession. A guilty subject of such an examination soon accepts that his deceit has been discovered—that the cat is out of the bag, so to speak—and he may as well get this guilty knowledge off his chest. By the same token, a good operator will also use his experience and expertise to determine if the subject is actually telling the truth, so law enforcement resources and time are not wasted investigating and prosecuting an innocent person.

That, indeed, is what happened at Jonathan Heynes's polygraph test on October 9, 1975, three days after his wife's disappearance, despite his exceedingly strange behavior. A third of the way through the examination, Heynes told his examiner that he was feeling faint. Saying that he often feels faint when nervous, Heynes proceeded to lie down on the floor to regain his composure. Nevertheless, BCPO Detective Albert Hynes reported to his superior, Lieutenant Bert Allmers, that the polygraph results showed "indications of truthfulness when Mr. Heynes claimed that he had not participated in nor had any guilty knowledge of the disappearance of his wife, Susan."

Jonathan Heynes was in the clear. The search for Susan Heynes could proceed with his elimination as a suspect.

* * *

By Friday, October 10, Susan Heynes's contacts in the US, Canada, England and South Africa (where she and Jonathan worked for a time, before their marriage) had been spoken with, and no one professed knowledge of her whereabouts. Haworth police finally focused on the only remaining explanation for her disappearance: She had probably been kidnapped. But Bergen County Prosecutor Joseph Woodcock wasn't so sure; there just wasn't enough evidence either way, he said, to draw that conclusion.

Jonathan Heynes told reporters, "We're completely puzzled—puzzled is not strong enough—exasperated." *The Record* noted in its October 10 edition that the husband passed a lie detector test and was not a suspect.

Dozens of volunteers lined up four-abreast and tramped through acres of woodland near the Heynes home. Police called in search dogs, and, together with their handlers, they traversed every square foot of vacant land in the Borough of Haworth. Not one clue was unearthed, despite the hundreds of man hours expended. By Sunday, October 12, *The Record* was reporting that Haworth Police Chief Gaston Michel and his department were "proceeding on the assumption she has been either abducted or murdered."

Within a few days, after another young and attractive Bergen County woman disappeared under mysterious circumstances, it would become painfully clear that Chief Michel had it right.

Chapter 6

Help me, please. Help me—he's a maniac.

Impatient to get rolling that Tuesday evening, driver John O'Hanlon gripped the steering wheel lightly and tapped a steady cadence with his thumb. It was five minutes past his scheduled departure from the Port Authority's George Washington Bridge terminal on the New York side of the Hudson River. O'Hanlon took pride in being on time, but some regular riders were already grousing over the delay. His bus was crammed with commuters eager to get home after their workday, but the Red and Tan Line dispatcher was holding him up, trying to fill every seat before the bus departed on its "Route 20" run into New Jersey.

Three men got on, and O'Hanlon punched their monthly commuter passes. Recognizing two of the latecomers as regulars, he exchanged pleasantries with them as he waited for his seventieth and final passenger to appear. A moment later, he saw her hurrying toward his loading dock, an attractive girl in her early twenties, wearing a tan raincoat below her short, dirty blonde hair. She smiled at O'Hanlon as she stepped in, no doubt happy at having made his bus and saving herself a wait until the next Route 20 departure. O'Hanlon didn't recognize her—she was probably fresh out of college and just starting a job in the city or else she normally took a different bus.

The girl asked for a ticket to Demarest and held out a five-dollar bill. O'Hanlon smiled back, as he gave her the ticket and change. He yelled to the dispatcher that he was full and shut the door, then shifted into reverse and slowly eased out of the loading dock. A few passengers continued their grumbling, no doubt upset at the prospect of being late for the martinis awaiting them at home. O'Hanlon chuckled to himself and checked his watch. It was 5:50, and he was only six minutes late, after all.

After crossing to the Jersey side of the river, O'Hanlon's bus itinerary snaked along the winding, two-lane roads of Bergen County's Northern Valley area. His route took him in a northwesterly direction through one small town after another, bedroom communities for New York City workers. Like his own hometown of Ramsey in the western part of the county, these towns were noted for great public schools, low crime rates, and quiet living. Ideal for folks who wanted to escape the congestion and noise of their workaday world in the big city, yet remain within easy commuting distance.

O'Hanlon knew his normal drop-off points, of course, and usually began slowing even before a passenger pulled the stop cord to alert him. He passed through Tenafly and Cresskill using County Road, a main thoroughfare, and making stops along the way. He dropped one of the regulars at Ross Avenue, his first stop in Demarest, and continued along County Road, anticipating his next regular drop-off at Rodney Place. In between Ross and Rodney, though, just before he got to the point where County Road veers 90 degrees to the left and where Anderson Avenue runs into County Road forming a wide T-intersection, O'Hanlon heard the buzzer and slowed. It wasn't a regular stop. Glancing up, he saw a passenger walking toward the front of the bus—the pretty young girl in the tan raincoat, his last rider before leaving the terminal in New York. She had taken off her raincoat and was carrying it over her arm.

O'Hanlon pulled over 75 to 100 feet past Anderson Avenue, and the girl smiled and thanked him before alighting from the bus. As he shut the door, he saw her walk back toward Anderson. It was about 6:15, and he was making good time. Squinting into the setting sun, John O'Hanlon flipped down his visor and eased back into the flow of traffic, west on County Road.

The next day, October 15, 1975, O'Hanlon would be stopped by a Demarest policeman as he drove past Anderson Avenue's T-intersection with County Road. The officer asked if a young woman got off there on the previous evening. O'Hanlon said yes, he did drop off a girl in her early twenties just before sunset. O'Hanlon viewed a photo of Susan Reeve, but wasn't sure it was the same woman.

* * *

After finishing the dinner dishes, Mary and Joseph Fabrocini decided to treat themselves to an ice cream at Friendly's on County Road in Tenafly. It was a little before sunset on a pleasant autumn evening, and with the weather so balmy and delightful—the temperature had hit 71° earlier that day and was still in the mid-sixties—they thought they'd enjoy the mile and a half walk from their home in Demarest to the ice cream store. Besides, the exercise would do them good and burn off some of the calories they were about to indulge in.

They lived on Edward Street, which crossed Anderson Avenue a block north of where it intersected with County Road. Walking south on Anderson, just before getting to County Road, the Fabrocinis noticed a girl in her early twenties. She had "mousy blonde" hair and was dressed in what looked like business attire. The young woman crossed Anderson right in front of them and moved to the east side of that street, where there was a sidewalk. It was about 6:15, the Fabrocinis later recalled, still light enough to see clearly. The date was October 14, 1975.

Mary Fabrocini had a keen eye and good memory. When interviewed by investigators months later, she described the young woman's dress as being a light green V-neck, with a print pattern. It had a sash, she said, tied on the left side. The girl was carrying something over her arm, perhaps a raincoat. Mrs. Fabrocini was asked to draw a sketch of the girl's dress, which she proceeded to do, signing and dating the drawing. It would match almost exactly a sketch Susan Reeve's mother had made to show what her daughter was wearing the day she disappeared.

Mary Fabrocini's drawing of the girl's dress would later be used as evidence to track Susan Reeve's path of travel, after she got off John O'Hanlon's Route 20 bus and began walking north on Anderson Avenue toward her home on Orchard Road, about a half-mile away—a destination she never reached.

Later on, Joseph Fabrocini would also recall another important detail. As he and his wife reached the corner and stopped, looking for an opportunity to cross the roadway and continue their walk to the ice cream parlor, a vehicle traveling east on County Road made an abrupt left turn in front of them and headed north on Anderson Avenue, in the same direction as the young woman they had just seen. A man was driving. The vehicle was a small station wagon, very dirty, with lots of "junk" in the back. Joseph Fabrocini remembered the color as "maroon."

At the time of Susan Reeve's disappearance, Robert R. Reldan was the sole proprietor of an unincorporated, odd-job type business he called Triple R Construction Company. Registered in the company name was a dull red, 1969 Opel Kadett compact station wagon that Reldan had recently purchased second-hand. Reldan had used the two-door car, which had a roof rack, that very day at a house-painting job in Closter, not far from the intersection of County Road and Anderson Avenue. His helper at that job would later tell investigators that he and Reldan had knocked off work around 6:00 PM. They both departed shortly thereafter in separate vehicles. Reldan had worked the sandblaster most of the day, getting old paint off the house's exterior surface and, by the time the two men left, Reldan and his clothing looked pretty scroungy. The co-worker said the back of Reldan's wagon was cluttered with paint cans, tool boxes and other equipment. Reldan's route from the job site to his apartment in Tenafly would take him along County Road.

* * *

Seventeen-year-old Stephen Prato, a high school senior, was in a hurry driving south on Anderson Avenue in Demarest the evening of October 14, 1975. He was on his way to pick up a girlfriend, and they were then going to visit a mutual friend, a patient at Englewood Hospital. Stephen was probably going faster than the 40 m.p.h. speed limit, he later recalled, and, consequently, got just a glimpse of the two people alongside the road. Something about the scene made him uneasy—so much so he almost stopped to investigate. Almost.

A woman and a man were both walking on the west side of Anderson Avenue, heading north, but they weren't together. The woman, a girl in her twenties with "blondish brown" hair and neatly dressed as though coming from a business, was in the lead. She was wearing a light-colored dress and carrying something over her arm, maybe a raincoat. A white male followed, about 15 to 20 feet behind the woman, almost as though stalking her. He appeared to be in his late twenties, was 5' 10" to 6' 1" in height, and well built. He was good looking, Prato later recalled, with thick, dark hair, but he was dressed in some sort of "rough workman's clothing."

Prato knew that stretch of Anderson Avenue. He lived in Alpine, which was to the north of Demarest, and often used Anderson in his travels. The area where the woman and man were walking was perhaps one-tenth to one-quarter of a mile south of Orchard Road and had no sidewalks on either side of the road. It was rather desolate, in fact. Nothing but woods and an abandoned house were on the side where the two individuals were and, on the opposite side, were the Alpine County Club grounds, deserted at this hour and time of year. It was odd that the two were walking in that part of Anderson, Prato thought. Dusk was approaching, which added to the eeriness. Clearly, the man did not belong with that woman. After he drove past, Prato tried to keep sight of them in his rearview mirror, but they disappeared from view.

* * *

Raymond W. Lozier, Jr., left his home in Closter about 6:15 or 6:20 on the evening of October 14, 1975. He remembered the date because he specifically went out to pick up his daughter at the Dwight School in Englewood. He'd traveled that route many times: McCain Court to Hickory Lane, then a right on Anderson Avenue to head south. Anderson Avenue ran from Closter into Demarest, where it ended at its wide T-intersection with County Road.

Traffic was light that evening, which may account for Lozier's attention being drawn to a strange scene—one he would recall years later.

Five minutes or so after leaving home and soon after getting into Demarest, he noticed a car parked on the east side of Anderson Avenue, facing north, in the vicinity of Alpine Country Club and opposite Orchard Road. In all the years he'd lived in the area and traveled that roadway, he couldn't recall anyone parking a vehicle in that particular location. There were no houses or businesses right there.

The car was the first thing that caught his attention, but activity outside the car was the really strange part. Although it was around sunset, the remaining daylight was bright enough for him to see perfectly well.

Between the curb and the sidewalk, two people stood on the grass strip next to the parked car—a man closer to the car, which had its front passenger door wide open, and a young woman, slightly apart from the man and closer to the sidewalk. She was staring at the man, seemingly oblivious to anything or anyone else. Both seemed rooted to their spots, not moving in the slightest. Lozier was so disturbed by the scene that he slowed his vehicle to half its previous speed as he approached them.

The woman had blonde hair of moderate length and appeared to be in her early twenties. She was wearing clothing with a green pattern. The man was taller, Lozier later said, and "his appearance was the way a workman might look at the end of the day."

Approaching, Lozier saw that the car was a smaller station wagon with a roof rack and distinctive grille, but he couldn't identify the make and later had trouble remembering its color. When Lozier came abreast of the vehicle, the man turned his head and looked directly at him. They made eye contact, and Lozier felt his blood chill. It was a piercing, menacing stare. Lozier slowed some more and thought about pulling over behind the other vehicle to investigate what was happening, but then remembered that his daughter was waiting to be picked up. He decided not to stop. Newspaper accounts of the missing woman in nearby Haworth were still fresh in his mind, and he didn't want his daughter left alone at her school in the dark.

Lozier arrived at Dwight School shortly after 6:30, and his daughter was waiting. He returned home by the same route and, on the way to Anderson Avenue in Demarest, explained to his daughter what he had seen earlier, hoping the young woman would still be there, safe. But when they passed the Alpine Country Club, about a half-hour after Lozier's first transit of that area, the car, the sinister-looking man, and the girl were gone.

Two days later, when he heard on John Gambling's morning radio show that Susan Reeve, a 22-year-old living with her parents at 160 Orchard Road in Demarest, was missing, Raymond Lozier realized the bizarre scene he had witnessed on Anderson Avenue, opposite Orchard

Road, was probably the abduction of Susan Reeve. He got dressed and went to work.

Later, he and his wife discussed whether he should contact police. His wife told him "to keep quiet about what he saw," Lozier later testified. They had "enough problems," his wife said. It would be "a lot easier" if he didn't say anything.

Raymond Lozier followed his wife's advice. It was weeks before he finally reported his observations to police. By then, Susan Reeve's body had already been discovered.

* * *

Louisa Pittaluga had just picked up her 15-year-old son Mark at his cousin's house on Ross Avenue in Demarest, where he had dinner, and they were driving back to their own home in Demarest. She came out of Ross Avenue and made a right turn onto County Road. After a quarter-mile or so on County Road, she slowed at the ninety-degree, left curve in County Road and then she proceeded straight ahead in a northerly direction on Anderson Avenue. It was about 7:30, and Louisa had her headlights on.

Just north of the Alpine Country Club and Orchard Road, she had to swerve to avoid hitting what appeared to be a large rock in the middle of the road. Realizing the danger to other motorists, Louisa pulled over. There was no traffic directly behind her, so she told Mark to walk back and move the rock to the side of the road. She watched in her rearview mirror and saw her son pick up the object, but instead of dropping it to the side, he brought it back to the car.

It wasn't a rock, after all. They didn't know exactly *what* it was. It was made of rust-colored, canvas-type material and was a hooded mask of some type, to be worn over the head. The part that would be over the eyes of the person wearing the mask was open, but it looked as though a protective-glass plate belonged there. The glass was missing. The Pittalugas brought the mask home and kept it in their garage.

Weeks later, during the height of publicity about the two missing women, Louisa would phone police and tell them about the mask they found on the roadway. It would turn out to be a sandblasting mask. Mark later told investigators the date he found the mask was October 14, 1975. He knew it because the next day at school, he learned that schoolmate Gus Reeve was upset over the disappearance of his older sister, Susan, the night before—the night Mark and his mother came upon the mask, a block from the Reeve residence. The mask would become a crucial piece of circumstantial evidence that linked Robert Reldan to Anderson Avenue at about the time Susan Reeve was abducted.

* * *

It wasn't like Susan to be late and not call, thought Arthur and Barbara Reeve. If she missed her usual bus or had to work late at Grey Advertising in the city, she invariably called to give them her new schedule. Sometimes, she decided at the last minute to see her fiancé, Danny Omstead, a graduate student at Columbia University, before coming home, but she would call and tell them not to hold dinner for her. Susan was their oldest child. She'd graduated from Hollins College in Virginia in May, and Arthur and Barbara sent their daughter on a monthlong tour of Europe, accompanied by her cousin, as a graduation gift. The two girls returned in the end of June, and Susan started working at Grey Advertising soon thereafter. She loved her job and had a future bright with marriage and career prospects.

It was now past 7:30, and Susan was more than an hour late. Arthur Reeve, a prominent Bergen County attorney and former municipal court judge in Demarest and Closter, was getting more worried by the minute. Susan always took the Route 20 bus from the bridge terminal and got dropped off at County Road and Anderson Avenue; then, she would walk the approximate half-mile from that intersection to their home. It took her no more than eight or 10 minutes.

If the weather was bad, Arthur or Barbara would pick Susan up when she got off the bus. In fact, Barbara Reeve had driven down Anderson Avenue to the County Road intersection at six o'clock that evening with the thought of giving Susan a ride home. It was warm for October, and she wanted to save her daughter the walk. Susan wasn't on that earlier bus, though, and Barbara had to turn around and drive back without her. Arthur, himself, had driven down Anderson along Susan's walking route closer to 7:00 PM, and he, too, had returned home without her.

* * *

Nineteen-year-old Eileen Dalton worked as a toll collector at the George Washington Bridge. Her father, who was the Fort Lee police chief, helped get her the job, but she was a conscientious employee and earned her pay.

On October 14, 1975, she was assigned the 4:00 PM to midnight shift at lane 40 on the Interstate Toll Plaza section, which was on the New Jersey side of the Hudson River. Between 7:30 and 7:45, a car with a male driver—the only occupant as far as she could see—entered lane 40 and stopped at her booth. It was dark by then, but the toll plaza lighting was bright enough for her to see clearly. The driver appeared to be in his late twenties or early thirties, of medium build, good looking and well groomed, with dark, medium length hair. He had his radio on at moderate volume and his driver's side window was rolled down. The vehicle was a light green, two-door coupe, Eileen would later recall.

Just as she reached out to accept the man's toll payment, she heard a voice come from the rear of the vehicle, a woman's voice. It was more like a scream, but when Eileen looked toward the back of the car, she saw no one. The man apparently heard the sound, too, because he seemed startled by it at first but then deliberately raised the volume of his car radio. He turned back toward Eileen and gave her an "icy glare" before driving off.

As the vehicle left the toll booth, Eileen realized there was someone in the trunk of the car. A woman was screaming, "Help me, please. Help me! He's a maniac." The female voice repeated, "Help me," as the car sped off.

All Eileen could do was yell after the vehicle, "Wait!"

But the vehicle did not stop. It headed toward the bridge and the New York side of the river at a high rate of speed. Eileen called to Jim Lillis, a 21-year-old co-worker manning the toll booth at lane 42, next to her. "Did you hear that?" she asked. Yes, Jim said, he'd heard a woman's voice, too, but he couldn't make out the words, except maybe the word "maniac."

Eileen and Jim called their supervisor and reported the incident.

* * *

Arthur and Barbara Reeve could wait no longer. They'd phoned Danny Omstead, but he hadn't heard from Susan and had no idea where she might be. They'd also phoned Susan's close friends; she did not have a large social network and kept pretty much to herself. No one knew of her whereabouts. Susan didn't belong to clubs and had no hobbies other than cooking and sewing, two activities she loved to pursue in the comfort and safety of her home. Something was dreadfully wrong. Arthur Reeve picked up the phone and dialed Demarest police to report his daughter missing. It was 11:15 PM.

Days later, as the search for his missing daughter continued, a grieving Arthur Reeve would tell reporters that Susan was "prompt, organized and clean cut. By modern standards, you wouldn't recognize her, she's such an old-fashioned gal," he said. "That's what gives us so much concern," the father added. "She wouldn't have gotten into a stranger's car or stopped off for a drink. It's absolutely inconsistent with her character. We know something's happened to her."

Chapter 7

He has the same kind of piercing eyes.

The last sure indication police had of Susan Reeve's whereabouts on the day of her disappearance—witness observations along Anderson Avenue would come later, after media coverage raised public awareness—was a brief chat she had with a co-worker at the elevators as she was leaving Grey Advertising in New York City, shortly after 5:00 PM. If she followed her usual routine, Susan would then have ridden the subway to the Port Authority Terminal at the bridge, where she normally took the 6:04 PM bus to her stop in Demarest. But, in the early stages of the investigation, there was no proof that scenario played out on October 14, 1975.

It was true, a Red and Tan Line bus driver told police he'd dropped off a young woman on County Road in Demarest, just past Anderson Avenue, around dusk on October 14, but after viewing Susan Reeve's college yearbook picture, he couldn't say it was the same girl.

Investigators had to consider the possibility that Reeve never made it back to New Jersey, and that meant one thing. The full resources of the Federal Bureau of Investigation, including its acclaimed forensic laboratory in Washington DC were now at the disposal of the Bergen County Prosecutor's Office, at least for the Reeve case. If a crime crossed the jurisdictional lines of two or more states, federal authorities had the power to act.

When BCPO Investigator Ed Denning went to Fort Lee on October 17, 1975, to interview Eileen Dalton, the young toll collector, he was accompanied by three FBI agents. Ms. Dalton recounted what she had observed *and heard* on October 14—the actions and description of the male driver, as he stopped at her tollbooth between 7:30 and 7:45 that evening, and a woman's heartrending screams emanating from the vehicle's trunk. Denning showed Dalton a photo array of six men that he'd put together using photos of known sex offenders recently paroled. Eileen studied the pictures before pointing to photo #6. That one "strongly resembles" the driver of the vehicle, she said. It was an older photo, Eileen noted, and the man she saw a few days earlier looked somewhat different now. But she was reasonably sure it was the same man.

"He has the same kind of piercing eyes," she said.

Photo #6 was a mug shot taken by the Bergen County Sheriff's Office. It depicted a man arrested in April 1967 for the rape of a Teaneck woman, Bernice Caplan.

* * *

As lead investigator on what was still the Heynes/Reeve missing person's case, BCPO Investigator Denning had to coordinate efforts of not only his own agency, but also the FBI and Haworth and Demarest police departments. A central command had been set up in Demarest. Scores of leads had to be followed, dozens of people interviewed.

Susan Reeve's fiancé Danny Omstead, for example, had to be cleared of any involvement in her disappearance. (He passed a polygraph test on October 21.) Reldan was one of several former sex offenders to be checked out. Much of that effort would yield nothing—dead ends and false trails—but it was the grind-it-out-, leave-no-stone-unturned type of police work that every good detective learned as a rookie. It was the stuff that solved cases.

Late in the day on October 21, 1975, a week after Susan Reeve went missing and four days after Eileen Dalton picked Robert Reldan out of a photo lineup, Ed Denning tracked Reldan down through his parole officer and asked him to come in for a talk. Denning disclosed the reason for the face-to-face meeting—he was investigating the disappearances of Susan Heynes and Susan Reeve—and Reldan agreed to come in the next day, October 22. He had no choice; as a condition of parole, Reldan had to cooperate with any police agency investigating any crime. He could refuse to say anything by claiming his Fifth Amendment right not to incriminate himself or his Sixth Amendment right to have an attorney present, but he *did* have to appear.

Reldan showed up at the appointed time, alone, and the interview began. It was recorded, with Reldan's knowledge, so there is a lasting record of what was said. Investigator Denning handled the interrogation masterfully, getting the maximum any investigator could expect from a suspect in what looked, increasingly, like a double-murder case.

Right off the bat, Reldan informed Denning he was expecting the call-in.

"Listen, I know I was coming," Reldan said on October 22. "I called my therapist as soon as the second one [Susan Reeve's abduction] went down. I said, when they run out of leads and everything else they're checking out, they're going to start picking up known offenders. I'm gonna be notified."

Denning asked Reldan if he knew Susan Reeve or Susan Heynes. Reldan denied knowing either woman, but was quick to comment on the *Susan* connection.

"That, oh yeah, here's the other coincidence that I told what's his name about this last night," he told Denning. "I said they both have to be named Susan and I got a sister named Susan, so now they're going to start looking for a psychopath who hates his sister." Reldan claimed to have a close relationship with his sister Susan, something she would later confirm.

Asked about his financial condition, Reldan said he and his wife were pretty secure, with $13,000 or $14,000 in the bank. His parents sold their Closter house two months earlier and gave him $10,000 of the proceeds, and Judy Reldan saved the rest of their nest egg while he was in prison. Although his business was slow because it had rained a lot lately and, consequently, contractors weren't hiring him to do work, Reldan said he did not need money. Besides, Judy had a good secretarial job with an architectural firm.

Remembering Eileen Dalton's description of a light green vehicle at her tollbooth the night of October 14, Denning asked Reldan what type of car he drove. Reldan said he bought a used red Opel wagon from a Tenafly teacher a few months back; it was registered in the name of his business, Triple R Construction. The Opel's importance to the case wasn't yet apparent, as Raymond Lozier and the Fabrocinis had not reported their observations to police by then. Denning, probing further, found out that Judy Reldan drove a 1974 Hornet, which Reldan had also used before he got the Opel. Judy's Hornet was light blue, not green.

Reldan produced a notebook and allowed Denning to inspect it. Because of his status as a paroled sex offender, Reldan said he began keeping a diary in July or August so he could protect himself with a log of his comings and goings, without having to rely on memory. This was a rare opportunity—a suspect who had recorded a day-by-day account of his activities—and Denning took advantage of it. If Reldan had valid alibis for the times the two women were abducted, he could be eliminated as a suspect. The more likely circumstance, Denning thought, would be Reldan making self-serving and false claims as to his movements at the relevant times, and investigators being able to prove the lies. They might also get other information from Reldan to aid the investigation. Things worked out just the way Denning thought they might.

Denning asked Reldan to refer to his diary, starting with September 1, and take him chronologically through each day's activities. The investigator had little interest in September, but it was a good place to start, without revealing too much to the suspect. As Reldan's recitation of his mundane daily routine reached the month of October, Denning's interest heightened.

On Wednesday, October 1, Reldan was at Bergen Lighting in Bergenfield getting fixtures to install at a job. Then he went to Demarest to pick up supplies. He took his wife to a drive-in movie on Route 303 in

New York State that night. The next day, October 2, he was home with a cold and worked around the house. He did the laundry and went shopping. In the evening, he and Judy took her son Eddie to a church carnival. On Friday, the third, he installed a part on his Opel, then worked up a job estimate in Englewood. In the afternoon, he stopped at his wife's office to say hello and got his car washed. That night, he played basketball.

On Saturday morning, October 4, two days before Susan Heynes's abduction, Reldan took Eddie to a "punt, pass, and kick" contest and watched him compete. That afternoon, Reldan traveled to Rahway State Prison for his regular, first-Saturday-of-the-month counseling session at the treatment center for sex offenders.

"It was a condition of the parole," Reldan explained, "and which I would sign anything just to get the hell out. Although, at this stage of the game, Mr. Kuhn [his parole officer], my therapist, and Prendergast all say it's ridiculous, that I don't need it and shouldn't be there, and he is about to make a recommendation in writing to be discontinued."

Amazingly, if Reldan is to be believed, William Prendergast still viewed Robert Reldan as his personal triumph, a rehabilitated sex offender—not only someone who should *not* be locked up, but also someone who had no need for therapy.

"I told [Prendergast] I wanted to come back anyway," Reldan said to Denning, "just to keep a finger in, see what the hell's going on. Because I do have some friends down there, so it should give me a chance to say hello." This may have been Reldan's way to rationalize his continuing with therapy—a recognition that he needed it, without having to admit that fact.

Reldan offered to give investigators permission to speak with his therapists, and Denning was quick to accept, getting it in writing. Undoubtedly, Reldan felt these folks, with whom he had a close relationship, would do him no harm. He was right, to a certain extent, but they did provide insight into their patient's psychological demons.

William Prendergast, when interviewed a week later, told BCPO investigator Jay Berman that "Reldan's problem was not sexual in nature," although the psychologist did suggest Reldan "might have latent homosexual tendencies." Reldan's prior attacks, according to Prendergast, "were merely the outward expression of hostility toward women." Ever the chief apologist for his favorite patient, Prendergast expressed doubt Reldan was responsible for the Bergen County crimes. "The circumstances surrounding the girls' abduction, murder, and discovery" [by the time of the interview, both bodies had been found], he told Berman, "were not consistent with Reldan's type of behavior." Because of strong guilt feelings, Prendergast said, Reldan couldn't hide his involvement, had he committed those crimes.

Peter Gartner, another of Reldan's therapists, praised his conduct during recent group therapy sessions, especially his "encouraging other patients to deal with their problems." Gartner felt Reldan "would be capable of committing a rape-murder," but believed "he would probably act in a manner that would lead police to him." Gartner said Reldan's problem was "his relationship to his wealthy aunt and, to a lesser extent, his mother." He was especially hostile toward older, wealthy women, Gartner said, and might lash out "in an impulsive fit of rage" at a woman he thought to be "snobbish." *

At the October 22 interview in the prosecutor's office, Reldan continued recounting his daily activities. "Sunday, October 5, it rained," he said. "We was home all day." Monday, October 6—the day Susan Heynes disappeared—was, of course, one of two dates that most concerned Denning. Reldan had lots of detail in his notebook for October 6, 1975.

"Took my dog in to the vet's at 10:30," Reldan read from his notes. "Benjamin Brothers picking up supplies, went back to see this guy in Englewood about the job, trying to get the job."

Reldan gave the name of the Englewood job contact, a Charles Wolthoff, and said he was there at noon. Then, "around two-ish," he went to visit his cousin, Candace Thompson, who worked at Closter Jewelers. Reldan said he knew the owner of that store, John Truncali, quite well. Reldan spelled out the last name for Denning.

Investigators would later learn that Reldan tried to sell Truncali a woman's ring that looked very much like the distinctive engagement ring Susan Heynes wore. Truncali would become a key prosecution witness in the murder trials. Charles Wolthoff would also tell police Reldan offered him a similar ring. Without these leads supplied by Reldan, himself, investigators probably would not have found out what Truncali and Wolthoff knew.

Still on his October 6 activities, Reldan tried to nail down an alibi for late afternoon, which, of course, he knew was the relevant time. After visiting his cousin at Closter Jewelers, he told Denning, he went to have

---

*One has to wonder, based on this particular revelation by Gartner, if Susan Heynes's English accent might have ignited in Reldan that "impulsive fit of rage" and been a factor in her death. As far as anyone knew, Heynes was the first time Reldan had killed a victim. Perhaps it was something as simple as a perceived "snobbish"-ness that pushed him over that edge. Or, perhaps Robert Reldan learned, after victims Bernice Caplan and Blanche Mate were able to bear witness against him, that his best interests lay in making sure he left no one alive to tell the tale.

the Opel's engine steam cleaned. First, he tried a garage in Closter, around the corner from the jewelers. That place couldn't accommodate him at the time, he said, but they directed him to another garage that possibly could—F&S Friendly Service, a Citgo station in Hillsdale, New Jersey.

Reldan said he was at F&S Friendly Service about 3:30 or 4:00 PM and that it took 45 minutes to have his engine steam cleaned. Incredibly, Reldan then handed Denning a receipt for the steam cleaning, and it showed the cost ($12.50 paid in cash) and the October 6 date, but did not have a time of service. Reldan had provided details about dozens of activities he'd engaged in during September and into October, yet the only one for which he produced a written receipt was the one on the afternoon of October 6, when he knew he needed an alibi.

FBI Special Agent Albert Chestone would question employee John Quick at F&S Friendly Service two weeks after Reldan's BCPO interview. Quick remembered doing an engine cleaning on a red Opel wagon in early October. The station wasn't doing many steam cleanings at the time, so it stuck in his mind. He started on the Opel about 2:00 PM, he said, and the job took 40 minutes to an hour. Quick estimated that the male driver of the Opel—he didn't remember what he looked like—left the Citgo station around 3:00 PM.

Reldan's alibi for the evening of October 14 was as shaky as his October 6 lie. He told Denning that he had a house-painting job that day for Dr. Maniatis at 11 High View Court in Closter. He said he picked up equipment at Taylor Rental Center in Closter at 8:30 AM, without specifying the type of equipment. John Rudolph, a co-worker of Judy's, helped with the job. They were there all day, except for lunch at Burger King in Closter. That much of Reldan's story was true. John Rudolph later verified it, including the time they both left the job site, 6:00 PM or thereabouts.

Reldan, still reading from his notebook, told Denning that, after leaving the Maniatis job, he headed toward his apartment, which would cause him to travel through Demarest, then Cresskill for a short stretch, then Tenafly—all on County Road. Reldan said he had a sudden desire to stop and have a drink, so he phoned his wife using a pay phone and told her he'd be home late. The Orbit Inn was on County Road in Tenafly, Reldan said, and he stopped there at 6:20 PM to have a gin and Bitter Lemon mixer, his "standard drink." After having just one drink, he said, he went home, where he stayed for the rest of the night.

Reldan never stopped at the Orbit Inn. Investigators interviewed the bartender and owner, both of whom were tending bar between 6:00 and 7:00 PM on October 14. Shown photos of Reldan, neither could remember him as someone they'd ever seen in the place. In fact, for all the days and nights of recorded activities in Reldan's diary, he had never once stopped for a drink after work and had never patronized the Orbit Inn, just blocks from his apartment. But the key factor in proving this particular lie was that Reldan volunteered too much information—namely, the specificity about *what* he had to drink and the fact that it was his standard drink, which he always ordered. Trying to cover their tracks, criminals commonly think that providing details makes their story more believable. But, instead, it gives investigators more ways to disprove the authenticity of their stories. The Orbit Inn did not stock Bitter Lemon mixer.

Denning asked Reldan if he'd be willing to take a polygraph test, specifically on the Heynes and Reeve abductions. Reldan knew what a polygraph was, and offered excuses regarding why he didn't think taking a lie-detector test was such a good idea.

"I have to talk—I have to talk to a lawyer," Reldan said. "And then I would have to talk to Mr. Gartner. Because in my background there is small things of guilt. A lot of the stuff I did to myself was because I felt guilty about things, and going to jail was more like punishing myself."

Reldan promised to get back to Denning if his lawyer and therapist said it was okay to take the polygraph. Not surprisingly, Denning never heard from Reldan on this issue, and no polygraph examination was ever administered to him.

It would take time for investigators to follow up on the assertions Reldan made during the interview, but Reldan let slip one remark that was an instantaneous "tell." At one point, he told Denning, "I sure hope no more girls get killed." Denning's instincts were sounding loud and clear that he had the right man. This was still a missing-persons case. The bodies of Susan Heynes and Susan Reeve had not yet been discovered.

* * *

There are two aspects of the Heynes/Reeve investigation that have troubling implications, at least from the vantage point of hindsight, some 35 years later.

First, prosecutors would never be able to prove Reldan owned or had access to a light green car the night of October 14, and so, they discounted the whole episode at the bridge toll plaza. In none of Reldan's three murder trials would they call Eileen Dalton as a witness to describe what she saw and heard that night. That may have been a missed opportunity.

Piecing things together now, it was possible—perhaps probable— that Eileen Dalton correctly identified Robert Reldan as the man driving the car with a terrified woman in its trunk. Judy Reldan's Hornet was *light* blue—a color Dalton could easily have mistaken for light green under the artificial lighting of the tollbooth, amid the excitement of hearing a woman scream for her life. Moreover, the tollbooth encounter occurred within an hour and a half of Susan Reeve's abduction and, perhaps most important, no other woman from the area was reported abducted or kidnapped that evening. There were too many connections for this to be mere coincidence.

After Reldan became the prime suspect, investigators would execute a search warrant on November 13 for Robert and Judy Reldan's Central Avenue apartment in Tenafly and also for Judy's vehicle, but they were looking for jewelry and personal effects belonging to the two murdered women—items large enough to be spotted with the naked eye. They found no jewelry or other belongings of Susan Heynes or Susan Reeve, but did come across one California driver's permit bearing Reldan's picture and a fictitious name, along with several blank birth certificates that could have been used by Reldan to create new identities. They also seized Reldan's address book, which contained the name of a former girlfriend, Roberta Gimbel, who would later provide crucial information linking Reldan to the sites where the two bodies were found.

By the time of the November 13 search, the investigative team had already concluded that Eileen Dalton's observations the night of October 14 had nothing to do with Reldan, even though Dalton had picked him out of a photo lineup. Consequently, when they searched Judy's Hornet, they did not try to collect microscopic evidence from the trunk for lab analysis—things like hair or blood traces that might have been left there by a bound but struggling woman.

Reldan could have transferred a subdued Susan Reeve from his Opel wagon, which he knew several people had seen that night, to a secure location nearby. Weeks later, in fact, police would learn of just such a location—a vacant Closter house in which Reldan had stored some belongings. Reldan's aunt, Lillian Booth, owned that house, which was less than 2.5 miles from the spot where Susan Reeve was abducted. Reldan could have stashed the young woman there, gone home to quickly change clothes and vehicles, swapping the Opel for his wife's Hornet, and then returned to the safe house to collect his victim, putting her in the Hornet's trunk, bound and carelessly gagged but still alive. He then likely transported the terrified girl to the place where he would rape and strangle her, before dumping her body in New York State.

A month after her disappearance, investigators would obtain credible evidence that Susan Reeve had, indeed, been inside the vacant Booth house—evidence never used at any trial.

There was a second instance when the prosecution may have overlooked an important detail, this time in the Heynes case. After Reldan became a suspect in Susan Heynes's abduction and murder, investigators couldn't figure out how he came to choose her as a victim. They assumed he saw her in the backyard of her home taking in the laundry, or perhaps in her driveway as she was about to go out to mail her mother's package. There was even speculation Reldan may have spotted one of the "nursing position wanted" cards she had posted in hospitals and other places in hope of finding a job.

The Heynes backyard was not clearly visible to someone driving by the house, so Reldan could not have first sighted Susan Heynes there. With trees and other vegetation along both sides of the driveway at 359 Schraalenburgh Road, a person driving past that address at normal speed would have had a restricted view. While possible, it was also unlikely Reldan first saw Heynes in the moment she walked from the door of the house to the garage. As far as Reldan targeting her through the employment cards she had tacked up on bulletin boards, that manner of choosing victims was so unlike anything he had ever done as to be highly implausible.

Prosecutors didn't have an answer as to how Reldan selected Susan Heynes and, consequently, they never put forth a theory on this aspect of the case. But if John Quick, the Citgo station employee, was right about the times he gave Special Agent Chestone, one can deduce how Susan Heynes's path just happened to cross that of Robert Reldan, on the unluckiest day of her life.

Reldan had a history of choosing his victims at random, while he was driving. It was as though his brain clicked into predatory mode at certain times—times when he encountered a lone woman, someone appearing to him as vulnerable. He *just happened* to be waiting at a stop sign when he saw Bernice Caplan drive past, alone, on her way home from delivering Passover cookies to her mother. Blanche Mate *just happened* to catch his eye when she drove past him, alone, as he was leaving JFK Hospital after visiting Prendergast.

Reldan's abduction of Susan Reeve fit his MO perfectly. Joseph Fabrocini saw Reldan's Opel wagon turn abruptly off County Road and head north on Anderson Avenue, in the direction that Susan Reeve was walking. She was certainly visible to Reldan as he came to that wide intersection—a single girl walking alone—and his instant decision to follow her in his car fell squarely within the man's pattern.

Again, with the benefit of hindsight, here's what investigators may have missed about the Heynes abduction. Susan Heynes had gone out in her car *before* 3:30 PM, the time when Mrs. Slater saw her in the backyard. A *Record* news story said she'd been to Westwood between 2:30 and 3:00 PM, trying to get a dental office job. Investigators never focused on that fact. Westwood is right next to Hillsdale. Robert Reldan, after departing

F&S Friendly Service in Hillsdale at about 3:00 PM, would have driven through Westwood to get to his apartment in Tenafly.

In fact, Reldan and Susan Heynes would have traveled along a common route—Old Hook Road—for almost three miles before Heynes turned right on Schraalenburgh Road to get to her house. Instead of continuing on Old Hook Road a few more blocks, his most direct route to Tenafly, Reldan followed Heynes south on Schraalenburgh, until she turned into her driveway. Reldan circled back and drove past the house a few more times, just to be sure, before entering the driveway himself.

By then, Susan Heynes had taken in and folded the wash and was leaving for the post office. She went out the kitchen door, locking it behind her. She placed the parcel she intended to mail to her mother in England on the front passenger's seat of her vehicle, still parked in the open garage, and tossed the house keys alongside it. As she was about to get in her car, she saw an unfamiliar vehicle slowly pull into her driveway.

Reldan came up with a quick deception, one like the "Brantley" ruse he had used on Bernice Caplan, to catch Heynes off guard. Perhaps he posed as a lost motorist, asking with a friendly demeanor for directions. He likely waved a map or scrap of paper—something to draw his victim closer to him. Susan Heynes, wanting to be helpful, dropped her car keys on the driver's seat and approached the stranger. Given the fact that there were no signs of a struggle at the scene, he probably used a gun, though he was strong enough to do it with his familiar chokehold. After Reldan gained control of her, he drove off with her lying immobilized on the floor of his car, taking her to a location where he'd feel safe in first sexually assaulting, then killing her.

In support of this hypothesis, a disturbing fact would come to light four years later, too late for it to be used effectively against Reldan in court. It would place Reldan's red Opel wagon in Susan Heynes's driveway and would involve the grossest dereliction of duty imaginable by a high-ranking police officer.

Chapter 8

To his horror, he saw a hand protruding above the weeds.

Matthew Shaindlin, a 20-year-old living with his parents and two younger brothers in Valley Cottage, New York, had dog-walking duty the evening of October 27, 1975. Although the month had started out warmer than usual, a chill in the air promised an end to the wonderful Indian summer the area had been enjoying. Matthew grabbed a jacket before leashing the dog and going out at about 5:00 PM.

Instead of taking the dog for the usual back-and-forth along Old Mill Road, the street where the Shaindlin family resided, Matthew thought he would try the wooded area near the Lake DeForest reservoir for a change, while it was still light enough to see clearly. It was only a few hundred yards from home, and he hadn't been down that way in more than a month.

A water company owned the heavily treed property and allowed locals to fish the lake, but didn't advertise that fact. You really had to be from the area to know about it. There was a small, unpaved parking area, from which a dirt path, not more than three or four feet wide, led down the gentle slope to the lakefront, some 250 feet from the road. The area was so secluded that it offered teenagers a perfect location for skinny-dipping and beer parties. Indeed, as Matthew headed down the path with his dog, empty beer cans and other litter marred the pristine setting.

Matthew was halfway to the lake when he was enveloped by a terrible odor, like that of a dead animal. He continued on to the water's edge, but there was nothing there that would account for the smell. Backtracking, Matthew stopped where the odor seemed strongest and peered down an offshoot of the main path. Twenty yards in, he could just make out what seemed like a store mannequin, partially covered by a branch. He made his way into the narrower, less traveled pathway, brambles whipping against his face with each step. As he got closer to the object, the odor got stronger and Matthew knew it was a human body, unclothed and lying prone in the dirt. He took a few more steps forward, but seeing the partial decomposition of the body and feeling his gorge rise, ventured no closer. He hurried home to call police.

Clarkstown police—the hamlet of Valley Cottage was part of the Town of Clarkstown—responded within ten minutes. After waiting in the parking area, Matthew Shaindlin led them to his grisly discovery. Veteran officers reeled at the sight. The victim's head and neck were almost completely decomposed and covered with maggots. The nude body appeared to be that of a woman, but it was difficult to tell for sure. Animals had eaten away the left buttock and calf of the right leg. A six-foot section of branch covered the back, in an apparent attempt to hide the body. The branch had been broken off a cedar tree, 10 feet away.

Detective Lieutenant Schnakenberg directed that Rockland County's Bureau of Criminal Investigation be summoned to take photos and assist in evidence collection. He also put in a request for the Medical Examiner's office to respond to what was, almost certainly, a homicide scene. Dr. Frederick Zugibe, chief medical examiner for Rockland County, or an assistant would be responsible for conducting the autopsy and determining the time and cause of death. It behooved the ME, therefore, not only to observe the crime scene intact but also to supervise removal of the body, which was crucial to preserving evidence. With less than an hour of daylight left, arrangements were made to bring in battery-powered portable lights, which would suffice for a cursory search and recovery of the body, but were not ideal for collecting evidence.

Nothing was touched until BCI technicians took photos from different angles and distances. An empty beer bottle was discovered a few feet from the body and bagged for fingerprint analysis. None of the victim's clothing was found. The ME's office personnel got there around 7:00 PM, and Dr. Zugibe, himself, arrived at eight o'clock.

It was readily apparent to the chief medical examiner that the victim had been dead for at least two weeks, a fact deduced from the presence of the maggots. There was a two-week life cycle between the time a mature fly laid its eggs in a host cadaver and the time full-grown larvae, or maggots, appeared, to do their work. After the autopsy, Zugibe would refine his estimate and conclude that death occurred within the three-day window of October 6 to 9, 1975.

Dr. Zugibe directed that plastic bags be placed over the victim's hands to preserve whatever fingerprints still existed. The body was then turned onto its back, revealing that the entire pelvic area had also been ravaged by animals and was missing. Zugibe noted the presence of a material around the skeletal neck of the victim, but because of the poor lighting, left it for closer examination during the autopsy. He ordered the body placed in a disaster pouch, a long zippered bag that would hold the remains relatively intact until the following day. His office personnel completed the removal of what was now determined to be an unidentified female and transported her body to their offices. Lieutenant Schnakenberg ordered officers to guard the scene in shifts until morning, when they would conduct a more thorough search of the area.

Back at Clarkstown police headquarters, Detective Brunjes received a phone call from Haworth, New Jersey, police officer Victor Pizza. An enterprising local newspaper reporter, knowledgeable about events earlier that month in New Jersey, had informed Pizza about the discovery of a woman's body in Valley Cottage. After learning that the body had not been identified, the Haworth officer provided details on two missing Bergen County women, Susan Heynes and Susan Reeve. Lieutenant Cono Delia of the BCPO also called Clarkstown police that night to see if there was a connection with the case his investigators were working. Lieutenant Delia promised to get dental records and forward them to Dr. Zugibe's office to assist in identifying the victim.

* * *

Tallman Mountain State Park, a 700-acre preserve off Route 9W in Rockland County, New York, was under the jurisdiction of the Palisades Interstate Park Commission, which kept gates to the facility open 24 hours a day to allow access for overnight campers. Robert Conklin, an 18-month employee of the Park Commission, was just back from a two-week vacation that Tuesday morning, October 28, 1975. Among Conklin's duties was the taking of water samples from a pipe, which drained a sewage treatment pump house and emptied into a swampy area adjacent to the Hudson River. The samples, which were used to monitor water temperature and chlorine levels, had to be collected once a week, by either Conklin or co-worker Michael Bettmann.

At 9:15 AM, Conklin started down a path toward the pump house to take the samples. The path's only purpose was to provide access to the sewage treatment facility; it led to no other park recreational feature or destination. Partway down, Conklin saw that a poplar sapling had been bent over, so as to block the path. He didn't think much of it at the time, but stopped to straighten the tree as best he could before continuing to the pump house.

Squatting to draw water at the drainage pipe, Conklin noticed a patch of ground where elephant reeds and cattails, the beautiful weeds that proliferated in the swampy surroundings near the pump house, had been flattened. As he began collecting water, Conklin glanced back toward the trampled area, about six feet away. To his horror, he saw a hand protruding above the weeds. Startled, he dropped the water samples and ran up the embankment to get his co-worker.

Together, Conklin and Bettmann returned to the area of the drainage pipe. Moving slightly closer, the two men saw not just the raised arm and hand, but also legs. The rest of the body was covered by weeds.

Bettmann had taken the water samples the previous week—on Monday, October 20, he recalled—while Conklin was on vacation, and he was certain that the body had not been there. They left the pump house to report their discovery. Police were duly summoned, as was the medical examiner for Rockland County.

* * *

Dr. Frederick Zugibe, in his capacity as a forensic pathologist, had performed more than 5,000 autopsies and he was used to dealing with bodies in even worse stages of decomposition than that of the female discovered in Valley Cottage. Before he could begin that autopsy on October 28, 1975, his office received a call from Palisades Interstate Parkway police that the nude body of a second young woman had turned up. Zugibe stopped preparations for the Valley Cottage victim's autopsy and hurried to Tallman Mountain State Park, site of the second grim discovery. Zugibe wasn't a believer in coincidence when it came to criminal investigations. Nude bodies of two young women, found within a day of each other and less than five miles apart? The veteran ME, already thinking serial killer, shuddered at the thought. He hoped he was wrong.

Dr. Zugibe had been chief medical examiner for Rockland County since 1969. His initial appointment to that position was used as a political football by some of the county commissioners, but Zugibe would go on to serve 33 years, distinguishing himself to the extent that the office would be renamed upon his retirement as the Dr. Frederick T. Zugibe Forensic Unit. He had a PhD in anatomy and microbiology from the University of Chicago and an MD from West Virginia University. Zugibe was qualified as a forensic pathologist, a specialty that included crime scene reconstruction and investigation of homicides and other violent deaths. He had published more than 80 peer-reviewed papers in that specialty and had authored a textbook on diagnostic pathology that was used around the world.

An experienced and competent forensic pathologist reaches his or her conclusions about the commission of a murder, including time and cause of death, not just from autopsy results but also from information gathered at the crime scene. Dr. Zugibe's presence at Tallman Mountain State Park to observe the body's removal would demonstrate the importance of that maxim.

Much of the second body, Zugibe saw, was covered with flat elephant reeds that had been hand-cut and purposely placed to conceal. The only body parts readily visible were those seen by Conklin and Bettmann, the two park workers. An arm was raised almost perpendicular to the ground, fixed in that position by later stages of rigor mortis, the stiffening of body parts after death due to contraction of muscle fibers. The time lapse for rigor to set in—and its lasting effects—varied with the weather, the degree of muscle exertion just before death, and other factors.

BCI photographed the scene from different angles, both before and after removal of the reeds. The victim was on her back. She had what appeared to be pantyhose wrapped around her neck. Decomposition was not as advanced as with the body discovered the day before.

The position of the raised arm in rigor mortis was the first indication Zugibe had of an incongruity. After death, arms and legs fall level with the ground, unless some other force or object holds them up. There was no such factor here that could account for the girl's arm being raised. Also, lividity, the gravitational effect that causes blood in a dead body to seek the lowest level, had set in. About two hours after blood settles, it forms a gel-like substance that stays in place, even after the body is moved. This process causes a permanent, reddish discoloration of the skin, at least until decomposition occurs. With this victim, Zugibe observed, the lividity was not consistent with the position of the body.

Zugibe was sure the body had been moved to the location some time after death, a fact he further substantiated during the autopsy. Willow leaves were embedded in the skin, stuck there during initial stages of decomposition. There were no willow trees anywhere near the place where this second victim's body was found.

Dr. Zugibe, himself, conducted both autopsies on October 28, one right after the other, starting with the Valley Cottage body. The material around that victim's neck—Zugibe had observed it at the scene, but the lighting was too poor to identify it—turned out to be pantyhose, with a stick double-knotted into the material as a garrote, a twisting aid to the killer so he could tighten the pantyhose noose with even greater force.

There are two main types of strangulation, Zugibe would later testify: one done using just the hands and the other by means of a ligature—a fiber, wire, or rope wrapped around the neck, as with a hangman's noose. In the case of the Valley Cottage victim, Zugibe determined the killer used a combination of the two methods to commit the murder, manual- and ligature-type strangulation. He reached this conclusion because, during the autopsy, he found a fractured hyoid, a delicate, U-shaped bone in the neck. In ligature strangulation, it is "very, very rare," Zugibe would later testify, for the hyoid to be fractured. A fractured hyoid is ordinarily a tip-off for manual strangulation, the pressure of hands on the neck accounting for that result. Here, the killer had to have used both strong hand pressure and the pantyhose noose to achieve this same result. As Zugibe put it, the combination was achieved by "a compression of the neck with the ligature . . . ," while, "at the same time, putting pressure on the neck with the hand, which fractured the hyoid bone." The person committing this act had to exert a lot of force with his hand, Zugibe said. He had to be very strong and . . . very driven.

Through the use of dental records and fingerprints, the Valley Cottage body was later confirmed to be Susan Heynes. Because of the missing pelvic area, Zugibe could not determine if she had been raped before being killed. There was nothing left to provide clues in that regard.

The body of the woman discovered in Tallman Mountain State Park still had gold filigree earrings in its pierced ears, which Zugibe gently removed before proceeding with that autopsy. This victim would later be positively identified as Susan Reeve, using records supplied by her dentist. Susan's mother would also identify the distinctive gold earrings as being the same earrings her daughter wore to work the morning of October 14.

The ME observed that the pantyhose ligature was knotted around this victim's neck in a way similar to the Valley Cottage victim, with an important exception. There was no stick double-knotted in the pantyhose to serve as a garrote; but, if the body had been moved, as Zugibe thought, that could account for the absence of a stick, which could have fallen out. This victim's hyoid bone was fractured in exactly the same place as the hyoid bone in the first victim, causing Dr. Zugibe to conclude that this, too, was a "combination strangulation," one employing both manual force and the pantyhose ligature. The cause of death for both women was listed as asphyxiation due to strangulation, which caused cardiac arrest.

One other crucial fact differentiated the Reeve case from the Heynes case. Dr. Zugibe found a contusion and an abrasion on the vaginal wall of Reeve's body. The contusion, or bruise, and the abrasion, a wearing away of skin from friction, enabled the ME to conclude that Susan Reeve was forcibly penetrated before she was killed. Zugibe also found traces of human semen in the girl's vagina. This proof of vaginal penetration in a forceful manner would lead to a reasonable conclusion that Susan Reeve had been raped before she was strangled to death. That fact—the commission of an additional felony with the killing—elevated her murder to a crime of the *first* degree, which would warrant a mandatory life sentence.*

---

*At the time of the Heynes and Reeve murders, the death penalty did not exist in New Jersey. Capital punishment had been declared unconstitutional by the US Supreme Court in June 1972. As a result, all state death penalty statutes, including New Jersey's, were invalidated. It wasn't until 1976 that the Supreme Court approved new death penalty guidelines, thereby allowing states to create new capital punishment statutes, which New Jersey did in 1982. Robert Reldan's crimes fell within that window of no operable death penalty statute in New Jersey, and, consequently, he never faced that sanction. New Jersey would later repeal its death penalty law, without ever executing anyone since its reinstatement.

Dr. Zugibe estimated the date of Susan Reeve's death to be on or about October 14, which was, of course, the date she was abducted. The fact that Michael Bettmann had taken water samples from the pump house site on Monday, October 20, with no dead body visible near the drainpipe, confirmed Zugibe's conclusion that the young woman had been killed earlier and her body dumped in another location, before being moved to Tallman Mountain State Park.

* * *

Roberta Gimbel dated Robert Reldan, even while he was married to Judy. Investigators got her name from Reldan's address book, which would be seized in the November 13 search of his apartment, after he became a suspect in the murders. In an interview shortly thereafter, Gimbel told investigators that she and Reldan had picnicked in Tallman Mountain State Park in August 1975. She accompanied investigators to the site, less than 100 yards from where Susan Reeve's body was found. In September 1975, Gimbel said, she and Reldan took a drive along Old Mill Road in Valley Cottage, New York, and Reldan pointed out to her the nearby apartments where he had once lived with Judy Rosenberg. They stopped to stroll through woods and feed ducks at a pond, though she couldn't remember the precise location. The Lake DeForest reservoir property, where Susan Heynes's body was found, fronted on Old Mill Road.

Ms. Gimbel, who was friendly with Reldan's family and would become less cooperative as time wore on, also revealed to investigators that Reldan had phoned her from jail after he became a suspect in the murders. She informed him that police were coming to interview her.

"Don't take them to Old Mill Road or Tallman Park," Reldan told her. "It would look real bad for me."

Chapter 9

A danger to any young, attractive woman walking alone.

The Record, New Jersey's largest-circulation evening newspaper in the mid-1970s, had a reach well beyond Bergen County. As one might expect, the mysterious disappearances of two young women from the paper's home county, within days of each other, touched a nerve, and the paper rightly pounced on the story. In today's 24/7 cable news environment, coverage would have been nationwide for the Heynes/Reeve abductions and murders, which had the sensational elements cable stations thrive on. But, in 1975, when the cable-TV phenomenon was in its infancy and New York City-based broadcast media gave short shrift to happenings across the river, print media were the major source of local news for New Jersey residents.

The Susan Heynes disappearance received its share of attention, but it wasn't until the second girl's abduction that *Record* readers really focused on what appeared like a crime wave in the making—one that could conceivably affect them, personally. When the two bodies were discovered right next door in Rockland County, New York, newspaper coverage, and the public's fear factor, exploded. *The Record* began referring to the murders as the "*Susan* strangulations," and any woman so-named took special precautions. Dr. Frederick Zugibe actually fueled public apprehension about the horrendous crimes in a bit of uncharacteristic, loose-tongued speculation. "The murderer could strike again," he was quoted as saying. "This type of individual is mentally ill and is a danger to any young, attractive woman walking alone."

Susan Reeve's body was identified first, because of easier access to her dental records. Susan Heynes last saw a dentist in South Africa, where she and Jonathan Heynes had both worked before their marriage. Her records had to be flown in from that country, causing a slight delay in confirming her identity.

The worst fears of the victims' families were borne out late on October 29, 1975, when the Rockland County ME's office confirmed both identifications. These were no longer missing persons cases; law enforcement efforts shifted to finding the murderer or murderers, rather than finding the two women. *The Record*'s front-page, above-the-fold headline in its October 30 edition noted the change: "Police retrace steps of strangled women." A second reference appeared in the same paper, with side-by-side photos of Arthur Reeve and Jonathan Heynes. The caption read, "The waiting is over, but not the torment."

There is always a question of how much public disclosure police agencies should engage in during an investigation. They want to encourage potential witnesses to come forward with information. An individual may not recognize the importance of a seemingly unconnected fact, like a sandblasting mask found lying in the roadway, while such a discovery might be hugely relevant to police, who have the big picture before them. There is also a responsibility to keep the public informed about anything affecting safety, like a perpetrator's description or a killer's method of targeting victims.

By the same token, investigators do not want to give out too many details. Holding some facts from the public, police can debunk the false confessions that inevitably turn up in a notorious murder investigation from sick individuals craving the spotlight, no matter what the circumstances. Prosecutors also have an ethical responsibility *not* to try a case in the newspapers by releasing information designed more to inflame than to inform. An overzealous prosecutor mustn't taint potential jurors by disclosing too much to the press before a trial even begins. There are also the sensibilities of a victim's family to consider. It was not necessary, for example, to comment in explicit detail about the condition of Susan Heynes's body when found or about evidence showing that Susan Reeve had been raped before she was murdered.

Bergen County Prosecutor Joe Woodcock placed a lid on anyone connected to the case giving out information without his permission. As chief law enforcement officer of the county, he had that authority. And, for the most part, police agencies participating in the investigation complied with his orders. It was possible to publicize just enough to inspire helpful citizens to come forward with information. Indeed, during early stages of the investigation, the BCPO needed all the help it could get.

The first big lead came from a telephone call Louisa Pittaluga placed to Demarest Police at 6:39 PM on October 31. She reported that her son Mark had found a mask of some type on Anderson Avenue the night of October 14, at a spot just north of Orchard Road. Mrs. Pittaluga didn't know if this mask had anything to do with the murder investigations, but decided to call, she said, "just to be on the safe side." Demarest Patrolman Richard Ross went to the Pittaluga residence and picked up the mask. He tagged the item, taking care to handle it as little as possible to preserve any fingerprints, and placed it in the detective bureau safe.

The next day, BCPO Investigator Jay Berman and other officers interviewed Louisa and Mark Pittaluga at their home and learned the circumstances surrounding their finding of the mask. Mark was able to fix the date as October 14 because of a conversation he had with his friend Gus Reeve, Susan's brother, at school the next day. Mark said he and his mother found the mask around 7:30 PM. The officers noted the missing glass faceplate and asked Mark about it. The boy said it was that way when he picked it up from the roadway. Police also took the Pittalugas to Anderson Avenue and had them point out exactly where they found the mask. Photos were taken of the location by Detective Thomas Prime of Demarest.

Investigators knew the mask was going to be sent to the Latent Fingerprint Section of the FBI lab in Washington to determine whose prints, if any, were present. Mark's and his mother's prints were taken so they could be excluded as known individuals who may have touched the mask. The fingerprint analysis would come to naught, however; lab technicians detected no useable prints on the mask. The rough surface of the canvas-type material wasn't conducive to retaining latent prints.

Investigators had already interviewed Elliott Pickens, owner of Taylor Rental Center, on October 29, based on Reldan's mention of that business in his October 22 interview. They knew Reldan rented sandblasting equipment on October 14 and returned everything but the mask on the morning of October 15. Reldan paid a $29.50 charge for the lost mask, and Pickens told them he ordered a replacement that same day, since he only kept one on hand at a time.

Before showing Pickens the mask found by the Pittalugas and asking him to identify it, if he could, investigators decided to re-interview John Rudolph, Reldan's helper at the October 14 house-painting job. Rudolph confirmed that Reldan used sandblasting equipment that day, including a protective mask, to take old paint off Dr. Maniatis's house. He said Reldan dropped the mask, and the glass eye-protection piece became dislodged and couldn't be refitted. Rudolph last saw the broken mask in Reldan's red Opel wagon late in the day. After speaking with Rudolph on November 5, investigators went to see Pickens that same day. He recalled that Reldan had returned just the glass piece, which Pickens discarded because it was useless without the mask. When investigators showed Pickens the mask that was recovered from the Pittaluga family, he said it was the same type mask he rented to Robert Reldan on October 14.

* * *

Reldan began feeling pressure, no doubt, during and after his October 22 interview with Investigator Denning. That may have been what motivated his decision to move Susan Reeve's body from its original location—most likely near the Heynes disposal site in Valley Cottage, which abounded in willow trees—to Tallman State Park, as Dr. Zugibe deduced. Reldan correctly assumed the discovery of two bodies in a common dumping ground would lead any competent detective to conclude that the same person committed both murders. By moving Reeve's body to a location five miles distant, he undoubtedly hoped to eliminate that connection between the two crimes. It was a futile hope, given other similarities—most notably, the method of strangulation.

Reldan was also following events through newspaper reporting. Judy Reldan would later tell investigators that her husband once remarked while reading the paper, "Jesus Christ, they found one of the bodies in Valley Cottage," a reference to where they'd lived together while Reldan was out on parole for the Caplan rape. He was feigning surprise for his wife's benefit, but may also have been expressing his own shock at the relatively quick discovery of this victim's body, which he had taken pains to conceal.

In a bizarre turn of events, Reldan committed two daylight burglaries—on October 30 and 31, 1975—in a way that strongly suggested he wanted to be caught. Prendergast and Gartner had alluded to this psychological need in Reldan when Jay Berman interviewed them. The burglaries might have been Reldan's attempt to throw investigators off his scent by casting himself as just a petty, two-bit burglar—decidedly not someone who should be suspected of murder. This possible motive is supported by Reldan's claim of a healthy financial condition at the time. He boasted to Investigator Ed Denning on October 22 of having upwards of $14,000 in the bank. He didn't need money, he said. If, indeed, the two October burglaries were a smokescreen, the subterfuge didn't work. By this time, Reldan had become the case's sole "person of interest."

The October 30 crime was an attempted burglary of the Muino residence in Norwood, another small town in the northern valley region of Bergen County. Reldan pulled his red Opel into the driveway at two o'clock in the afternoon and brazenly parked it there. He then placed a milk crate against a shed and climbed to the shed's roof, using that perch to reach the second floor of the residence. Reldan didn't get farther than the second-story window of the master bedroom: Mrs. Muino surprised him in the act of entering, and he immediately jumped to the ground and drove off.

As Reldan fled the scene, Mrs. Muino got a fleeting look at his vehicle, describing it as a red, foreign-make station wagon, but a neighbor working in his yard nailed it cold. The vehicle was a 1969 Opel Kadett wagon, he said. Mrs. Muino would later pick Reldan out of a photo array. She said he was wearing a blue ski jacket and orange gloves when she saw him.

On October 31, shortly after 10:30 AM, police were called to the home of Richard and Natalie Leeds at 1 High View Court in Closter. Mr.

Leeds told officers he heard his wife leave to walk their dog. Minutes later, he went into the kitchen and there stood a stranger, holding a fistful of money in one hand and Mrs. Leeds's pocketbook in the other. Leeds was startled and didn't know what to make of the confrontation. He actually engaged the man in a brief, almost comical conversation. "Excuse me," he said. "What are you doing here? Can I help you?"

The stranger, whom Leeds later identified as Robert Reldan, replied, "Gee, no. That's okay." Reldan then turned and ran out the door, with Richard Leeds in hot pursuit.

The chase lasted a few blocks before Leeds gave up and returned home to call police. By then, Mrs. Leeds was back with the dog. She said she hadn't noticed anyone in the vicinity when she went out, except for the man painting Dr. Maniatis's house across the street at 11 High View Court. Police went looking for the workman, but he was nowhere to be found. His car was still there, though, in the driveway of the Maniatis home: a 1969 red Opel Kadett station wagon, with a blue ski jacket stuffed in the front passenger's seat. Orange gloves were in the jacket's pockets. Closter police towed the vehicle to their garage and impounded it.

A warrant was issued for the arrest of Robert Reldan, who turned himself in later that day accompanied by his lawyer, Frank Lucianna. Prosecutors were able to get bail set at $750,000, an extraordinary amount for two burglaries. The supposed justification was Reldan's status as a parole violator and the added risk of his fleeing the jurisdiction.

At ten o'clock on the night of October 31, within five hours of Reldan's arrest on the burglary charges, investigators obtained a search warrant for the 1969 Opel Kadett station wagon, ostensibly to look for evidence pertaining to the two burglaries, but really wanting to find anything that might help their double-murder investigation. In their opinion, they didn't have probable cause to obtain a search warrant based on the two murders. So, in the search warrant application, no mention was made of the Heynes/Reeve case. That omission would cause significant problems for the prosecution later on.

The warrant was executed at 10:00 AM on November 1, while the Opel was in the Closter police impound garage. FBI Special Agents Hilverda and Robinson joined the search, supported by BCPO personnel and local officers. It would be the first time the technical expertise of the FBI laboratory in Washington DC would be brought to bear in the case.

What investigators were looking for, in effect, was anything that might tie the two murdered women to Reldan's vehicle. All the floor mats, front and rear, were placed in secure containers, properly tagged to document the chain of evidence—a requirement in any criminal investigation. Evidence must be accounted for during every step of the

71

process, from its initial collection to its ultimate use as a courtroom exhibit. The carpeting was removed from the front, rear, and cargo area flooring, and similarly bagged and marked. Every inch of the vehicle's interior was vacuumed with special apparatus used to collect microscopic particles that might have evidentiary value, such as hairs, fibers, and blood traces. The vehicle was dusted for fingerprints, inside and out. Soil samples were taken from the four wheel wells. All collected materials were forwarded to the FBI lab for detailed analysis.

It would be two months before the results became known.

* * *

The initial widespread newspaper coverage attending the discovery and identification of the bodies was followed by new stories reporting Robert Reldan's arrest for the two residential burglaries. The thing that guaranteed above-the-fold, front-page coverage for what otherwise would have been a relatively minor criminal episode—burglaries are fairly common and unremarkable—was a leak from an unnamed, informed source, duly reported by *The Record*: Robert Reldan was a prime suspect in the Heynes/Reeve murders. These articles also requested the public's assistance in the continuing investigation.

This renewed publicity generated an almost immediate response. Mary and Joseph Fabrocini came forward and made known their observations on the evening of October 14. They identified Susan Reeve by photo as the girl they encountered on Anderson Avenue, just before the County Road intersection. From memory, Mrs. Fabrocini later drew a sketch of the girl's dress that almost exactly matched a sketch drawn by the girl's mother. There was no doubt about whom they saw walking north on Anderson Avenue that evening. Even more important was Joseph Fabrocini's recollection of the small "maroon" station wagon, loaded with junk, that suddenly turned in front of them and headed in Susan Reeve's direction.

Stephen Prato called Demarest police and told them about the girl he saw on the west side of Anderson Avenue walking north toward Orchard Road and about the man in rough workman's clothing walking in close proximity behind her. Prato had no recollection of a vehicle parked in the vicinity and he could not identify Reldan from a photo array; but his description of the girl and the man left little doubt as to who they were—Susan Reeve, being stalked by Robert Reldan.

One can surmise what took place from the time Reldan first caught sight of the lone girl and made his abrupt turn off County Road to follow her. He probably drove slowly past Susan Reeve as she was walking in a northerly direction on the east side of Anderson Avenue. (The Fabrocinis placed Reeve there, saying that she crossed in front of them to get to the east side of Anderson, which had a sidewalk at its lower end.) Then, Reldan drove on ahead, pulling over and parking his vehicle across from Orchard Road, where Raymond Lozier would see it shortly thereafter. Reldan sat a few minutes, glancing in his rearview mirror to watch the girl's approach and devising his plan to abduct her. He then got out of his car and proceeded south on Anderson, walking on the east side of the roadway toward the approaching woman.

At some point, Susan Reeve, still walking north on the east side of Anderson, must have seen the stranger coming toward her, dressed in "rough workman's clothing" that may have been out of place in the neighborhood. Perhaps alarmed, but at least wanting to put space between that man and herself, Reeve crossed Anderson and began walking on the *west* side of that road, the side Stephen Prato saw her on. Reldan observed this, but continued in a southerly direction past the girl, before he, too, crossed the street to the west side and turned to walk north, 20 to 30 yards behind the girl. One can imagine Susan Reeve casting nervous glances behind her; she had to have sensed she was being followed. But it was still light out and she was only a quarter-mile or so from Orchard Road, the street where she lived. And so, she continued on, hoping the twinge of fear she felt was unwarranted.

After the spate of publicity following Reldan's burglary arrest (and his being named a suspect in the murders), Raymond Lozier finally contacted police in early November and told them what he saw on Anderson Avenue the evening of October 14. How Susan Reeve and Reldan got from the place where Stephen Prato saw them—on the west side of Anderson, a quarter-mile south of Orchard Road—to the place Raymond Lozier saw them—on the east side of Anderson, directly opposite Orchard Road and next to Reldan's parked vehicle—is open to speculation.

Given Reldan's history of using a pretext or ruse to get close to his female victims, one can assume he did the same thing that evening, perhaps calling to Susan Reeve and, posing as a lost motorist to put her off guard, asking for directions. Once he got next to her, Reldan probably used a handgun to gain control over the girl. He couldn't chance overpowering her right there, more than a hundred yards from his vehicle, with the brute force of a chokehold. Too many people might have seen him and intervened. Also, Raymond Lozier did not see a struggling Susan Reeve standing next to Reldan; rather, she was frozen to her spot, he said, staring directly at Reldan, perhaps transfixed by the point of a gun. Reldan had a prior record of carrying a handgun in a motor vehicle. It was not likely a habit he abandoned.

Lozier's descriptions of the two individuals he saw were vague, but he was close in his description of Reldan's vehicle—not exact, but close. He said it was a small wagon, with a roof rack and distinctive front grille. He couldn't recall if it had two or four doors and was unclear about its color. He gave investigators a sketch of the scene and vehicle.

Six weeks after his initial interview, Raymond Lozier went to Closter police headquarters to get fingerprinted for his job as a licensed securities salesman. He passed through the police garage, where Reldan's 1969 red Opel Kadett wagon was still under impound for the October burglaries. Lozier was taken aback, absolutely certain that this was the same vehicle he'd seen parked on Anderson Avenue the evening of October 14. The distinctive grille cinched it for him. He immediately called Special Agent John DiMarchi, the FBI agent who had interviewed him on November 3, and reported this information.

* * *

Among the personal effects found in Reldan's Opel during the November 1 search was a small red notebook. It had been sent to the FBI laboratory along with everything else, but when it was determined that the notebook held no useful trace evidence—fingerprints, hairs, or fibers—it was returned to the BCPO. The notebook did contain partial names and phone numbers, one of which led Investigator Ed Denning and Detective Ralph Cenicola to the home of a 17-year-old girl in Bergen County. After an initial reluctance to talk about her connection to Robert Reldan, the girl finally broke down and related the following story to the officers.

She was introduced to Reldan in mid-August 1975 by a mutual friend. The girl, her male friend, and Reldan chatted briefly in a coffee shop near a job site where Reldan was working. Reldan looked and acted much younger than his 35 years. The talk turned to the quality of marijuana Reldan and the girl's male friend had recently smoked. About a week after this initial encounter, the same friend phoned the girl and asked if she wanted to accompany him and Reldan on a marijuana-buying trip to New York City. The girl said she felt like getting high and agreed to go along, but the trip never happened. The friend ended up having to work, and the girl drove with Reldan, alone, to his apartment in Tenafly. This was Reldan's residence with Judy, whom he had married just two months earlier. Reldan told the girl he wanted to pick up some "grass" at his apartment, and she accompanied him inside.

They both drank beer and smoked a joint in the apartment, and, after a while, Reldan began talking about his wife and stepson. The girl asked Reldan if his wife minded his bringing girls to their apartment, and he replied she "was cool" about such things. Then, Reldan turned the discussion to sex. He told her that, when he was younger, he was attracted to "guys," but he'd had lots of experience with women, too, and had received compliments from them on his sexual prowess. The girl said she became very nervous at this point and didn't respond to Reldan's comments. When he said he wanted "make it" with her, she replied that she'd come to his apartment only to smoke.

Reldan wouldn't take *no* for an answer and began touching and kissing her. They were seated on an open sofa bed, and Reldan forced her shoulders down on the bed. The girl told the officers that Reldan "was very strong and [she] could not get out of his grasp." Reldan told her he was not trying to hurt her—he just wanted to "make her feel good." She threatened to scream, but Reldan scoffed and told her to go ahead and scream, that no one would hear her. She became increasingly terrified; the more she resisted him, the stronger he got. As they struggled, she noted that Reldan "had a crazy look in his eyes."

She began to cry hysterically, and Reldan told her to stop, that "this is supposed to feel good. You look like you're enjoying it." She eventually reached a point where she was so fearful that her life was in danger that she decided not to resist further. She allowed Reldan to undress her, whereupon he sexually assaulted her for about 20 minutes. When he was finished, he asked if she wanted to take a shower. She said no, she just wanted to go home. They both dressed and Reldan drove her home. That was the last time she had any contact with Robert Reldan.

During the drive to her home, Reldan said, "Now that wasn't so bad, was it?"

* * *

Deputy Attorney General Charles Buckley joined the Division of Criminal Justice—the criminal prosecution arm of the New Jersey Attorney General's office—in 1972, after working two years as an assistant prosecutor in Bergen County. Buckley tried cases the way he lived his life—as a nose-to-the-grindstone, blue-collar type of guy, with all the best characteristics a working class background implies. He would spend 25 years as one of the Division's top trial prosecutors before his retirement in 1998. For most of that time, he acted as a modern-day legal Paladin—"have briefcase, will travel"—crisscrossing New Jersey to try the most difficult cases on behalf of the State. Most criminal prosecutions are handled by local county prosecutors, except when they have legal conflicts or when a state grand jury, rather than a county grand jury, issues the indictment. In those instances, the Division calls upon its best legal guns—men and women like Charles Buckley.

Buckley put away the acting boss of the Philadelphia/Atlantic

City based Bruno-Scarfo crime family, as well as the Genovese crime family soldier in charge of the Hudson County waterfront in a trial that took six months to complete. In the first televised trial in New Jersey, he convicted a sitting Camden County judge accused of accepting bribes to fix sentences. Other public officials who felt DAG Charles Buckley's brand of justice included a state official who took bribes relating to bridge and road construction, a mayor and three planning board officials in a Bergen County town who took bribes from real estate developers, and, in separate trials, a Hudson County police chief, a Passaic County detective, and two City of Paterson cops—all convicted of misconduct involving organized crime.

Buckley also served as Acting County Prosecutor—the chief law enforcement officer—in five New Jersey counties, while the process to appoint a permanent prosecutor may have been stalled for any number of reasons peculiar to New Jersey politics.

Buckley was born on May 31, 1933, and grew up in Kearny, New Jersey, a diverse Hudson County town noted for high percentages of Scottish and Scots-Irish immigrants. Besides fielding some of New Jersey's best soccer teams, Kearny was renowned for its fish and chips shops, chief among them the Thistle and the Argyle. After high school, Buckley worked for Western Electric making telephone equipment for Ma Bell. He enlisted in the Navy in 1954, spending most of his two-year tour aboard the *USS Lloyd Thomas*, an anti-submarine destroyer.

Upon his honorable discharge from the service, Buckley began night school at Fairleigh Dickinson University, while working full-time. In time, he was able to switch priorities, going to school full-time and working part-time. It took five years to get his undergraduate degree, part of which he spent at Rutgers Law School in Newark, the state university. Rutgers accepted students back then with three years of undergraduate work. Buckley got his law degree in 1963, but had to serve a nine-month clerkship with a practicing attorney, an apprentice-like program no longer required by the New Jersey Bar. He handled negligence cases for Allstate Insurance Company before finding his niche as a trial prosecutor.

In 1975, Buckley lived in Norwood with his wife Ruth and two sons. He was following the Heynes/Reeve murder case closely that autumn, not only out of professional interest but also because the crimes, including Reldan's strange daytime burglaries, were happening right in his family's backyard, so to speak—the northern valley region of Bergen County. Ruth Buckley shared her husband's interest in the case and, during one evening discussion, asked him if there was a chance he'd be involved in the prosecution. Buckley reminded her that the County Prosecutor's office, not the Division of Criminal Justice, handled crimes like these.

No, he assured her, there was no chance he would be involved in this prosecution.

Ten years later, after the case took a tortuous path no one could have predicted, Deputy Attorney General Charles Buckley would take over as lead prosecutor in the matter of the State of New Jersey v. Robert R. Reldan, the indictment charging Reldan with the murders of Susan Heynes and Susan Reeve.

Chapter 10

I've got to have the ring. I've got to have that ring.

Neither Reldan nor his parents had funds to post the $750,000 bail that had been set for the Norwood and Closter burglaries; the amount was clearly based on his status as prime suspect in the Heynes and Reeve murders.[*] And, apparently, Aunt Lillian refused to pay the 10% cash bond fee or to put up her extensive real estate holdings as collateral, which could have sprung Reldan. One of the few times when Lillian Booth failed to come to her Bobby's rescue, the incident may have contributed to his growing resentment toward her.

With Reldan tucked safely away in jail, BCPO investigators could proceed at a deliberate pace in building their case against him for the two murders. All they really had so far, thanks to publicity-driven leads that were coming in to the command center, were important but circumstantial bits and pieces tying Reldan solely to the Susan Reeve case. It would be a while before they had lab results from the search of the Opel station wagon. Although there was enough to focus everyone's attention on Reldan as the only suspect in both crimes, there was certainly not yet enough to indict him for either crime, let alone to obtain a conviction at trial.

Circumstantial evidence is often disparaged, especially by defense attorneys, as being inferior to direct evidence. That has become the public perception, as well, thanks largely to law-and-order, "ripped from the headlines" television shows that perpetuate the fiction. In fact, circumstantial evidence can be equally if not more powerful in getting at the truth.

Take, for example, eyewitness identifications, a common form of direct evidence. They are subject to a range of factors that might diminish their validity—the lighting conditions under which a crime is viewed, obstructions to the view, the amount of time an observation lasts, any eyesight limitations a witness has, racial or ethnic differences between the witness and the person he or she is identifying, the distraction a gun or other weapon might cause, and so on. Actor Joe Pesci's cross-examination

---

[*]This amount of bail is grossly above what would normally be set for two burglaries, even considering Reldan's record. Word had to have been quietly passed to the judge (the Honorable Morris Malech, who would preside at a subsequent Reldan trial) that Reldan was a suspect in two murders and had to be kept off the streets. Being a suspect, without charges lodged, is not a legal basis for setting bail amounts.

of the eyewitnesses in the 1992 movie, *My Cousin Vinny*, was a humorous but realistic example of the limitations of such testimony. ("How many fingers am I holding up now, Dear?" Vinny asked an elderly eyewitness, whose Coke-bottle-sized lenses apparently were not strong enough.) Increasingly aware of the potential for eyewitness unreliability, courts are now allowing defense attorneys to present experts at trial to cast doubt on this type of direct evidence.

Circumstantial evidence, on the other hand, can be highly probative. If a surveillance camera, for example, shows a suspect entering a secure location at 11:00 AM and exiting 30 minutes later, with no other traffic in or out, and if a crime, like robbery or murder, is shown to have been committed within that secure location during the 11:00 to 11:30 AM timeframe, then it's a pretty safe bet—even without an eyewitness—that the suspect shown on camera did the deed.

Investigators were beginning to build a strong circumstantial case against Reldan for the Reeve abduction and murder. His own statement to Investigator Ed Denning on October 22 placed him in the immediate vicinity of the abduction at the relevant time. His lie about having a drink at the Orbit Inn—creating a bogus alibi for himself, in other words—showed that he had something to hide. Two witnesses, Joseph Fabrocini and Raymond Lozier, saw a small station wagon—Reldan's vehicle, or one very similar—on Anderson Avenue in Demarest at about the time of the abduction. Stephen Prato and Lozier saw a man fitting Reldan's description in close proximity to a woman fitting Susan Reeve's description, and both men concurred in the sinister implications of what they had observed. Roberta Gimbel established Reldan's familiarity with the remote location where Reeve's body was found; she and Reldan had picnicked less than 100 yards from the site. The damaged sandblasting mask, found 50 yards or so from the Reeve abduction scene, was still another link in what was turning out to be a convincing chain of evidence.

In contrast, investigators had almost nothing tying Reldan to Susan Heynes's abduction and murder. True, the body was dumped in a secluded area of Valley Cottage—where Reldan once lived—and both victims were killed in a signature way, pointing to Reldan. But the evidence was not even close to sufficient. Investigators needed a break in the Susan Heynes case, something to connect Robert Reldan to her tragic end.

On November 10, 1975, they got their break. Shortly after five o'clock that evening, James McBride, Director of Security for Macy's Herald Square department store in New York City, phoned the Bergen County Prosecutor's Office. When the phone was answered, McBride said that he had information pertaining to Robert Reldan. He was immediately put through to Lieutenant Cono Delia, head of the homicide squad.

McBride told Delia that an individual identifying himself as Robert Reldan sold a woman's engagement ring to the jewelry brokerage department at Macy's on October 21, 1975. He was paid $100 for the ring. That same man returned to the store on the twenty-third, two days later, demanding the ring back. McBride explained that, under New York law, any jeweler buying secondhand pieces from private individuals must keep the items for 15 days before reselling them or breaking them down into their component parts for reuse. The idea behind the law was to give private sellers the opportunity to change their minds and get their pieces back. Also, it provided police with a reasonable opportunity to recover stolen goods. McBride told the lieutenant that the ring was located on October 23 and returned to the customer.

Lieutenant Delia recognized immediately the importance of the information and informed McBride that he would have investigators follow up with Macy's employees who were involved in Reldan's transaction. He arranged for a meeting that very night.

Earlier in the investigation, Jonathan Heynes had told police that his wife always wore an unusual engagement ring, which they picked out together at Harrod's, England's world-famous department store, on January 18, 1975. Even though it wasn't the most expensive ring they looked at, Susan fell in love with its distinctive design, which Harrod's described as "18-karat white gold, with 15 brilliant-cut diamonds (total weight 1.08 carats) arranged in a cluster." Jonathan paid 370 British pounds for the ring, or about $885.

When Susan Heynes's body was found, the ring was missing. Police rightly assumed that her killer took it. They didn't know if it had been taken as a trophy—the common practice of serial killers to collect things from victims for their own, ongoing gratification—or for the profit it might bring when sold. Before getting the call from McBride at Macy's, the police had anticipated that the ring's design might have investigative importance later, so, through Jonathan Heynes, they had already requested a detailed sketch of the ring from Harrod's. Indeed, Saunders Jewellery Limited in London, the company that made the ring and wholesaled it to Harrod's, produced the sketch on November 7, and arrangements were underway to have it sent to investigators in New Jersey.

FBI Special Agents William Klotz and Thomas Byrnes, along with Haworth Police Lieutenant Louis Herouart, were dispatched to Macy's in New York, where they met with James McBride and Julius Herrmann, manager of the fine jewelry department at the Herald Square store. Herrmann related that an individual, who identified himself as Robert Reldan, came into the store on October 21 with several pieces of jewelry to sell. To verify the man's identity, he presented a New Jersey driver's license; the state did not use license photos back then. Melvin Norman, an associate manager in the department, took care of him. Norman looked over the several items Reldan wanted to sell, and purchased just one—the fancy woman's engagement ring—for $100. A Macy's check was issued to the man, who left the store, only to return on the morning of October 23, when he asked that the sale be canceled and the ring returned to him. He said "his wife" had changed her mind about selling it. He had $100 in cash to pay back the money he had received for the sale.

When Reldan came back on the twenty-third, the ring couldn't be immediately located. Melvin Norman had somehow incorrectly marked the envelope in which the ring had been placed, and other jewelry not connected to Reldan was in that envelope. Norman wasn't in the store at the time. Reldan became irate, demanding his ring. In a voice loud enough to call attention to himself, Reldan declared, "I've got to have the ring. I've got to have that ring."

Reldan was persuaded to return to the store after noon, when Melvin Norman was scheduled to begin work, and, indeed, that is exactly what occurred. Reldan came back, Norman was there, and the ring was located. Reldan returned the $100 in cash and got the ring back.

Clearly, the motivation behind Reldan's retrieval of the ring was his interview with Investigator Ed Denning on October 22, when he found out that he was a suspect. He realized that he had shown identification when he sold Macy's the ring on October 21, producing a record that tied him definitively to Susan Heynes. He had carelessly used his true driver's license, rather than one of the bogus forms of identification he possessed. Reldan had to get the ring back and try, if he could, to erase the entire transaction. His antics at the store—when the Macy's employees couldn't locate the ring right away—only served to fix him more indelibly in the minds of those who witnessed the scene. In fact, one employee remembered the fuss Reldan made, and, when that employee later read a newspaper article mentioning Robert Reldan's name as a suspect in the two murders, he brought the information to the attention of his supervisor. That's how McBride learned of it.

There was a suspicion that Melvin Norman purposely removed the engagement ring from Reldan's envelope at Macy's and substituted the extraneous jewelry items, so that he, instead of his employer, could profit from the transaction. Norman must have recognized the ring's value when he first examined it. Jonathan Heynes had paid the equivalent of $885 for the ring in England and Norman, after striking a deal with Reldan to obtain it for $100, may have decided to put it aside for his own private sale. Despite that, Melvin Norman was the primary link to the most damning piece of evidence that prosecutors had, tying Reldan to the Heynes murder. He was, after all, the only person who had examined Susan Heynes's ring in detail *after* the woman's murder. Someone else, though, may have got a look.

Investigators learned that John Truncali, the owner of Closter Jewelers, had also been approached by Reldan regarding a possible purchase of what was most likely the Heynes engagement ring. Reldan had offhandedly given the jeweler's name to Investigator Denning during the October 22 interview, not in any particular context but as someone Reldan knew through his cousin, who worked in Truncali's store. Investigators began interviewing the store owner, even before the call came from Macy's security chief McBride. They spoke with him several times in early November and established that he was a regular buyer of jewelry offered up by Reldan. Truncali had an amazing lack of curiosity as to where Reldan was getting these items. When he bothered to ask, he was content with Reldan's vague explanations of having won various pieces "in a crap game" or at cards. Reldan even claimed he found jewelry and other valuables in houses where he was hired to do salvage work. Apparently, John Truncali didn't care.

The frequency of these purchases came dangerously close to putting Truncali in the role of Reldan's fence, a buyer of stolen goods, but investigators never proved such a relationship and never brought charges against the owner of Closter Jewelers. Instead, they welcomed him as a cooperative witness. In fact, at the request of BCPO investigators, he drew a rough sketch of a missing engagement ring the second victim, Susan Reeve, had been wearing when she was abducted. It was a family heirloom of Susan's fiancé, Danny Omstead, and his family still had the similarly designed, wedding ring mate of the engagement ring, which Truncali used as a guide. In case it might prove useful in the investigation, a physical copy of the missing engagement ring was crafted using Truncali's sketch, and made with materials matching the wedding ring version, but no leads were ever developed to track down Susan Reeve's ring.

John Truncali did provide useful information, however, regarding Susan Heynes's engagement ring. On November 11, he told Investigator Ed Denning that Reldan had approached him the month before, in the parking lot near his store. Reldan had an old style engagement ring that he wanted to sell. Truncali didn't have a loupe—the eyepiece jewelers use—with him and could only give the ring a cursory look. He offered $50, which Reldan refused as too low. Truncali said that this encounter occurred between October 7 and 21, but he couldn't be more specific as to the date. He later inquired about the ring, and Reldan told him he'd sold it in New York City for $100, which comported with actual events at

Macy's. Denning asked Truncali to draw a sketch of the engagement ring that Reldan had tried to sell him, and the jeweler did so from memory, providing a rough depiction that was close but did not exactly match the Heynes ring.

BCPO investigators interviewed Melvin Norman on November 11, showing him a blow-up of a photo taken at Susan Heynes's wedding. The enlargement showed Susan's right hand, where she wore her engagement ring. Norman said the ring looked similar to the ring he had purchased from Robert Reldan on October 21. He couldn't be more definitive, because his notes relating to the transaction were not accurate. He had described the ring as "14-karat white gold, fancy ring, 15 diamonds, three-quarters of a carat." Presumably, he had examined the ring with a jeweler's loupe, yet the only correct information in his description was a "fancy ring" with "15 diamonds." The ring was 18-karat gold, according to Harrod's, and the diamond weight was 1.08 carats. During that same interview, Norman picked out Reldan from a photo lineup. Later, investigators would determine that a Macy's check for $100 had been deposited into Reldan's bank account. There would be no mistake about the identity of this Macy's customer.

Two days after his initial interview, Melvin Norman viewed the newly arrived sketch prepared by the ring's manufacturer, Saunders Jewellery. Again, he could only say the ring's design in the sketch was "similar" to that of the ring he bought from Reldan.

On November 13, Special Agent Klotz and a Haworth officer met with Truncali and showed him the Saunders Jewellery sketch. Truncali said the ring depicted in the sketch was, to the best of his recollection, similar to the one Reldan had tried to sell him the prior month. Once again, he had only taken a brief look—without his jeweler's loupe—at the ring Reldan offered.

Evidence connecting Robert Reldan to the Susan Heynes abduction and murder had been established, but only if the credibility of witnesses John Truncali and Melvin Norman held up in court under cross-examination. A big "if," considering their own questionable activities: Truncali as a regular buyer of Reldan's seemingly inexhaustible supply of used jewelry, and Norman as a shoddy recordkeeper, not only for the Reldan transaction but also for other dealings—a series of errors that caused Macy's to terminate his employment soon after the Reldan incident.

* * *

In the course of their frequent visits to Closter Jewelers to speak with owner John Truncali, investigators also interviewed two employees of the establishment to see what, if anything, they may have observed regarding Reldan. Florence Candace Thompson, Reldan's cousin, provided no useful information, except for a comment she made about Judy Reldan's car. When asked to describe that vehicle, Thompson remembered it as being "blue or green." The comment was telling, if only to illustrate that the actual light blue color of Judy's car might easily have been mistaken by a casual observer for light green—a mistake toll collector Eileen Dalton apparently made on the night of October 14.

Investigators also spoke with Millicent Williams, who managed the jewelry store for Truncali. Ms. Williams told police she remembered Reldan coming into the store on October 10, or thereabouts, and asking if her boss had a tarpaulin he could borrow. He said he needed it to "move some leaves," an unlikely chore for an apartment dweller. A tarpaulin is also useful for concealing the transportation of a dead body, particularly moving a body from a vehicle in a public parking area, like the one in Valley Cottage where Reldan would have parked before taking Susan Heynes's body down the path toward Lake DeForest. He surely would have done this at night, but it would have been prudent for him *not* to carry the nude body of a dead woman openly, especially in an area he knew to be a popular hangout for young people.

Ms. Williams made a second, more significant observation. She said Reldan came into the store to see Truncali on October 15, 1975, the day after Susan Reeve's abduction. The jeweler was not present, but Millicent Williams noticed "a great big scratch on the side of [Reldan's] face," so startling that she exclaimed, "Bob, what did you do to your face?"

Reldan looked at her "kind of funny," Williams later recalled to investigators. He then said, "I cut it shaving."

* * *

Thomas McGinn, a nationally known dog trainer, operated a Philadelphia-based company called "Search and Rescue 9," which provided trained dogs for law enforcement. His biggest client was the FBI. Indeed, he and his dogs worked on the Patty Hearst case. The newspaper-chain heiress was abducted from her California home on February 4, 1974, and then she was brutalized and brainwashed into becoming a member of the very gang that took her. McGinn and two of his scent dogs established that Hearst had been inside a Pennsylvania farmhouse during her captivity—a fact later confirmed by fingerprints. The FBI also employed McGinn's company in a less successful attempt to locate Jimmy Hoffa after his July 1975 disappearance.

On November 17, 1975, Thomas McGinn's help was sought in the Heynes/Reeve murder investigation. He was asked to determine if Susan Heynes or Susan Reeve was ever in Reldan's Opel wagon, which was still impounded at the Closter police garage, and if either woman was ever inside a vacant house in Closter owned by Reldan's aunt, Lillian Booth. The Booth house was used only for storage, and Robert Reldan had previously put personal belongings there. Still believing her nephew had nothing to do with the murders, Lillian Booth remained cooperative and had given investigators written permission to search the house.

McGinn selected "Veed" and "Drux"—two German shepherds that had worked more than 1,000 cases between them, including the Hearst case—to work the Reldan investigation. He handled the dogs himself, using the established procedures of his profession.

First, Susan Reeve's family supplied the police with clothing—a sweater, nightgown, and such—that Susan had worn. Veed was placed in an enclosed room with the clothing. In a process called "priming," the dog was left alone in the room with the clothing (and no distractions) for three hours. After being primed, Veed was taken to Lillian Booth's vacant house at 61 Carlson Court in Closter.

A dog is trained to indicate the presence of a primed scent in one of two ways: by sitting down or by lying down, in each case where the scent is strongest. At the vacant house, Veed, primed with Susan Reeve's scent, indicated in two locations—inside the attached garage, about ten feet from the driveway door, and in a second-floor bedroom, directly above the garage. McGinn would later say that the second floor bedroom indication, positioned as it was above the garage, might have been a false positive because of the strength of the garage scent. Veed indicated very quickly in the garage and it is possible that the scent wafted upwards—a tendency with scent molecules—and got into floorboards of the room above. According to McGinn, Veed had never made a mistake in all the cases he had worked. McGinn was absolutely sure that Veed had correctly identified Susan Reeve's scent in the garage, but wasn't sure the second floor bedroom indication was valid because of its location directly above the spot of the garage indication.

Veed was then taken to the Closter impound garage, where he was allowed to wander among the vehicles stored there. After a few minutes, Veed entered an open door to Reldan's Opel station wagon, went to the back seat area of the car, and lay down, indicating that Susan Reeve, or clothing she had recently worn, had been in that location.

The entire process was then repeated. Veed was "re-primed" with Susan Reeve's clothing for two hours, then taken back to the Closter house and back to the impound garage and Reldan's Opel station wagon. The results were identical. Veed indicated in the same two places in the vacant Booth house and in the same place in the Opel wagon.

Drux would have his chance, too. Less experienced than Veed, he was primed for 11 hours with clothing of Susan Heynes—from 9:00 PM on November 17 until 8:00 AM the next morning. The clothing had been kept in a sealed plastic bag until it was removed for the priming process with Drux, who was trained to sit when indicating the presence of a primed scent. As a test, Drux was taken to the Heynes home at 359 Schraalenburgh Road in Haworth. Like all of McGinn's dogs, Drux was trained to indicate at the spot where a primed scent was strongest. At the Heynes home, Drux went to the couple's bedroom and jumped on to the bed, sitting where Susan Heynes usually slept. Drux was next taken to the vacant Booth house, but gave no indication that Susan Heynes had been there. He was then taken to the Closter impound garage, where he walked around before entering Reldan's Opel. Drux sat down in the back seat area of the wagon.

One doesn't have to be an experienced trial lawyer to understand the devastating effect Thomas McGinn's testimony would have at Reldan's murder trial. Courts across the United States have ruled that evidence produced by dogs specially trained in scent work and under the control of experienced handlers using correct procedures is admissible at trial.

Contemplating the strategy that might be used in the Reldan trial, McGinn would be called to the witness stand and asked to give his credentials as an expert in training and handling scent dogs, including hundreds of cases he'd worked with the FBI. He would be offered as an expert witness, a finding the defense could not challenge, as well as a fact witness. Then, McGinn would be asked to describe the training of his dogs and the procedures he employed. In other words, he'd be used to educate the jurors on this unusual but proven law enforcement tool.

After the jury gained an appreciation for the reliability of evidence obtained from scent dogs, an astute trial prosecutor would have sought the court's permission for a demonstration. The night before McGinn's testimony, Veed could have been primed with an article of clothing borrowed from a prosecutor's office employee. The clothing would then have been left on the courtroom floor, right in front of the jury box, for most of the morning before being removed. The prosecutor would explain this set up to the jury and then McGinn would bring Veed into the courtroom during the trial, letting the dog loose in the area in front of the judge's bench and the jury box. When Veed lies down in the exact spot where the clothing had been left, the significance of McGinn's subsequent testimony about details in the Reldan case would hit home for the jurors.*

After the demonstration, McGinn would then describe the exact procedures used in the Heynes/Reeve case and the results obtained with Veed, showing that Susan Reeve or her clothing had been inside the vacant Booth house—most likely just in the garage—and in the rear seat area of Reldan's Opel wagon. Further, McGinn would then relate the additional results obtained with Drux, showing that Susan Heynes or her clothing had also been in the rear seat area of the Opel wagon.

* * *

The FBI crime laboratory's painstaking analysis of every item seized in the November 1 search of Robert Reldan's Opel Kadett station wagon, after it was impounded for the two late-October burglaries, was completed on January 2, 1976. Prosecutors hit pay dirt, of a sort, with two conclusions reached by the FBI examiners. Regarding Susan Reeve, the report stated, "Light brown head hairs of Caucasian origin which exhibit the same microscopic characteristics as the known hair of Susan Reeve were found on the right front floor mat, in the debris recovered from the rear seat, and in the debris from under the rear seat of Reldan's car." Regarding Susan Heynes, the report stated, "Brown head hairs of Caucasian origin which exhibit the same microscopic characteristics as the known hair of Susan Heynes were found in the debris from under the rear seat of Reldan's car." Others who might have ridden in the Opel wagon—Reldan, his wife, and Roberta Gimbel, for example—gave control samples of their hair (by court order, in Reldan's case) and the FBI lab ruled them out as the source of these particular head hairs.

Continuing, the lab report cautioned that the analysis of human hair does not offer a sufficient number of unique microscopic characteristics to be positively identified with one individual to the exclusion of all others, as fingerprint evidence might accomplish. Again, these events took place before DNA analysis was an accepted scientific technique. Bureau examiners were prepared, however, to testify about the extreme unlikelihood of finding matching hair samples from both murder victims in the same location—Reldan's vehicle.

---

*Courtroom demonstrations can backfire, of course, as prosecutors in the O.J. Simpson trial found out when they asked Simpson to try on the blood-stained glove. ("If it doesn't fit, you must acquit," Johnnie Cochran, one of Simpson's lawyers, repeated again and again in his summation—and the jury did just that.) Here, a prudent prosecutor would have tested Veed's ability to perform in a crowded courtroom atmosphere before attempting it in front of the jury.

* * *

    The scent evidence relating to Susan Reeve, together with the fact that specimens of what was likely her hair were found on the right front floor mat taken from Reldan's Opel wagon and in debris vacuumed from the rear seat area of that vehicle, fit squarely within the hypothesis presented earlier in this book: that Susan Reeve was forced into the front passenger-seat floor area of Reldan's Opel when she was abducted on Anderson Avenue in Demarest on October 14, 1975. (Raymond Lozier said that that particular door was open when he saw the sinister-looking Reldan and motionless Reeve, apparently under Reldan's control, standing next to the vehicle at about 6:20 that evening.) Then, Reldan transported Reeve less than two miles to Closter and the vacant Booth house, where he gagged and restrained her, perhaps with duct tape, and placed her on the garage floor. This enabled Reldan to go home—his Tenafly apartment was less than ten minutes away—to get rid of the Opel wagon; he knew that Lozier had paid close attention to the car, and also wanted to change out of his dirty work clothes, which also might have been observed. He then drove Judy's light blue coupe back to his aunt's vacant house and placed his subdued victim in the trunk of his wife's car, before hightailing it out of the area.

    The fact that Reldan crossed the George Washington Bridge, where toll collector Eileen Dalton saw him and heard screams coming from the trunk, is a bit strange. However, it could have been the same scenario he followed in his abduction of Susan Heynes, except that, with Heynes, he used his Opel wagon throughout instead of Judy's car; as far as he knew, no one had observed the car. Eileen Dalton's observations on October 14 (7:30 to 7:45 PM) fit squarely within time parameters—the time of Reeve's disappearance and the time it would have taken Reldan to switch cars, change clothes, and retrieve his victim from the Booth house.

    It isn't clear where Reldan raped and killed Susan Reeve, or, for that matter, where he most likely raped and killed Susan Heynes. When one contemplates that crime, too, and realizes that Reldan never entered the Heynes residence, where nothing was disturbed, it becomes a reasonable assumption that he had a place where he felt safe in taking two abducted women, where he could rape and strangle them. It's unlikely that he did those acts outside, in the places where the two bodies were initially dumped; it would have been too dangerous, offering opportunities for the women to cry out or for a witness to appear. It could have been done in New York at a "safe house" that he had access to. While this would explain his trip over the George Washington Bridge, it would have been difficult for him to take Reeve out of the Hornet's trunk unobserved, or Heynes out of the back seat area of the Opel wagon, while in the city. Another possible explanation is that his safe house was in New Jersey, but that he was spooked at having been observed with Susan Reeve and wanted to put time and distance between the abduction and his eventual rape and murder of the girl. A while later, he could have backtracked to New Jersey, in the case of Reeve, and gone to the same place where he had terrorized and killed Susan Heynes.

Wherever he was, after killing both women, it would be a simple matter for him to drive to the Valley Cottage site. If he stayed on the Hudson's east side, he could have re-crossed to the west side of the river, where Valley Cottage was located, at the Tappan Zee Bridge. If he did both crimes in New Jersey, Valley Cottage was less than a 30-minute drive north, and he would not have needed to cross the river. After his October 22 interview with BCPO Investigator Ed Denning, Reldan moved Reeve's body from its initial dumping site near the Heynes body to Tallman Mountain State Park, transporting it in the back seat of his Opel, where hair and scent evidence remained.

Neither Assistant Prosecutor Leaman nor Deputy Attorney General Buckley would use the Eileen Dalton observations in their prosecutions. That episode left unanswerable questions, and Buckley felt that it would only confuse the jury to introduce it. He believed he already had a strong enough case, without adding to his burden by trying to explain to jurors why, for example, Reldan would take a subdued but alive Susan Reeve across the George Washington Bridge. "It would require too much conjecture," Buckley explained, "to make Eileen Dalton's observations believable and relevant."

Thomas McGinn's testimony, Veed's demonstration (if the judge allowed it), and the FBI lab technician's report of the hair evidence would have conclusively nailed Robert Reldan, removing all doubt as to his guilt. Unfortunately, this perfect scenario never played out. Although he did testify before the grand jury, McGinn was never called to testify in any of Robert Reldan's three trials for the murders of Susan Heynes and Susan Reeve. And the hair evidence would not be used until Reldan's third murder trial, 10 years later.

Chapter 11

The thing I'm trying to find out is, is my son a killer.

Irene Lippert claimed to have survived imprisonment in a Nazi concentration camp in Poland as a young girl, so it was ironic that she, herself, took a job as a prison guard in 1974. She rose in rank to become food services supervisor at Rahway State Prison. In that capacity, she oversaw day-to-day operations of the officers' dining room (ODR) and the adjoining "VIP" dining room, used when dignitaries or other special guests visited the prison. Lippert supervised a staff of inmates assigned to her as cooks, waiters, and office clerks, the choicest assignment. The head clerk and his assistant got perks that the general prison population was denied, like the same food the guards ate and even alcoholic beverages from time to time—not legally but on the sly, when no one was paying attention and the VIP liquor cabinet could be jimmied. The duties were light—typing menus, inventory reports and internal memos, mostly—and Irene Lippert was away from the office for hours at a time, leaving the staff largely unsupervised.

After entering into a plea bargain for the two burglaries he'd committed the previous October, Robert Reldan was sentenced in June 1976 to concurrent two-to-three-year terms at Rahway State. His pleasant, ingratiating manner might very well have landed him a cushy prison job in the ODR, but he already had an "in." During the latter part of Reldan's previous imprisonment, after his Blanche Mate conviction, he and Irene Lippert were at Rahway contemporaneously—he as a prisoner, of course, and she as a guard—and they got to know one another. It wouldn't have taken long for Lippert to arrange Reldan's assignment to her staff. He served briefly in the kitchen until Lippert cleared the way for him to become her head clerk. An inmate familiar with the ODR and food services office later suggested Lippert and Reldan had more than just a working relationship; if true, it may simply have been friendship. She later admitted taking a liking to Reldan, personally, and she testified on his behalf at subsequent trials, which is rare for a prison guard.

In early December 1976, Reldan and his assistant clerk, Albert Barber, were sitting up front in the prison auditorium awaiting the start of the Saturday night movie, when Barber felt a tap on his shoulder. It was Allison Williams, an old friend from Atlantic City, whom Barber hadn't seen in years. The two men, smiling broadly, jostled each other in a show of playful exuberance. Allison explained that he and his brother Cliff, still seated at the back of the room, had just been transferred to Rahway to begin serving five-to-seven-year sentences for a burglary they had done together.

Barber, gesturing for Reldan to join him, started to walk with Allison to greet Cliff. "I have two friends I want you to meet," he told Reldan.

Barber was in awe of the two brothers, whom he had known for 12 years and who had near-celebrity status in the prison culture. They had pulled off some of the biggest heists of jewelry and cash in recent New Jersey history, but didn't limit themselves to the Garden State for their criminal enterprises. Cliff and Allison Williams were known as the "Dinnertime Socialite Bandits," primarily because of the high-end clientele they targeted. They had once targeted the wife of an elite Mexican official and also cased the ski-resort digs of the Duke and Duchess of Windsor for a possible jewelry score, though things didn't click and they never pulled it off.

After making the introductions and chatting a while, Barber asked if Reldan could get jobs for his friends in the ODR. Reldan said that it would not be a problem, but the favor would cost $100, a small price for a plum prison job. The brothers readily agreed with no hard feelings; quid pro quo was a fact of life in prison. The four men sat together and watched the movie, after which they went to the food services office, where Reldan typed the paperwork to get Cliff and Allison Williams assigned to the officers' dining room. He said he would have Irene Lippert sign off on the request first thing Monday morning.*

With Al Barber vouching for the trustworthiness of both Williams brothers, the ordinarily cautious Reldan began almost immediately to feel comfortable in speaking openly to them, even to the extent of revealing snippets of information about his past crimes.

In the prison environment, snitches were then and still are an ever-present danger. Truly, there isn't much honor among thieves. Almost any inmate will "dime out" a fellow inmate by contacting a prosecutor or investigator (the phrase comes from dropping a "dime" in a pay phone) to trade confidences—some real and some fabricated—in exchange for preferential treatment. This occurs so often that one has to wonder at what seems like sheer stupidity on the part of those who do the confiding.

---

*Reldan later instructed Barber to tell the Williamses to send the $100 fee to "B. Rosenberg" and gave the name and address of the architectural firm where his wife worked as a secretary. There was never an explanation for the use of "B. Rosenberg"; the first initial may have been some sort of code between Reldan and his wife, who was still known at her job by her former name, Rosenberg.

Whether it is a top-this-if-you-can competitive attitude or merely a need to attain status by building up one's criminal resume in the eyes of other prisoners, the opportunities to "rat" on a prison cohort for personal gain are rife.

Reldan certainly knew of this propensity among the prison population. Indeed, in September 1976, not long after arriving at Rahway but months before meeting the Williams brothers, he went so far as to write a self-serving declaration, which he had validated and sealed by a prison notary public. The statement read, in part: "I am stating unequivocally that I have not discussed any aspect of my case except on the most superficial of levels, nor will I discuss it at all after this date with anyone except my attorney or my wife."

It isn't clear what Reldan hoped to gain by this officious undertaking, but it does give insight into how his mind worked. He may have let slip an off-handed comment in the presence of another prisoner, then scrambled to have it neutralized, at least in his own mind, in case that prisoner turned on him. No one proffered information in September 1976, but Reldan's resolve to keep quiet about the ongoing murder investigation would fall apart within three months. In late December 1976 and January 1977, not only would Robert Reldan open up to Cliff and Allison Williams about his involvement in the Heynes and Reeve murders, he would also solicit their help to pull off a shocking new crime—the robbery and murder of his wealthy aunt, Lillian Booth, and her male companion, Misha Dabich.

* * *

After receiving the FBI lab report in early January 1976, prosecutors took no action on the Heynes/Reeve murder case for one year. Despite the accumulation of strong circumstantial evidence relating to both victims, they were looking for more. Once indicted, Reldan would have been entitled to a speedy trial under New Jersey law. The clock would start ticking as soon as a Bergen County grand jury handed up its formal charges. The prosecutors were certain that Reldan was their man for the two murders. But, since he was doing time for the Norwood and Closter burglaries, prosecutors—decided to wait, hoping more evidence would turn up. They didn't want to go to trial with what they had. If they could not prove Reldan's guilt beyond a reasonable doubt, Reldan would be acquitted and he couldn't be tried again for the same offenses because of the double jeopardy provision of the Fifth Amendment. The prosecutors opted to wait until they were sure they had enough.

The families of the two victims were willing to wait, too. The Bergen County prosecutors would have explained the risk of proceeding prematurely to the families, conveying their certainty that Reldan, who was behind bars and off the street for the foreseeable future, was the murderer. But no additional evidence did turn up.

In early January, 1977, prosecutors learned that Reldan would be eligible for a parole hearing on the two burglaries that very month, because he'd been given concurrent sentencing as part of a plea bargain. His hearing would be held on January 19, in fact, although a decision could take months longer. Given Reldan's history of success with parole boards, the BCPO decided it could not wait any longer. It needed to secure an indictment.

But, in the hurried decision to present the case to a grand jury, there was another factor, one Reldan would make much of later on. Joe Woodcock wanted to be governor of New Jersey, and the election was less than a year away. Not only would Reldan's indictment be a feather in his cap, announcing it on television would bring a welcome spate of new publicity, after more than a year of inactivity in the case. There would be risk involved in moving the case to the front burner right then: Getting an indictment through the grand jury would be easy, but getting a conviction at trial would not be. Unconcerned about the perceived weakness of the case because he wouldn't be around for the trial, Woodcock would resign as Bergen County Prosecutor and announce his candidacy for governor within a month.

Assistant Prosecutor Dennis Kohler presented the case against Robert Reldan to a Bergen County grand jury on January 20, 1977, the day of President Jimmy Carter's inauguration. To obtain a "true bill of indictment," the formal charge necessary to bring Reldan to trial for the murders of Susan Heynes and Susan Reeve, Kohler would have to convince 12 of the 23 grand jurors that Robert Reldan *probably* committed the murders. In other words, a simple majority of the panel had to agree that the State met a very low threshold. Indeed, that threshold was so low, one has to wonder what protection it actually affords against potential abuse of the system.

There is absolutely no indication that AP Kohler, or anyone else, abused the grand jury process in Reldan's case. The assistant prosecutor followed every established procedure in presenting the State's case, but grand jury procedures are clearly stacked against any defendant, no matter how honorable or scrupulous the State's representatives are in presenting evidence.

Although constitutional and procedural protections assure defendants of certain rights in trials before juries, those protections are *inoperable* before the grand jury, where defendants do not even have the right to be present. Defendants and their attorneys are excluded from the grand jury room when evidence is being presented. In fact, they have no say in what evidence a prosecutor decides to bring before the grand jurors. A prosecutor is not even required to introduce potentially exculpatory evidence, if there is any, and defendants are not allowed to call their own witnesses or confront the witnesses against them, by cross-examination or any other means.

Prosecutors are able to introduce hearsay evidence before the grand jury—that is, evidence that doesn't come from actual observers of events but from third parties to whom the actual observers have related their information. Since all proceedings are recorded and a transcript is provided to defendants upon indictment, prosecutors prefer not to call civilians before the grand jury. Civilian witnesses can inadvertently blurt out inconsistencies, which the prosecutor or another witness would correct afterward. But defense counsel can use such mistakes to impeach a witness's credibility during trial; prosecutors avoid this by putting civilians' testimony into the record through hearsay.

Prosecutors can also ask leading questions of witnesses before the grand jury. In effect, the State's entire case can be presented in the words of the prosecutor, where he or she tells a police witness what the evidence is, using leading questions (such as: "Isn't it correct that . . . "), so that witnesses simply answer "yes" or "no." Prosecutors always ask questions so that the answers are always "yes." An oft-repeated saw among the defense bar claims that prosecutors could "indict a ham sandwich" if they wished to do so. That is not too far from being true.

Kohler called 11 witnesses to testify before the grand jury. All but two—dog trainer Thomas McGinn and Dr. Frederick Zugibe, the Rockland County Medical Examiner—were police officers, BCPO investigators, or FBI agents. Using the economy of leading questions, hearsay, and other prosecutorial shorthand, the entire matter of the State of New Jersey versus Robert R. Reldan was accomplished in one day of testimony, after which the grand jury returned a two-count true bill of indictment. That very same day, January 20, 1977, Prosecutor Joe Woodcock appeared on television to announce the murder indictment.

The first count of the indictment charged Reldan with felony murder of Susan Heynes; the second count charged him with felony murder of Susan Reeve. If the State could prove Reldan committed an additional felony, in conjunction with the murders, the crimes would become first-degree offenses, with mandatory life sentences for each. Dr. Zugibe's autopsy provided the prosecution with evidence that Susan Reeve had been raped before she was killed, but the condition of Susan Heynes's body precluded any such finding. Still, if the State could show Heynes was forcibly abducted from her home—a logical inference, given all the circumstances—kidnapping could become the additional felony needed to constitute first degree murder in her case; if not, the Heynes murder, if proven, would likely be downgraded to second degree.

Back then, a "life" sentence did not mean that the defendant would be put away for *life*. First-degree murderers became eligible for parole at some point. The best the State could hope for would be two first-degree convictions, in which case Reldan could receive consecutive life sentences. A second-degree conviction on either count would limit the maximum sentence to 30 years for that count.

Although Robert Reldan knew that he was under investigation for the two murders, he was in shock over the indictment. When fellow inmates ran up to say that the Bergen County Prosecutor was on television talking about him, Reldan couldn't quite believe it was happening. He had maintained, consistently, that investigators didn't have enough evidence to indict him. Why else would they have taken so long to bring the charges? He even thought that the question of jurisdiction would be a problem. The bodies, after all, had been found in New York State, where Bergen County officials had no authority. Reldan wondered aloud if "the ring" had done him in.

On January 24, 1977, four days after the murder indictment was handed up, Reldan was transferred to Trenton State Prison. It was a far cry from the easygoing atmosphere at Rahway State, where Reldan had been hoping to be designated as a minimum-security prisoner, which would facilitate his escape if things turned bad. Clearly, prosecutors were taking the murder indictment seriously. The stakes had been raised.

Reldan's family rallied to his support. His father William, 70 years old at the time, worried that his son was suicidal. He had a contact in the office of Edward Bennett Williams, the renowned Washington DC lawyer whose list of clients read like a "Who's Who" of the powerful and elite in America—people like Frank Sinatra, Jimmy Hoffa, Senator Joe McCarthy, mobster Frank Costello, and *Playboy* publisher Hugh Hefner. In later testimony, William Reldan would tell of sitting in Edward Bennett Williams's Washington office, almost begging the great man to take his son's case.

"The thing I'm trying to find out is, is my son a killer," William Reldan told the lawyer. "Before I die," he said, "I want to find out."

Edward Bennett Williams took the case.

Representation like that would cost plenty, but Aunt Lillian was back in Bobby's corner. She put up the initial retainer—there were conflicting versions of the amount, either $50,000 or $75,000. It would take hundreds of thousands more to defend the murder case through trial but, at least for now, Reldan had the best defense team that money could buy. And, as any expert in criminal law will attest, the chance for an acquittal in a murder case is directly proportional to the quality of the attorneys championing a defendant's cause. With legal talent like Edward Bennett Williams on his side, Robert Reldan was confident that he would beat the rap. The only question? Would Aunt Lillian stick by him, or would she pull the plug on her money, as she did when she refused to post bail for the Norwood and Closter burglary charges, if the going got tough?

Reldan had already initiated a contingency plan to avoid that snag.

* * *

BCPO Investigator Ed Denning was attending to one of the many other files on his desk—nothing to do with the Reldan case—when a call was put through to him on Thursday, February 17, 1977. With Reldan indicted for the Heynes and Reeve murders and the preliminary skirmishing between defense lawyers and prosecutors well underway, investigators were on standby, as far as the Reldan matter was concerned. There wasn't much to do until it came time to gear up for the trial or until the inevitable pre-trial defense motions started.

Denning picked up the phone and a woman's voice asked if he was involved with the Robert Reldan case. Denning responded in the affirmative, and the woman then identified herself as Emily Williams. Her husband was Clifford Williams, she said, an inmate at Rahway State Prison. She gave his prison number, 58741, to provide verification that she was who she said she was. Denning asked how he could help the woman.

Her husband wanted to meet with someone from the prosecutor's office, she said, as soon as possible. He had information on Robert Reldan and two rape-murders in Bergen County.

Chapter 12

I'm an investigator for the Buzzard.

Ed Denning would meet with Rahway inmate Cliff Williams and his brother Allison a dozen times over the ensuing months, but his first encounter with Cliff on February 18, 1977, one day after Emily Williams's call, convinced Denning he was on to something that could seal Robert Reldan's fate and insure that the double-murderer would never see the outside of a prison again.

Cliff Williams started out by giving Denning the background—how he came to be at Rahway and the circumstances surrounding his meeting Robert Reldan. Williams explained that, with the close proximity of their prison work assignments—Cliff and Allison Williams in the officers' dining room and Reldan in the nearby food services supervisor's office— they had plenty of free time to socialize most days. The back dining room, called the VIP room, offered a private place for them to relax, drink coffee, and chat, with little chance of being overheard.

Reldan began bragging about his involvement in two Bergen County rape-murders less than a month after Cliff Williams met him. One comment Williams remembered clearly was Reldan's regret at having dumped the two bodies so close to each other in New York State. He had done so, Reldan said, to avoid Bergen County, where he was well known. By transporting the bodies to New York, Reldan thought he could throw his old nemeses in the Bergen County Prosecutor's Office off his scent. Williams also said Reldan was concerned about "the ring." That's all Cliff knew about that. Something about a ring.

These two items were enough to arouse Denning's interest, but the experienced investigator knew they were of marginal value by themselves. Every prison snitch comes with baggage. The information they provide is usually an admission of guilt or disclosure of an incriminating fact by a fellow prisoner, useful but subject to challenge at trial, given its source.[*]

---

[*]The informer always wants something from the prosecution in return for his cooperation, an inevitable bargain that causes jurors to look askance at such evidence—and rightly so. Also, to call the informer's credibility into question, defense attorneys can use an informer's prior conviction record, a criminal history that may even dwarf the defendant's wrongdoing by comparison. Jurors frequently conclude that a career criminal is not entitled to be believed.

Even so, prison snitches sometimes give information that has a strong claim on the truth, despite the unsavory backgrounds of the purveyors. Cliff Williams's mention of "the ring" being a concern of Reldan's was a case in point. The facts surrounding Reldan selling Susan Heynes's engagement ring to Macy's had not been widely publicized, and no one in prison was likely to have known about the importance of the ring, except Reldan—and anyone he mentioned it to. Denning knew he had something, but the next revelation by Williams nearly floored the investigator.

Prior to Reldan's indictment, Cliff Williams said, Reldan asked him if he could get someone on the outside to rob his aunt's house; after the indictment, though, the talk turned to killing the aunt and her boyfriend. Reldan claimed that his aunt was wealthy and that she kept $100,000 to $150,000 worth of jewelry in the house. Whomever Williams got to do the job could keep all the jewelry and cash found in the home. All Reldan wanted out of the deal, he explained, was his inheritance. He said that he, his mother and his sister were the aunt's sole beneficiaries, and he needed money to pay his lawyers. Reldan promised to take care of Cliff out of his inheritance.

The possibilities were almost endless, Denning thought. Even though the value of a snitch's testimony was marginal, Reldan's scheme to have his aunt murdered, if handled properly, could constitute a whole new second front in the BCPO's efforts to keep Reldan behind bars for the rest of his life. The investigator's mind was spinning.

He asked Cliff Williams what he expected in return for his cooperation. Denning had already warned Williams that he could make no promises without consulting the assistant prosecutor in charge of the case.

Williams said that he and his brother Allison, who also had information and would also cooperate, were facing trial on March 7, 1977—three weeks away—on B&E charges in Camden County. Williams wanted their case postponed and wanted the BCPO to intervene and get them a plea deal that would make any sentence concurrent to the term they were already serving in Rahway. In other words, they wanted a free pass on the Camden County crimes.

In taking his leave, Denning reiterated that he could make no promises, but said he would see what his superiors were willing to do. Later, after checking with AP Kohler back at the BCPO, Denning reached out to Deputy Attorney General Barry Goas, who was in charge of the Williamses' Camden County case. Goas listened politely to Denning's request for consideration for the two Williams brothers, if they cooperated in Bergen County's murder case and, now, its new conspiracy-to-murder case. DAG Goas turned Denning down flat. There would be no plea deal, no trial postponement, and no leniency of any sort shown to Cliff Williams or his brother Allison.

Dealing with a colleague who was well versed in the value of collaboration and support among law enforcement agencies, Denning was shocked. What could account for such a hard stance on a request from another prosecutor? Given the extensive criminal records of both Williams brothers, Goas explained, he couldn't justify leniency, especially with the circumstances surrounding their past crimes. In at least two previous prosecutions, key witnesses had been murdered to prevent their testifying against Cliff and Allison Williams. Although he couldn't prove it, Goas believed the Williams brothers were behind those hits. And he wasn't about to show them the slightest preferential treatment, even if it meant disappointing a colleague.

Limited in his ability to trade for the Williams brothers' cooperation, Ed Denning headed back to Rahway State Prison on February 22 to give Cliff the bad news: There would be no deal in Camden County. Surprisingly, Williams did not withdraw his offer. He said he and his brother would still cooperate, but asked only that the BCPO make their cooperation known to the Camden County judge hearing their case. Denning made a quick call to Dennis Kohler and got the go-ahead to make that promise to Cliff Williams. They were in business again.

At the February 22 meeting and in subsequent meetings, Cliff Williams fleshed out for Denning the conversations he'd had with Reldan about the two murders in Bergen County and Reldan's scheme involving his aunt. The plan to rob Lillian Booth was actually the subject that Reldan broached first, according to Williams. Later, after the indictment, Reldan broadened the plot to include his aunt's murder. Denning asked how Reldan came to trust the Williamses with so incriminating a plan, that could cause Reldan serious trouble if it came to light.

"Well," Cliff Williams explained, "I suppose Al Barber gave him the big buildup about my brother and myself as being people who could handle things of this nature, and he has known us for years, and we were all right and he could trust us and things of that nature."

Denning asked where these conversations took place.

"He used to come over to the officers' dining room and have coffee," Williams said. "And we would go in the back [VIP] room, which was private there." Williams went on to say that he and his brother, at times, also went to the food services office, where Reldan worked as head clerk and Al Barber worked as his second clerk. "Sometimes, Mrs. Lippert, mostly she wasn't there when we went over. She had left and would do something else." Williams estimated that he, brother Allison, Al Barber, and Reldan had these private conversations dozens of times.

"That's how we got into the robbery of his aunt," Williams told Denning, "and then into the murder, and during the course of these conversations [Reldan] discussed different little phases of his problem that he thought he was going to have with Bergen County." When Reldan first brought up the two murders of women in Bergen County, Williams said, neither he nor his brother knew anything about them.

Around the holidays in December, Williams said, Reldan had been drinking and started talking about the two women he killed. He told Williams that "it was a mistake" taking the two bodies to New York State and "leaving them so close to one another." He transported the bodies to New York, Reldan told Williams, to take "the heat off himself in Bergen County." Reldan didn't see how Bergen had jurisdiction or evidence to charge him, but "did mention something about a ring that he was very concerned with . . . that it might get him into trouble," Williams recalled, but could provide no other details.

In a later interview, Allison Williams would tell Denning about Reldan's preoccupation with sex in these discussions they had. It was not unusual for prisoners to talk about sex, but according to Allison Williams, Reldan's obsession took on a sadistic bent.

Reldan never admitted that he had raped the two Bergen County women, Allison Williams said, but he "did discuss rape, forcing girls into sexual intercourse, and inflicting pain and so forth during intercourse, and he was very demonstrative about that, and it seemed to give him a great deal of excitement when he discussed that subject and the methods of causing pain and how to do that and so forth."

Denning asked Allison if Reldan ever elaborated on his methods of inflicting pain during sex. "He described whipping and choking," Allison said. "You know, holding them that way to keep them quiet." Cliff remembered similar comments by Reldan about his sexual preferences.

"Well, he was a person that had a very strange attitude toward girls," Cliff Williams told Denning. "He seemed to feel as though they liked to be beat. He used to mention it to me and my brother. I remember on occasions he said, 'Boy, you should try to beat them. They really like that'." Williams also remembered a VIP dinner that they had all worked together. An attractive young woman was part of the party being served dinner, and Reldan spent most of the evening fantasizing aloud about how he would like to "grab her"—the object being rape.

Allison Williams told Denning that, after the indictment was announced but before Reldan was shipped off to Trenton State Prison, Reldan seemed "nervous" and "depressed." Allison said to him, "Bob, you told me you didn't have anything to worry about."

"Yes," Reldan replied, "but you never know what they might come up with, what they might discover. I covered myself good, I have a good alibi, my wife is my alibi, they can't break that," Reldan said. "But you never know these people down in Bergen County. They're something else in their investigations."

Before the indictment, Reldan had boasted to the Williams brothers, "There's no way they can pin [the two murders] on me." Reldan said that he'd been interviewed by the prosecutor's office, but that they would not be able to "break his story." He was confident that he had put one over on them, according to Allison Williams. Reldan had "conned" the investigator, he said, and was confident "there was no problem at all" with that interview. Reldan told Allison that, because of his college education, he "could usually cover himself if he got in a conversation." Cliff Williams also recalled Reldan saying his wife Judy was a stand-up person, implying that she would provide him with any alibi he needed, even if it meant lying about it.

Reldan's tune changed after the indictment. The cockiness was gone. Allison almost felt sorry for him and wondered if Reldan was looking for someone to lean on for support. He seemed "under tremendous pressure," Allison told Denning, like he felt himself "doomed."

Regarding the robbery of Lillian Booth, Cliff Williams told Denning that Reldan brought this matter up in mid-December 1976, before he started talking about the two Bergen County murders. At first, Williams said, Reldan spoke only in terms of robbing his aunt, who was very rich and had an unbelievable amount of jewelry and cash in the house.

"It would be a simple job," Reldan promised Cliff Williams. If Williams could recruit someone to do it, all that the guy had to do was knock on the front door and say he was from the police. His aunt had been interviewed several times already by police in connection with the ongoing murder investigation against him, Reldan said, and she would let Williams's guy in without questioning the visit. Reldan described his aunt's house and street as being in a secluded area and said she lives with a man, but he is away a lot on skiing trips.

As discussions progressed after his indictment, Reldan began talking about murdering the aunt and her male companion as part of the deal. Earlier, both Williams brothers recalled, Reldan had expressed an aversion to leaving witnesses behind when he engaged in criminal activity. That may have been part of Reldan's motivation in turning the Lillian Booth plan from just robbery to robbery and murder.

Reldan's January 20, 1977, indictment for the murders of Susan Heynes and Susan Reeve and transfer to Trenton State Prison four days later interrupted the planning of the Lillian Booth matter. By that time, the

Williams brothers were playing along with Reldan and may have already formed the idea to trade the incriminating information to prosecutors for help in Camden County. Cliff agreed to help Reldan, and arrangements were made to communicate with him after he was at Trenton State through Al Barber, who remained behind at Rahway with the Williamses. They would use regular mail, if the message could be hidden in language that wouldn't be picked up by prison censors; otherwise, they'd keep in touch with "kites," illegal written or oral communications using go-betweens—fellow prisoners being transferred from one prison location to another and willing to carry the messages in their personal papers.

As a result of his first meeting with Cliff Williams, Denning and his superior officers at the BCPO had already started thinking about the possible use of an undercover officer to pose as the hit man Reldan wanted Williams to get. Lieutenant Cono Delia had just the man in mind for the job: Detective Nick Gallo, a tough, no-nonsense cop, but also something of a prima donna.

Nick Gallo had the brutish, big-framed look of a hit man. He stood six feet tall and, at the time, weighed more than 200 pounds. He had successfully played the role of a hit man in a previous murder-for-hire prosecution the BCPO conducted, and he frequently went undercover in carrying out assignments for the office's gambling squad. Besides the look, Gallo had one other important talent that suited his undercover activities: He was a good bullshitter, able to think fast on his feet and cover himself when a situation got dicey. And his ego and temper both matched his physical size.

Ed Denning was back home after his February 22 meeting with Cliff Williams when he got a message from Emily Williams the next night. She said that her husband needed to see Denning again. She didn't say what it was about, but Denning made the trip back to Rahway on February 24. Denning met again with Cliff Williams, who asked once more that the BCPO intercede in Camden County. Denning said he would give it another try. Williams then gave Denning an undated, typewritten letter that was signed, "Bob." Williams said that Al Barber gave him the letter, which came from Reldan, down in Trenton State Prison. Examining the letter and signature, Denning recognized Robert Reldan's handwriting. He was familiar with Reldan's writing from the materials seized in the search of his and Judy's apartment the preceding November.

The salutation in the letter read, "Dear moth-eaten buzzard," which Williams explained was Al Barber's prison nickname. In the first paragraph of the letter, Reldan brought Barber up to date on the murder charges on which he had been indicted. "The prosecutor is jerking my attys. around and told them they have to wait 30 days until they can get the discovery together—all this after having the case over 18 months," Reldan wrote. "So my lawyers told them that they didn't recognize their jurisdiction anyway since the victims were found in NY and that I would not plea so the judge entered a not guilty for me and now they have to wait for the discovery and then they will begin their motions."*

Continuing the "moth-eaten buzzard" letter to Barber, Reldan made a cryptic reference to the scheme to have his aunt robbed and killed. "Now as far as our project goes," Reldan wrote, "you know how very paranoid I am especially about that—especially with this other thing [the murder indictment] hanging and there is no way I can make myself put anything down on paper in any form. It is just too hot if it ends up in the wrong hands or going bad," Reldan continued. "Something like this has to be word of mouth for everyone's benefit. I don't trust these mails for spit. I know it will be complete and I will be satisfied when alls done but until we can find a foolproof way to exchange info, I guess it will just have to hang for a while." (Underlining in the original.)

After giving Denning a chance to read the letter, Cliff Williams advised the investigator that he had taken it upon himself to tell Al Barber how to respond to Reldan's requirement for a "foolproof way to exchange info." Williams said that he and Barber had discussed who could be the hit man for the job— someone "heavy"—in prison parlance, someone who had the guts to commit murder. They had both agreed on a mutual acquaintance as fitting the bill, a hard case by the name of Jimmy Parcells. Barber and Cliff Williams decided they would have Parcells visit Reldan in person at Trenton State Prison to make arrangements. Obviously, Parcells couldn't use his real name for the prison visit, which would require him to sign in and present identification, so Cliff Williams suggested that Parcells use an alias. Barber agreed. Cliff Williams never explained to law enforcement or anyone else how he came up with the fictitious identification that he picked for the hit man, who would be Frank Parisi of 1919 Walnut Street, Philadelphia, PA. Williams told Barber to communicate this information to Reldan, including the instruction to put Parisi down on his visitor's list at the prison.

---

*In New Jersey, as in most states, defendants in any criminal case are entitled to receive "discovery," or copies of every document the prosecution has in its files pertaining to the case. This prevents defense attorneys from being surprised by evidence in the midst of a trial. However, as we shall see, it also gives defendants the chance to formulate strategies—invent a defense, to put it bluntly—that fit known facts but still offer what defendants hope are believable and, more importantly, potentially exculpatory stories that juries might buy into.

Denning was somewhat taken aback that Cliff Williams had assumed the authority to proceed with the plan without consulting with him beforehand. Indeed, it would lead to conjecture later, during the trial, that the Williams brothers were actually planning to go ahead with the hit—in cahoots with Reldan—but that they got cold feet and switched from co-conspirators to prosecution witnesses, hoping instead to benefit from informing on Reldan. When Denning first met Williams on February 18, the inmate said nothing about the elaborate hit-man plan. Six days later, not only had Barber received the undated letter from Reldan, but Cliff Williams and Barber had discussed the names of possible robbery/ murder perpetrators, *and* they had already communicated their decision to Reldan. Something wasn't quite right, but the BCPO decided to go with the arrangements, anyway, the way that Cliff Williams had set them up.

On March 1, 1977, Denning made another trip to Rahway to meet Cliff, and, this time, he brought Nick Gallo. Denning informed Williams of DAG Goas's continuing refusal to postpone the Williams brothers' Camden County trial, still scheduled to begin March 7. Apparently, Williams resigned himself to that fact. (A postponement would actually happen, but not out of consideration for the Williams brothers.) Cliff again asked that the BCPO let the judge know of his and his brother's cooperation, and Denning said that would be no problem.

Nick Gallo was particularly interested in learning about the background of the whole scheme from Cliff Williams, firsthand, to fix the details squarely in his own mind—with no loose ends. They needed to decide on a word or phrase that Gallo could use as a password when he met Reldan for the first time—something that could be communicated to Reldan beforehand, something that would put Reldan at ease when he met with "Frank Parisi." They decided that, upon meeting Reldan at the prison, Gallo would introduce himself by saying, "I'm an investigator for the Buzzard." Al Barber would like that little touch of using his prison nickname as part of the code.

Two days later, Denning and Gallo returned to Rahway. Cliff Williams handed them another typewritten letter, also undated, from Reldan to Barber. Reldan had taken the bait.

"Parisi sounds good," Reldan wrote, "and I will have him down as of Monday. He can come any day but Wed. because that's when Judy usually comes. I don't know if they had 'yard' visits when you were here, but that is a contact visit for an hour and a half during the week . . . . I have put down one for Friday, 3/11 so if you want to call him or tell him about that o.k. He has to be here by 8:45 AM the latest though and the visit is from 9 to 10:30."

In expressing a preference for Frank Parisi to meet with him face to face in an outdoor yard visit, Reldan was being his cautious self. The next line in the letter showed his reasoning.

"If he can't make that [yard visit] then it will have to be a phone visit although I am paranoid about a tap there too," Reldan wrote. "Just let me know and I will set something up." This other option for a visit would not be a contact visit, but indoors, in a room monitored by guards. Separated by a partition, the prisoner and his visitor would see each other through a small window opening that allows a restricted view of each other. Communication would be by phone.

At the top of the letter from Reldan to "Buzz," a handwritten note read "(1919 Walnut, Phila)," a reference to Parisi's address, which Barber had previously sent. Under that notation, Reldan handwrote the word, "description." Reldan wanted to know what "Parisi" looked like. Cliff Williams told Denning and Gallo he had instructed Al Barber to reply to Reldan's request for a description of Parisi. Both Williams and Barber knew the "real" hit man was supposed to be Jimmy Parcells, using the alias of Frank Parisi. Barber knew Parcells well; that's why he and Williams had settled on him as the heavy. Barber sent Reldan a description of Parcells: five feet, nine inches tall, 170 pounds, brown wavy hair.

Gallo was three inches taller and at least 30 pounds heavier than the man he was supposed to be representing. He could fake the hair with a hat, but there was no way he could finesse the height and weight differences, if Reldan had a sharp eye. Back at the BCPO, Lieutenant Cono Delia asked Gallo if he wanted out of the undercover operation, given the new wrinkle. If need be, Delia could find another investigator who more closely fit the description that Barber had communicated to Reldan.

"No way," Gallo replied. He was confident he could play the role. Besides, if they could work the meeting between "Parisi" and Reldan to be a window visit, where both he and Reldan would be seated on opposite sides of a partition, communicating by closed-circuit phone, the height difference would be less apparent. In fact, with the window providing a restricted, 18-inch-by-18-inch view—Delia had already checked out the visiting room at Trenton State—even the weight difference may not matter.

Height and weight discrepancies would turn out to be the least of the problems they would face in the undercover operation. Later that month, before the second of two prison visits that eventually took place between Robert Reldan and Detective Nick Gallo—posing as Parcells, who was posing as Frank Parisi—the real Jimmy Parcells would be indicted for a $1,000,000 postal robbery. His name and face were plastered across the pages of every newspaper in the state.

Chapter 13

He moved his fingers across his throat in a cutting motion.

Arrangements were set for Nick Gallo to make a window visit to Robert Reldan on Tuesday, March 8, 1977. Ed Denning obtained a Pennsylvania driver's license in the name of Frank Parisi, with the address of 1919 Walnut Street in Philadelphia, and gave it to Gallo. A special phone line and number were also prepared so that the number would ring in Gallo's own home, in case Reldan wanted a way to contact Parisi. Given Reldan's paranoia about communicating by telephone, it was unlikely they'd be needed, but it was better to be ready, just in case. Gallo, Denning, Lieutenant Delia and Investigator Ken Nass all piled into one of the BCPO's unmarked vehicles and made the trip to Trenton State Prison.

Nass was a former Bell Telephone employee and had been with the BCPO for about four years. His prior training with Ma Bell and experience with electronic devices were invaluable assets to the gambling squad, which used wiretaps extensively in its investigations. Before leaving the BCPO that morning, Nass had outfitted Gallo with an Alpha I miniature recorder—ideal for undercover work—and jury-rigged it so Gallo could record both ends of his conversation with Reldan on the prison phone system. The self-contained cassette recorder was taped to Gallo's side with an induction coil running up his back, connected to a tiny microphone that Nass positioned behind the detective's ear—the ear he would hold the prison phone to. Gallo's hairline covered the ear, effectively hiding the microphone. Before hooking everything up to his colleague, Investigator Nass tested the device using the BCPO phone system. The set up, which Nass, himself, had devised, worked fine.

At the prison, Nick Gallo entered the front gate and visitors' area alone, while the other three men waited outside in their vehicle. Because it was not going to be a contact visit, Gallo did not have to worry about being searched. He gave his driver's license—in the name of Parisi—to the sergeant at the desk, and the guard checked to make sure he was on Reldan's visitor list. He was, just as Cliff Williams had arranged through Al Barber. The guard kept the license and handed Gallo a phone and jack, telling him to sit and wait to be called. Several others were already waiting. Within 10 minutes, Gallo heard the guard call out, "Visitor for Reldan? Visitor for Reldan?" He walked into the visiting area, which consisted of glass and steel partitions with stools in front of each, and saw a man motioning to him through the glass, indicating that he should sit down at a particular booth. He recognized Reldan from photographs. Gallo complied, and both he and Reldan plugged in their phones.

"Frank?" Reldan asked, using the agreed-upon bogus first name for Jimmy Parcells.

"Yes," Gallo replied, adding the set code-phrase. "I'm an investigator for the Buzzard."

Robert Reldan and Nick Gallo, a.k.a. Frank Parisi, would talk for an hour during that window visit on March 8, but there is no transcript or recording of the conversation. The system Ken Nass had devised failed to work. Though it had been successfully tested back at the BCPO, the prison phone system was different and did not throw off the volume that Nass expected. Gallo's end of the conversation was faintly audible, but the words Reldan spoke were almost impossible to decipher. The tape would be unusable in court proceedings. Fortunately, the BCPO investigative team learned of the malfunction right after Gallo exited the prison. During the drive back to BCPO offices in Hackensack, Gallo immediately set to work trying to reconstruct from memory all that had occurred during the visit.

Reldan had begun the conversation by saying he didn't trust the prison phones—they may be bugged. Gallo said he doubted it, and hadn't Reldan, himself, picked the booth where they were sitting? Yes, Reldan said, but all the booths may be bugged. He then motioned to Gallo that he would write things down and hold notes up to the glass so that Gallo could read what he wanted to say. The two men agreed to do things the way Reldan felt most comfortable, but because Reldan didn't trust phones (he wouldn't call "Parisi" at the number Gallo had set up) or the mail, a subsequent *contact* visit in the prison yard would be necessary. Gallo said okay, but wanted it set up quickly.

"I'm in a hurry," Gallo said. "I need money." Gallo then asked, "What kind of deal is it?"

Reldan wrote something down on a piece of paper and held it up to the glass for Gallo to see. It read, "$100,000 to $150,000 in jewelry."

"How many people?" Gallo asked.

Not bothering to write, Reldan said, "One or two."

"What kind of hassle?" Gallo asked.

"No hassle," Reldan responded.

Gallo wanted to know who the people were, and Reldan told him, "a close relation of mine." Through the window, Reldan mouthed the word, "Aunt." He then wrote something and again held his writing up to the window: "female-50's, male-39 years."

"Will they be home?" Gallo asked.

"Yes," Reldan answered.

"What do I do with them?"

Again, Reldan began writing, and then he held his notation to the window. Gallo felt a chill as he read the words, "take out," as Reldan, his eyes cold and direct, moved his fingers across his throat in a cutting motion. The universal sign language meant only one thing. Reldan wanted them both dead.

Gallo acknowledged that he understood what Reldan was trying to convey. "How will I get into the house?" he asked.

"Introduce yourself," Reldan said on the phone.

"Introduce myself," Gallo mused, adding, "You got any ideas?"

Reldan wrote the words "cop, milkman, delivery man"—there was one other suggestion that Gallo couldn't recall. Gallo pointed to the word "cop" and asked, "What do you mean by this?"

"There's been many of them to the house because of B&E's," Reldan said. "I can tell you better when we're alone in the yard."

Gallo asked, "What's your end for this?"

Reldan wrote the words, "two years—will." He pointed to the "two years" and said, "I'll be out by then," and then he pointed to the word "will." Gallo acknowledged that he understood.

In his reconstruction of the encounter with Robert Reldan on March 8, Nick Gallo recalled an amazing amount of detail. He established that the house Reldan wanted him to rob was in Alpine, a ritzy town (with "Beverly Hills"-type homes) in Bergen County, New Jersey. He got directions and obtained a general description of the layout, including tennis courts, pool, garage, and the fact that there would be two Cadillac El Dorados parked in the driveway. Gallo said he'd "check out" the house beforehand, but Reldan didn't want him to. "It's not necessary," he said. Reldan then wrote down a phone number and held it up to the glass: "201-568-9833."

"I have to call this number?" Gallo asked.

"If she says yes, you go," Reldan said. "If she says no, work can't be done. But you have to call after 5 PM."

Gallo, as Parisi, had told Reldan that he did some contracting. Since this was the business that Reldan was in, the two of them disguised their discussion by using construction metaphors—words like "cabinets" to refer to the jewelry that Parisi was supposed to steal.

"Who is this?" Gallo asked about the owner of the phone number that Reldan displayed.

Away from the phone, Reldan mouthed the words, "my wife." It was the first indication investigators had that Judy Reldan might have been involved in the conspiracy, but that supposition was later ruled out when it was determined that Reldan intended to dupe her into participating. Using his wife to insure that both victims would be home for the hit, Reldan told Judy that "Frank Parisi" was a friend of his—an insurance salesman— whom he wanted his aunt and Misha Dabich to see. Reldan would also use

Judy to set up Parisi's future yard visit.

If he could, Gallo wanted to avoid making a yard visit, which would give Reldan a better opportunity to observe the differences between his appearance and that of Jimmy Parcells. Gallo intimated that he was afraid that the guards would recognize him if he came back again.

"Every time I walk in here," Gallo said, "they see me."

"Once or twice, it's the same," Reldan argued.

"Are you sure you can't call me or write?" Gallo tried.

But Reldan was adamant. "No," he said. "If someone reads the mail one time, we're dead. When you come [for the yard visit], I'll have . . . everything laid out."

Reldan didn't want his hit man to get cold feet. He wrote down "$50,000,000," held it up to the window, and said, "That's what we are talking about." Gallo understood that he was referring to the wealth of the people whom Parisi would be robbing and killing. "You can check these people out with Dun and Bradstreet," Reldan said. He pointed to a prior note, which said, "$100,000 to $150,000 in jewelry." Then, he wrote, "$98,000-8 ct." and pointed to his left ring finger, indicating that his aunt would be wearing a ring.

Reldan couldn't resist the impulse to let Parisi know he was dealing with someone serious. "Do you know what I'm in for?" he asked.

"I thought it was a B&E," Gallo replied.

"Well, yeah, but—" Reldan stopped and wrote, "two homicides." He held the note up to the glass.

Gallo expressed disbelief that Reldan thought he would be out of prison, collecting his inheritance, in two years, if he was in prison for two homicides. But Reldan, using a combination of writing and the phone, assured his visitor that he would be out. He showed Gallo the business card of his Washington DC attorneys, the Williams & Connolly law firm.

"How's it look for you?" Gallo asked.

"Real good," Reldan reported. "They [the prosecutors] wouldn't have waited 18 months if they had anything. I got the best, and we can beat it. As long as I am in here and the shelves get cut down [meaning the hit on his aunt and her friend goes down as planned], I'm all right."

"How come you didn't handle it before?" Gallo asked.

"I couldn't do it personally," Reldan explained. "I couldn't cover myself."

The visit ended with Gallo and Reldan deciding on how to arrange the contact visit for later that month. Trying to avoid complications by limiting the information that Reldan might convey to Barber and Williams, Gallo suggested, "Let's not go telling the other guys too much when you write." Reldan agreed to follow that suggestion.

On March 15, Ed Denning interviewed Allison Williams at Rahway State Prison and received confirmation that Gallo's undercover gambit worked. Allison gave Denning a letter that Reldan had sent to Al Barber and that Barber had given to him. Though the letter was undated, it did have "Friday" typed at the top, which indicated that it had to have been sent to Barber on March 11, three days after Gallo's Tuesday, March 8 window visit, which Reldan referred to in the letter. He wrote, "The investigator was down and will have to make one more trip but things are progressing nicely and I think everything will be under control soon."

As to his pending murder indictment, Reldan informed Barber, "Things are really moving with the case and the counsel seems to think that there is a better than 70% chance that the case will never hit the courts. I never believe shit like that but these guys are top of the line and they don't bullshit too much so we will see."

Reldan soon followed up with another typewritten letter to Barber, this one dated "3/16/77" and covering much the same ground. "I got a long letter from my lawyers," he wrote, "and they have all the discovery now and will be coming up [from Washington DC] to spend a full day next Tuesday, so I guess we'll know just what is what next week." Reldan also referred to Parisi, again by code: "The investigator will be back next week and we will have that done then we can move forward," he wrote. "Looks like everything will be coming together for both of us in the next few months and we will know where we are going."

Reldan ended his March 16 letter to Barber with an attempt at what he considered humor: "Hang in there and as one child molester said to the other, 'May all your problems be little ones'—ha ha."

On March 18, Investigator Ed Denning made a formal application before Assignment Judge Theodore Trautwein to place a tap on Judy Reldan's phone line. The application was made *in camera*—in the judge's private chambers—to preserve secrecy. Judge Trautwein granted the request, and BCPO Investigators Nass and Lange installed the tap that same afternoon, March 18, 1977. That evening, just before six o'clock, Nick Gallo called and got through to Judy Reldan. He introduced himself as Frank Parisi, "a friend of Bob's." Judy seemed to be expecting his call. Gallo asked if she would help set up a yard visit with Bob, and Judy said she would contact her husband to see when the visit should be made and then she would call Parisi back at the number he gave her—the dummy number that had been arranged to ring in Gallo's home.

Reldan's lawyers from the Williams and Connolly firm showed up at Trenton State as promised on Tuesday, March 22, spending most of the day with their client. It is certain that Edward Bennett Williams, himself, was not part of the entourage—a rainmaker attorney like him does not make house calls to out-of-state, non-celebrity murder defendants. But, apparently, Reldan was happy with the firm's efforts in his behalf. He wrote to Barber that same day and updated him: "my lawyers were here all day today and they just got the discovery items from the prosecutor so it will be quite a while until they finish with all the motions, etc. so it looks like I will be here for the duration or at least the next six months."

In that same March 22 letter, Reldan complained to Barber about the distance his wife Judy had to travel to visit him, but she most likely saw him between March 19 and 22 to deliver the message that Frank Parisi wanted to set up the contact visit. Reldan told Barber, "The investigator will be here Thurs or Fri and that should be the last trip."

On Wednesday, March 23, Judy Reldan called Gallo using the special phone line and told him the visit would be for either Thursday or Friday of that same week—March 24 or 25—and that Gallo should call the prison to make sure which day yard visits would be allowed. Since these visits were outdoors and depended on clear weather, the prison did not finalize the approved days for yard visits until a day or two before, when weather reports were more reliable. Gallo said he would follow that instruction. He called the prison and found out that Thursday, March 24, would be the yard visit day that week.

On the appointed day, the same group of investigators—Gallo, Denning, Delia and Nass—made the trip to Trenton State Prison. This time, Nass equipped Gallo with both a transmitter and a backup self-contained recording device. Gallo would have two "on" switches and two "off" switches to activate. Both devices were hooked up to a microphone hidden in Gallo's coat, which he would wear during the yard visit. It was chilly that March morning, so Gallo would not attract suspicion by keeping his coat buttoned. Also, because it was going to be a contact visit, Lieutenant Delia had contacted the Trenton State warden to arrange for "Frank Parisi" to get a pass on the body search. Guards would be instructed to fake the search so that other visitors going through the search process would not become suspicious.

The group arrived at Trenton State Prison just before 9:00 AM. They parked two blocks from the prison entrance. Gallo would go in alone, as before, while the others waited in the vehicle. From the transmitting device, Investigator Nass would monitor and record Gallo's conversation with Reldan. With the backup of a separate recording device on Gallo's person, there was every expectation there would be no equipment malfunction this time around. To be sure of convicting Reldan on a murder conspiracy charge, it was essential that they had a tape of the conversation in which he conspired with Parisi to murder his aunt and her companion.

114

Upon entering the prison's main gate, Gallo went to the visitors' area, presented his identification as Frank Parisi to the guard, and was told to wait in an adjoining room. About seven or eight other visitors—mostly women, but also a few children—were already seated in the waiting room. Ten or 15 minutes elapsed, before several corrections officers came in and told everyone to line up on one side of the room to be searched. The officers used a wand, presumably to detect the presence of metal. Gallo was passed through without incident, after which he switched on both the transmitter and self-contained tape recorder.

Along with the other visitors, Gallo walked through a long outdoor yard into a second yard where the contact visits took place. It was a large area, encompassed on three sides by 25-foot walls, topped off by concertinas of razor-barbed wire. The prison, itself, served as the fourth wall of the enclosure, which was spacious enough to afford a degree of privacy to each prisoner and his visitor. Gallo noticed a group of yellow benches off to the right of the yard entrance and took a seat in the sunniest section to await Reldan's arrival. He didn't have to wait long before he saw Reldan come into the yard.

"Greetings," Reldan said, as he approached Gallo and shook hands with his designated hit man. In the BCPO vehicle parked outside the prison, Investigator Nass and the others listened in, satisfied that the transmitter was working properly. Both sides of the conversation came through clearly.

Gallo started by complaining about the search. "*Ma Donna*," he said, using the familiar mob expression of exasperation, "they go over you like with a fine-toothed comb."

Reldan nodded. "They don't want you bringing a piece in with you," he said.

"This is too much, this is bad," Gallo said, showing dissatisfaction with the risk of the second visit. He was laying the groundwork, as he did not want to have to come back a third time, should Reldan get that idea in his head. He needn't have worried.

"Well," Reldan said, "this is the last trip. We'll work everything out."

Reldan told Gallo that he would have to delay the hit on his aunt for a month or so. He said his lawyers came to the prison to review his murder case and they needed to get a statement from his aunt to help with his defense.

The encouraging reports Reldan was getting from his lawyers raised his optimism to its highest level since the indictment, making him all the more eager to have Frank Parisi carry out the hit on Lillian Booth and Misha Dabich. That eagerness apparently blinded Reldan to the obvious discrepancy between the Jimmy Parcells description and the physical characteristics of the man now before him. Gallo remained seated for most of the contact visit, but there were times when both he and Reldan walked about, side by side. Reldan was six feet tall. He surely saw that Parisi was about equal in height and, even with a bulky winter coat on, was nowhere near the 170-pound stature of the real Parcells. Reldan had also heard about the $1 million post-office job that Parcells had pulled off—and been arrested for. Gallo side-stepped that issue by alluding to being out on bail, and Reldan, who was focused on beating his murder rap and getting his hands on his aunt's wealth, didn't press him. In fact, he got right down to business early in the visit.

"All right, now listen," he told Gallo. "You do this like I tell you, it's one, two, three, in and out, pop. As a matter of fact, I can get you right into the house. Your bit is that uh, good morning, I'm an investigator for the law firm of uh, Williams and Connolly, a law firm from Washington DC and we'd like to ask you some questions. She'll let you right in the door."

Gallo, trying to get Reldan to give him something in writing to serve as corroboration of the conspiracy, said, "You're gonna have this written down for me because I ain't gonna be able to remember all this shit."

Reldan demurred. He tore a few blank pages out of a small notebook and gave them to Gallo to take notes, but he wasn't about to put anything down on paper himself. Reldan then proceeded to lay out the plan for Gallo. He told him to expect no weapons in the house, and only his aunt, in her fifties, and her companion, a man about 40, would be there at the time. He referred to his aunt's companion as "a stone cold punk" and said, "She'll give you more problems than he will. I mean if it was gonna go to a knockdown fight, she'd jump on you before he would. Ya know what I'm telling you? The woman, the female is the deadlier of the species."

Gallo expressed uneasiness about carrying a gun on the job.

"Well, you gotta take it," Reldan said. "How else you gonna go there? I mean . . . ."

"Well," Gallo paused, "do I have to use a gun?

"It's the best," Reldan said.

Gallo continued to express reservations about carrying a gun. "What if I'm stopped?"

The men continued to discuss the issue of what weapon Gallo would use to do the job. The detective's mastery of the undercover role was clearly evident throughout the taped meeting with Reldan. On the fly, he drew out detail after detail about the robbery and murders that Reldan wanted Frank Parisi to commit on his behalf. The information Gallo elicited from Reldan would prove decisive later on, when Reldan was brought to trial for the conspiracy. Eventually, Reldan would win the argument about the choice of a murder weapon, but only after he became visibly agitated over the subject.

"Yeah, but if you see," Reldan argued, "if you get 'em, get 'em both, ya know, if they split up on you and you got one going this way and one going that way, you can't start to chase one way and then the other. Forget that part. Then you take 'em down, even if you don't take them out with the first shot, you take down. They don't get out of the house. They don't get a chance to get to that wire [the phone]. Ya know what I'm saying?"

"All right, all right," Gallo finally relented. "Then the worse, I'll have to dump it, that's all."

Reldan, showing relief, told Gallo that there would be plenty of good spots where he could dump the gun, including the Hudson River and Alpine reservoir. He went on to give Gallo directions to the aunt's house and a description of the secluded neighborhood. Gallo guided the discussion back to specifics about the expected loot from the job.

"Yeah, now what are we talking about now?" Gallo asked. "You know, you showed me a lot of figures before." Gallo was referring to the numbers Reldan had written down and showed him during the window visit on March 8.

"You're talking—the ring alone is worth $100,000," Reldan said. "The ring alone."

"She's gonna have this?"

"She wears it on her at all times," Reldan said. "She wears it to bed. She takes it off maybe to wash dishes, ya know. The jewelry—she's got a, she's got a star sapphire that's 40 carats, surrounded in diamonds. She's got—you're talking about another hundred thousand dollars minimum worth of jewelry. You're talking about a minimum of—you're talking about retail $250,000 worth of jewelry. Wholesale, uh—"

"What about cash in the house?" Gallo asked.

Reldan said Parisi might get lucky and find some cash. If he did, it would be in his aunt's pocketbook. She didn't have any other hiding places in the house, as far as he knew.

"Sounds strange," Gallo said. "She must be a weirdo."

"She is," Reldan agreed.

After further discussion about his aunt and how she inherited her wealth, Reldan told Gallo to contact his wife Judy when he was planning to do the hit, just to make sure that both his aunt and her male companion were home, since they traveled a lot. Judy, Reldan explained, called them frequently, so she'd be able to let Parisi know whether it was a "go" or "no go." Reldan mentioned again the necessary one-month delay to give his aunt time to help his defense lawyers on the murder case, which he expected to be completed by the end of April.

"Any time after May 1," Reldan said. "It's your party."

Reldan told Gallo he might have difficulty "moving" his aunt's 40-carat star sapphire, given its size, and provided the name of a fence in Chicago that might be able to handle it.

Gallo, playing dumb, again had Reldan review specifics about the hit, including directions to the aunt's house, what he would find when he got there, and how Reldan expected the victims to act. During the course of this exchange, Reldan went off on a rant about his Aunt Lillian, confirming the deep hostility for her that his therapists—Prendergast and Gartner—had related to BCPO investigators.

Drawing Reldan out, Gallo asked, "You got no qualms about this broad now?"

"Shh—I would have done it myself," Reldan said. "What qualms?"

"Well, you know," Gallo said. "That's why I asked if she's a relative."

"She's an aunt only by marriage [one of many lies Reldan told that day] and she's a real bitch," Reldan said. "Ya know, she's uh—she uses that money—she makes my mother's life miserable. See, I don't—I don't depend on her."

"Yeah," Gallo said.

"And—and all these other people, like every year she gives them a couple thousand dollars for Christmas and does her bit, but she dribs and drabs it out so she can control them," Reldan said. "And then, if you don't do something she wants, 'oh, you're not getting your check this month.' She told me that once. I said to her, 'You know what you can do with that fuckin' check. Stick it up your ass. I may blow it in a fuckin' poker game in one night.' "

"Yeah," Gallo said, encouraging him.

"That's why I say I'd be the first one they would come to," Reldan continued. "I'm barely on speaking terms with her." Reldan had previously told Gallo that a $75,000 initial retainer for his lawyers came from his own funds, not from his aunt, who actually put up the money. But his aunt's generosity in that regard wouldn't have fit into the story he told Parisi.

"Yeah, yeah."

"And she treats my wife like shit when I'm in here," Reldan continued. "'Oh, Robert shouldn't have done this,' and all he did to her. In fact, she can keep the fuck off my back."

"Yeah, I know," Gallo said. "But, you know, sometimes you get a little leery when you're gonna kill somebody's aunt."

"I would have done it myself, that's what I'm telling you," Reldan assured him. "I only did her house [Reldan claimed earlier to have burglarized his aunt's house when she wasn't home] and I would have done her if I would have known that the heat wouldn't come by doing it, ya know?"

"Yeah." Reldan was on a roll, and Gallo, like the good detective he was, just let his undercover mark keep talking, which he did.

"There's no way I could have set up an airtight alibi and do this thing at the same time," Reldan explained. "That's what I'm telling you. And they would have been dead in my ass."

"You must have a good rep," Gallo said.

"Yeah, I do," Reldan agreed. "You know, I had a good long run for years, then they knew I was doing shit. I was living on top of the world and never done no time, and then everything fell at once and I've been doing time for the last fuckin' 10 years or more."

"What the hell's your problem now?" Gallo asked.

"Because I stay in the area, see," Reldan explained. "I stay in Bergen County, and uh, I'm known. So every time they get a chance, they—they zap me."

"Yeah."

"And I'm like a chump," Reldan said. "I keep going back up there. Because, uh, I got so many connections up there. My family's up there, all my business connections are up there. So, I had my own construction firm up there this last time out. But everything's done now. I'm leaving."

Gallo then tried something ingenious, going with Reldan's conversation as he tried to draw him out by setting up an opportunity for Reldan to boast about getting rough with women.   "I stopped at this fuckin' bar," Gallo said. "I was with this fuckin' broad. I could have killed her. I hoped to make it with her. I go out in the car with her. I no sooner get out in the car, I make a move on the fuckin' broad, and don't you know a cop's car came by."

"Eeee!" Reldan reacted.

"And the fuckin' broad swings at me in the car!" Gallo said. "I thought she had got me, but she missed me. That's all I fuckin' needed. To have something happen."

"Yeah, that's rough," Reldan agreed.

"Hmmm, the fuckin' cunt," Gallo continued.

"That's rough."

"Oh, they are unbelievable," said Gallo.

"Yeah. Well, I've got no complaints," Reldan said. "I been lucky. I been living good. I'm only here through my own stupidity." Reldan would not talk about the abductions and murders of Susan Heynes and Susan Reeve, not even to burnish his tough-guy image with Frank Parisi. But he did begin talking to Gallo about a contingency plan, in case his Washington lawyers didn't come through. He told Gallo he had been contemplating an escape from Rahway when his indictment for murder came down, thwarting his hoped-for transfer to the minimum-security section of that prison. But he was nurturing another idea about how to bust out.

"That's something else I was gonna talk to you about," Reldan said. "Uh, either you or somebody else. If this thing [the murder charges] starts shaping up like it don't look good, ya know, I'll find somebody that's looking for a couple of hundred thousand, ya know, just to uh—"

"For what?" Gallo interrupted.

"To make a move to get me out," Reldan said. "Ya know, on a court trip, ya know."

"You're talking a lot of money and you talked about giving it all to your lawyer," Gallo said, since Reldan had told Gallo his case would end up costing over $175,000. "Where you gonna come up with—"

"Listen, to get out of here, before I'll give it to the lawyer, I'll give it to, ya know, to get out," Reldan explained. "That's what I'm saying. Well, they only got 75. The rest they don't get unless it goes to trial. Ya know?"

"Yeah."

"Now, if I see it's going to trial and it don't look good—" Reldan said. "They told me the other day, 'Listen,' they said, 'we can get all of this squashed. This is all illegal,' and they said, 'We're in good shape and we're very optimistic.' I said, 'Listen, you can be optimistic, because if you're wrong—' "

"You ain't shittin', because they're on the outside," Gallo said.

"Yeah, if you're wrong, you can go home," Reldan said.

"Yeah. Yeah. Yeah."

"But these guys are standup," Reldan said. "And they're qualified, so they don't bullshit too much, ya know? They're not like the average joker: 'Don't worry, I got everything under control.'"

"Yeah, right, right."

"So uh, when they talk, I listen," Reldan said. "But I don't listen all the way, and uh, I'm going to see what they do first. But uh, I'm looking for somebody . . . ."

Gallo didn't show further interest in Reldan's escape plan, even when Reldan bragged about helping two friends, one in Florida and one in Kansas, escape from custody under similar circumstances. "Um, well, all right," Gallo said. "Keep that in the back of my mind."

The rest of the yard visit was uneventful. Gallo continued to shmooze Reldan, selling himself as a regular guy whom Reldan could trust, but no significant revelations were in the offing. Reldan talked a lot about his Bergen County murder indictments, but only in the context of authorities having no case and his lawyers being confident that he would beat the rap.

"Everything that they got—that little bit of shit that they got, should be suppressed," Reldan said. "And if it does get to trial, they'll put it in front of a judge, rather than a jury, and, uh, you don't fuck with Edward Bennett Williams, ya know? You go— You look at that counsel table, you see eight fuckin' lawyers sitting there, and every time you open your mouth, there's an objection because they—"

"It's the guy," Gallo said.

"Yeah."

"It's the guy."

"That's what I'm saying," Reldan said.

"Right man to have," Gallo agreed.

"The only man to have."

* * *

Reldan's vision of the kick-ass, top-shelf defense in the double-murder case would vanish like a mirage in front of a thirst-crazed nomad. Within two weeks of Reldan's final meeting with undercover detective Nick Gallo, the lawyers of Williams and Connolly, including the great Edward Bennett Williams himself, would pull stakes and disappear into the cold desert night.

Chapter 14

There was no way her Bobby would ever want to harm her.

The rude awakening came at 11:00 AM on March 30, 1977, when BCPO Investigator Ed Denning and Detective Charles Lange showed up at Trenton State Prison and served Robert Reldan with an arrest warrant for conspiring to murder his aunt, Lillian Booth, and for advocating the deaths of both Booth and her male companion, Misha Dabich. Reldan appeared confounded, his usual glibness gone. Before he could overcome his shock, he was also handed a search warrant. Then, the officers gave Reldan's prison cell a thorough going-over. Denning removed 71 items in all, including a stack of letters and other writings, a diary, and a Smith Corona typewriter, which would be tested to see if Reldan had used it for the "Buzzard" letters that Denning had acquired through the Williams brothers.

When a search is done, the officer in charge normally leaves an inventory of what was seized. In this case, too much was taken for Denning to do the inventory on the spot, but he promised Reldan an itemized list at a later date. The investigators were also in a rush to conduct another search before the prison grapevine alerted that particular subject. They headed north from Trenton and arrived at 2:30 PM at Rahway State Prison, where they served an arrest warrant on Al Barber for participating in the conspiracy to murder Lillian Booth. Barber's prison cell was also searched, and items seized.

Among the letters they confiscated from Reldan's cell was one from his wife, Judy. Beginning with the salutation, "My love," it referred to the call she'd made to Frank Parisi on March 23 to set up the yard visit.

"I called Frank last night and he said he will call there and see you. He really sounds dumb," she wrote. "I had to explain it to him 3 times. He said, Oh, I can visit either Thurs. or Fri.? I said, No, they will tell you which day. Oh well. He sounded pretty nice though." Gallo was not being *dumb* but was manipulating a tapped conversation on a special line while he was working a suspect—Judy Reldan, who was, at the time, under suspicion for being involved in the conspiracy.

Judy enclosed a letter to Reldan from her son Eddie, for whom Reldan had genuine affection. She then asked a question about the murder indictment and whether the hair and blood samples Reldan was forced to give had implicated him in the crimes. Sounding like a wife who was trying to believe the stories that her husband had told her, she seemed to be finding it difficult. She told Reldan she was hurt by what she had learned about "Ronnie," a woman Reldan apparently had been seeing the last time he was out of prison, but said she took comfort in knowing that Reldan loved her and not Ronnie. In her letter, Judy made it clear that she was finally reaching a decision point about her future with Reldan, the man with whom she had fallen in love at first sight 10 years earlier and the man she had stuck with through the Bernice Caplan rape conviction, the Blanche Mate assault conviction, burglary convictions, a double-murder indictment, and multiple infidelities. One has to wonder at her forbearance.

"There are other ways I can resolve a lot of the negative feelings I've been having for so long," she wrote, "and I'll tell you about that when I see you. Don't worry, it won't take long. I promise to do very little talking, but there are a few things I must say. The rest I will say now.

"I love you very much for listening to me at all times, no matter what it is I have to say, for being patient and for being willing to discuss everything with me. I forgive you for all the wrongs, real or imagined, that I thought you had inflicted on me. That's about all I can say for now. I'm doing a lot of heavy thinking and I know I have to make a decision. I will not continue in this vacillating anymore; it hurts us both too much. I will know my decision by Sunday. I have to give myself that much time at least to decide if it's right."

Judy ended her letter by urging Reldan to watch *Scenes from a Marriage*, a television program that was airing that Sunday. "It shows a woman's feelings when she has been betrayed," she said. Signing off, she asked him again. "Watch it, please. I love you, Judy."

We don't know if Judy Reldan made her decision that Sunday, or later. We do know that by the following Thursday, March 30, when the conspiracy charges were formally lodged against her husband, whatever future Judy hoped to have with Robert Reldan was gone forever. At some point, she realized that and she left, moving to southern California. She eventually divorced Robert Reldan and changed her name back to Rosenberg. She would never testify at any of Reldan's later trials, as an alibi witness or anything else. Survived by her son Eddie, Judy Rosenberg died on April 24, 2007, in Palm Desert, Riverside County, California.

* * *

When word of the new charges against Reldan arrived at the Williams and Connolly law firm in Washington DC, consternation reigned. Most likely, the lawyers heard about it that day, March 30, via a phone call from their client. A call to the Bergen County Prosecutor by Reldan's lead attorney would have confirmed the messy details of the new charges. Most assuredly, Reldan, speaking with his lawyers, had neglected to convey those details—like the fact that the entire transaction was on tape.

By the next morning, the firm's managing partners were fully aware of the allegations contained in the arrest warrant and had reached their own decision point about continuing to represent Robert Reldan. Not only would these latest charges damage the firm's chances for success in defending the murder case, they would also dry up Reldan's funding source, Lillian Booth. The money already received was an initial retainer, a down payment on what would surely cost $200,000 or more, through the trial phase. No one expected Booth to pay for her nephew's defense on the charge that he tried to have her robbed and killed, let alone the continuing expenses for the Heynes/Reeve murder trial.

They had to make a quick decision whether to stay in the case and risk not being paid or to withdraw as counsel, which would require an application to the court for permission. Up to that point, Williams and Connolly had not become deeply involved. They had made a preliminary court appearance to gain approval for out-of-state representation, and, because they intended to challenge jurisdiction in the murder case, they had advised Reldan to stand silent at the murder indictment arraignment, allowing the judge to enter *pro forma* "not guilty" pleas on Reldan's behalf. They had also obtained discovery in the case and had begun to review it, but that was all. If they withdrew now, they could do so without prejudicing their client's ability to obtain other representation. If they continued to represent Reldan and began filing pre-trial motions, their ability to withdraw later—when payment for services was no longer forthcoming—would be severely limited.

It was an easy decision for the partners. Within 48 hours, the firm applied to the Superior Court in Hackensack for permission to withdraw as Reldan's attorney in the murder case. The application was granted on April 8, 1977. Reldan was on his own, at least for the time being.

* * *

Ed Denning picked up his phone shortly after 10:00 AM on April 11, 1977, and heard the excited voice of Assistant Prosecutor Dennis Kohler. "Ed, Ed," said Dennis. "Come over to my office. You won't believe what I'm holding in my hand." Kohler refused to tell him what it was over the phone. Amused at his friend and colleague's excitement, Denning put his work aside and walked to Kohler's office, in the Prosecutor's section of the nearby Bergen County courthouse.

Smiling as Denning walked in, Kohler waved what appeared to be a letter. "Close the door! Sit down and read this," he said.

As Denning began reading, he understood Kohler's excitement. It was a letter from Robert Reldan.

"This guy is crazy," Denning said, still reading. "He must be going off the deep end."

The handwritten letter was dated April 8, the same date the Williams and Connolly firm got approval to withdraw from the murder case. Addressing his remarks to Assistant Prosecutor Kohler, Reldan, in stilted legalese, wrote:

> I will be appearing pro se [without counsel] in all matters, pending and future, from this date forward.
>
> As such, I would appreciate it if you, or one of your representatives, could arrange to meet with me in the very near future.
>
> My hope is to save the State, your office, and myself, much time, trouble, and money by expediting any present or pending cases.
>
> I am fully aware of my rights and privileges under <u>Miranda</u>, et al, and you may take this letter as my acknowledgment, and waiver, of those rights at this time so that we may talk, on or off the record, and hopefully adjudicate everything as quickly as possible.
>
> Hoping to hear from you shortly, I remain
>
> Very truly yours
>
> Robert R. Reldan

An accomplished jailhouse lawyer, Reldan had matriculated in dozens of real-life courtrooms, doing his homework in prison law libraries over a 20-year criminal career. He was also a bright guy, as doctors at the Rahway diagnostic center noted 10 years earlier, when he dropped psychiatric and medical terms as if he understood what they meant. When he wrote the letter, Reldan knew—as Kohler and Denning did—that Edward Bennett Williams had cut him loose. He was also aware that he would soon be indicted on the conspiracy charges, and he wanted to engage the Bergen County Prosecutor's Office in a fishing expedition to see what they had and how confident they were of a successful prosecution. Still believing that he would eventually beat the murder charges, even without Williams at his side, Reldan must have realized that he was cooked on the conspiracy charge, having spilled his guts to Frank Parisi, his imposter hit man.

Kohler and Denning thought that they had nothing to lose by accommodating Reldan and making the trip to Trenton State Prison to talk to him, but they ran the decision by the newly appointed prosecutor, Roger Breslin. (Joe Woodcock had resigned in February to pursue what would be an unsuccessful bid for the governorship.) Breslin approved the meeting, so Denning, with Detective Ralph Cenicola and a certified court stenographer—who would make a verbatim record of the discussion— went to Trenton on April 11, the same day Kohler received the letter.

Remember, Denning and Robert Reldan had a history by this time. When Denning interviewed Reldan on October 22, 1975, for what was, then, a missing person's case, the investigator was the first person to suspect that Reldan was involved. And Denning was the BCPO representative whom Reldan boasted of "putting one over on." After his indictment for the murders, and after gaining access to discovery in the case—including a transcript of his October 22 interview—Reldan gained a new, not unfounded respect for Ed Denning. He still didn't like him, but he was smart enough to be on his guard with the investigator and to watch what he said.

Denning was all business. He began the interview by confirming, on the record, that Reldan had sent the April 8 letter to Assistant Prosecutor Dennis Kohler.

"You work fast," Reldan said.

"Is that a copy of the letter you sent down?" Denning repeated.

"Yes."

"That is why we are down here," Denning said.

Reldan said that he'd met with his attorneys the previous Friday, when they informed him that they were withdrawing from the murder case. "I would like to know . . . what you've got," he said, "and what I can do to get it knocked out of the box as quick as possible." Reldan knew from his attorneys that a grand jury action was pending on the conspiracy charges.

"That is going to tie up this whole other thing [the murder indictment]," Reldan said. "It's going to influence this other thing and I would just as soon move on it, get it out of the way. What have you got

127

and what do you need and what does the prosecutor want and what can we do?" Trying to negotiate a plea bargain on the murder conspiracy charge, Reldan seemed to want to concentrate solely on defending the Heynes and Reeve murder indictment.

Denning ignored Reldan's inquiry. Instead, he read Reldan his Miranda rights, point by point, getting his affirmative responses as he waived each of those rights. Denning also had Reldan waive his right to have counsel present, and then he read a written waiver form aloud and had Reldan sign that, too. With the housekeeping finished, Denning felt assured that, if Reldan was dumb enough to make any admissions during the interview, they could be used against him in court.

But, immediately, it became clear that Reldan was not willing to discuss the murder charges. All he wanted from Denning was an indication of what evidence the BCPO had against him in the conspiracy case, and what might be possible as a plea deal. Reldan also wanted to let Denning know that, in his mind, Bergen County didn't have jurisdiction to handle the new charges, since the conspiracy had occurred at Trenton State Prison, in Mercer County. Reldan was disputing the Bergen County Prosecutor's authority in the case, but he still wanted to try to make a deal with that office.

Denning rightly refused to disclose what evidence his office had for the conspiracy charges. He also refused to discuss the legalities of the matter. Reldan's legal analysis, however, was far off the mark, particularly regarding jurisdiction. The targets of Reldan's robbery and murder scheme—Lillian Booth and Misha Dabich—resided in Bergen County. More important, at least one overt act in furtherance of the conspiracy occurred in Bergen County; Reldan had used his wife, Judy, in Tenafly to set up the yard visit with his hit man, Frank Parisi. Therefore, there was no issue of Bergen County's jurisdiction.

Reldan and Denning sparred on the issue of plea bargaining. Denning didn't have authority to make a deal, but wanted to know what Reldan was after. Reldan wanted to talk with Kohler directly, but Denning said that there was no way that was going to happen. They also had a difference of opinion regarding how much time Reldan might face; Reldan thought his maximum exposure was 15 years on the conspiracy charges, but Denning explained that he was facing far greater time. Talking to the undercover Gallo on March 8, Reldan had advocated the deaths of Booth and Dabich—two victims—making two separate charges of advocating death. He did the same thing again, at the March 24 yard visit, thereby accumulating two more "advocating" charges, making four in total. Then, there was the additional charge of conspiracy to commit murder, so he faced five charges in all.

Reldan conceded Denning's math, but said he didn't care how many charges he pleaded guilty to, so long as the sentences all ran concurrently. He had ample experience with the wonders of concurrent sentencing. But Reldan required two other stipulations before he would agree to plead guilty: He wanted a maximum term of 15 years and an agreement that the prosecutor would not ask the sentencing judge to impose "habitual offender" status on him. Designated a habitual offender—which he certainly was—Reldan would face enhanced time, more than the 15 years he was bargaining for.

Having finally pinned Reldan down on what he was looking for, Denning left the room to call Dennis Kohler to see if the assistant prosecutor wanted to make the deal. After a short delay to check with his superiors, Kohler called back with an answer, which Denning related to Reldan.

"Unless you are willing to do something with respect to the murder indictments," Denning told Reldan, "he's not going to accept anything from you on the advocating the death of your aunt."

"What does he want to do with [the murder indictments]?" Reldan asked. "He wants a plea to those?"

"He wants a plea," Denning confirmed.

Reldan nodded to the court stenographer. "Make sure you put down I laughed," he said. "Is he kidding or what? A plea to what?"

"He wants you to plead to the murders," Denning said.

"What does he want for a plea?" Reldan asked. "He wants two guilty pleas, right?"

"What do you expect?" Denning asked.

"What does he want?" Reldan repeated.

"He wants a guilty plea."

"On two counts?"

"Yes," Denning said.

"First degree?" Reldan asked. "You wasted your time . . . . I don't know, guys, Jesus Christ."

"We are looking for a guilty plea," Denning said. "And he would be willing to give you concurrent sentencing on that."

"That's wonderful," Reldan said. "That's really nice of him. That guy is all heart. Listen, doesn't he understand that if I go to bat on that and blow [lose], do I give a shit about this second charge, the advocating?"

Denning acknowledged that Kohler probably understood that, but was unwilling to do anything on the advocating and conspiracy charges without a plea to the murders. Reldan, still convinced that he would beat the murder rap, made it clear that he had no intention of pleading guilty to those charges. He thanked Denning and Cenicola for responding so quickly to his letter. As he departed the interview room, Reldan sneered, "Nice talking to you."

Ten days after the fruitless plea bargain discussion at Trenton State, a Bergen County grand jury handed up a five-count indictment against Robert R. Reldan on April 21, 1977. The indictment included two counts of advocating the death of Lillian Booth (on March 8 and 24, 1977—the two dates when Gallo and Reldan met), two counts of advocating the death of Misha Dabich (same dates), and one count of conspiring to murder Lillian Booth. Albert Barber, named only in the fifth count, was indicted as a co-conspirator to rob and murder Booth.

Though the murder indictment preceded the advocating and conspiracy indictment by some three months, and the Heynes and Reeve murders occurred 15 months before the conspiracy, the Bergen County Prosecutor would elect to try the advocating and conspiracy charges first. Still doubting the strength of their evidence for the murder case, prosecutors wanted to go for the sure thing. With the advocating and conspiracy crimes laid out in detail on tape in Reldan's own words, prosecutors believed that particular trial would be a slam-dunk. The order in which multiple indictments against the same defendant are brought to trial is normally left to the prosecutor's discretion, so long as the decision doesn't prejudice a defendant.

Robert Reldan would be facing a jury for only the fourth time in his 20-year criminal career. All of his other crimes were disposed of by plea bargains, usually to his advantage. Indeed, in his three previous jury trials, Reldan had actually bested the State in two, achieving hung juries for the Anna Maria Hernandez trial and the first of two Caplan rape trials. He was banking on the special appeal he seemed to have with jurors, his ability to charm at least one of their number at any trial. If he could repeat that in this conspiracy case—even with the evidence and the odds stacked so heavily against him—he could get yet another hung jury, yet another *win*.

During the conspiracy trial, Reldan would have another ace up his sleeve, as Aunt Lillian would come through for him, yet again. By the time the matter came to trial, he would convince his aunt that the conspiracy to murder her was a hoax, something he had cooked up to embarrass the Bergen County Prosecutor's Office. Not only was Lillian Booth charmed into believing that preposterous story, she would eventually provide funds so that Reldan could hire a top-notch lawyer to fight the charges and, incredibly, she would even testify on her nephew's behalf. There was no way, she would tell the jury, that her Bobby would ever want to harm her.

Chapter 15

Bring on the Tsoris Morris.

After collecting almost all of the evidence they would ever get against Robert Reldan for the abductions and murders of Susan Heynes and Susan Reeve, it took prosecutors more than a year to indict him for those crimes. The delay arose out of concern that they didn't have enough evidence to convict him. That impediment did not exist with the new conspiracy charges against Reldan, and the indictment for those crimes was signed, sealed, and delivered in 22 days.

The undercover tape provided the smoking gun that prosecutors needed, and they felt confident that they would get a conviction in the conspiracy case, but other considerations actually accounted for their haste. When Reldan and Barber were informed of the new charges on March 30, 1977, the two Williams brothers immediately had to be transferred from Rahway State Prison for their safety. Though Reldan was at Trenton State, Barber was at Rahway, and Reldan had other friends in Rahway. He could communicate with them by prison kite. Knowing the Williamses had set them up and ratted on fellow inmates, Reldan and Barber could have used their contacts to retaliate—whether in an "accident" or some other means.

The BCPO arranged to temporarily remove both Cliff and Allison Williams to the Bergen County jail. Though the county sheriff, in charge of the jail, would take extra precautions, he didn't want the Williamses there too long as it presented a security nightmare for him. Prosecutors intended to call them before the grand jury to testify in person, as they were eager to get their statements under oath in a formal setting before the brothers could change their minds about cooperating. After all, they were career criminals, about as trustworthy as their extensive records indicated. Assistant Prosecutor Kohler was able to take Cliff's and Allison's grand jury testimony on April 14, allowing them to be shipped to Clinton Corrections Facility in western New Jersey shortly thereafter. A minimum-security prison for women, Clinton had a separate section for men, where the Williamses could serve their time with less risk. The indictment was handed up one week after the brothers testified, but then things stagnated.

If there is one universal truth about the criminal justice system in most states, it is that the wheels of justice turn slowly. Lawyers have to be retained; discovery has to be prepared and supplied to the defense;

and pre-trial motions have to be researched, filed, and argued. On May 6, 1977, Reldan and Barber were brought to the Bergen County courthouse for their arraignment on the conspiracy indictment, but it would be almost six months before this *expedited* case again saw the inside of a courtroom. Five new players would enter the drama—four at once and one later.

The Honorable Morris E. Malech was assigned to handle all of Reldan's pending matters, including the Heynes/Reeve murder indictment and the conspiracy indictment. A World War II veteran, Judge Malech was as sharp as they come, but his courtroom philosophy left many an assistant prosecutor clenching jaws and snapping pencils in exasperation over his rulings. Malech resolved all close calls in favor of defendants. If convicted, a defendant could appeal the judge's rulings and possibly get his conviction overturned based on judicial error, but the State had no right of appeal if a defendant were acquitted; it was a safer course for the judge to err on the side of the defense, with less chance of embarrassment from a higher court citing a mistaken ruling. On the other hand, prosecutors loved the judge when it came to sentencing. Having given a defendant every advantage in his trial rulings, Judge Malech was not averse to slamming the unfortunate soul once a jury lowered the boom. In the New York court system at the time, one judge was so lenient in his sentencing practices that he earned the nickname, "Turn 'Em Loose Bruce." On the other hand, convicted felons familiar with the Yiddish vernacular might well have tagged Judge Malech, "Bring on the *Tsoris* Morris."

Joseph Nackson, a prominent Bergen County defense attorney, took on Robert Reldan's defense—for both cases—in July 1977, but not as a privately retained attorney. The Bergen County Public Defender's Office assigned Nackson to represent Reldan, who had declared himself indigent, unable to pay for his own lawyer. Lillian Booth, uneasy about her nephew's plot, had not yet come to the rescue. Because Albert Barber was also represented by the public defender, the agency had to farm out Reldan's case to an outside attorney to avoid a conflict. Nackson was a good choice. A competent trial attorney, he was a conscientious man of integrity, as well. In fact, his integrity would cause complications six months into the case.

Frank Wagner, the head of the Bergen County Public Defender's Office, represented Al Barber. An assistant prosecutor in the 1960s, Wagner had enough political clout to be appointed chief of the Bergen County PD's office when the State of New Jersey created public defender offices in each of its 21 counties. Under Wagner's leadership, the Bergen office gained the reputation of being among the best in the state. Wagner, himself, often took on the most difficult, high-profile cases, instead of assigning them to less experienced deputies.

Wagner's courtroom style differed from that of most trial attorneys. He was loud and confrontational, especially after lunch, which he was known to take in liquid form. His forte was getting in the face of a witness who had damaged his client's case and screaming rapid-fire questions that drowned out any attempt by the witness to respond, all the while ignoring prosecutorial objections and judicial attempts at restraint. It wasn't pretty, nor was it especially effective, but when a case was over, Wagner's indigent clients were usually satisfied that their lawyer had given maximum effort, win or lose.

Assistant Prosecutor Richard Galler would represent the State, having taken over all Reldan matters from his colleague, Dennis Kohler. When it came to murder cases, the 1970s was the busiest decade in the history of the Bergen County Prosecutor's Office. With dozens of cases at that time, young prosecutors took on immense responsibilities early in their careers. Galler was in that group of prosecutors who earned their spurs the hard way—on their feet in the well of a courtroom, arguing points of law and persuading juries to dispense justice by convicting the bad guys. After gaining that experience, many went into private practice, as Galler would, and became stalwarts of the defense bar in Bergen County.

On October 17, 1977, the attorneys settled into Judge Malech's chambers to discuss the case informally but on the record. Robert Reldan had not been brought up from Trenton State Prison to attend the meeting, nor had Barber been brought over from Rahway. Defendants are supposed to be present at every critical stage of the proceedings, but, apparently, this particular meeting was not deemed to be such an occasion. The decision made at this meeting, however, would have the most significant consequences to date for Reldan's prospects of ever getting out of prison.

The group needed to resolve whether they would try the murder indictment against Reldan first, or whether they would give precedence to the conspiracy indictment, in which both Reldan and Barber were charged. Galler advised the judge that the prosecution would seek to try the conspiracy case against both Reldan and Barber first, holding back on the murder indictment with the intention of trying that case after the completion of the conspiracy trial.

Reldan's attorney had obtained all discovery materials from the Williams and Connolly firm and he was familiar with the State's evidence. Nackson objected to the prosecutor's preferred order of business. The murders occurred significantly earlier than the alleged conspiracy, he pointed out, adding that "the conspiracy indictment really grew out of a continuing investigation into the homicides with Reldan and that although the Prosecutor's office may have come up with something that they didn't think they were going to get, the investigation which resulted in this alleged conspiracy is part of their ongoing investigation of the murder cases."

Frank Wagner, for his part, wanted to get his client's trial over with as soon as possible. If Al Barber were acquitted of the one conspiracy count against him in the indictment, he would be eligible for immediate parole on the B&E conviction for which he was already incarcerated. Wagner thought he might prevail, and he didn't want his client in prison one day more than necessary. If the murder trial took priority, it would take months to complete; the prosecutor claimed to have more than 100 witnesses. The conspiracy trial could likely be completed in a week—two at the most.

Claiming that the murder case was too complicated for him to predict how much time he needed in order to prepare to try it, Nackson refused to give the judge an estimate. That worked against him. Judge Malech, like most judges, obsessed over moving cases. Having a courtroom sit idle was a cardinal sin, and in Bergen County, any judge who allowed that to happen had to answer to Criminal Assignment Judge Fred Galda (the former prosecutor who convicted Reldan for the Caplan rape 11 years earlier.) Galda ran the Criminal section of the Bergen County justice system like a benevolent autocrat: follow his rules, and he was an avuncular mentor; cross him, and he made Attila the Hun, Scourge of God, look like the Captain of the Love Boat. Judge Morris Malech wasn't about to cross his boss.

"I'm going to set down the case involving [Indictment] S-500-77 first, State vs. Robert R. Reldan and Albert H. Barber," Judge Malech declared, 'because that's what the prosecutor wants to move, the other attorney, the public defender is ready to go, and that one is not a long case. So, it would seem to me to make sense to move it." Malech then set January 9, 1978, as the trial date for the conspiracy indictment.

On October 28, 1977, the parties were back in Malech's courtroom for a pre-trial conference, when Nackson again raised the issue of having the murder trial—not the conspiracy trial—first. It was clear from the defense attorney's comments that he'd delved more deeply into the discovery for the two cases and had a firmer grasp on the potential prejudice to his client if the order of the trials stood as the court had previously decided. It was also clear that he had spoken to Reldan in the interim.

Nackson argued that, if Reldan were required to go to trial on the conspiracy case first, the fact that his client had a pending indictment for two murders would, of necessity, have to come into evidence to explain his alleged motive for the conspiracy—his supposed need for money to pay for his defense in the murder trial. Nackson argued that this would prejudice his client's chance for a fair trial by poisoning the jury's mind against him. Nackson also questioned the strength of the State's murder indictment, stressing the yearlong delay in bringing that matter to the grand jury. He suggested to the court that Reldan had a good chance of being acquitted for the murders and, thus, those charges would not be hanging over his head during the conspiracy trial if the order of trials were reversed.

Judge Malech tried to be accommodating. "Well, it's your thought that you want to try the homicide case on January 9," Malech said. "Is that it?"

"No," Nackson answered.

"Well, I don't understand then," Malech said. "I mean, you have to move the cases."

Nackson said that, because of the voluminous amount of preparation involved, he couldn't possible be ready to try the homicide case before April, 1978, but he wouldn't even commit to that time frame. Moreover, he suggested that pre-trial publicity may even require a change of venue for the murder trial or, at the very least, busing in jurors from another part of the state to hear the case. "I think those problems are best dealt with, in terms of the homicide case, with whatever relief the court may see fit," Nackson said. "And that might involve a delay of the trials, it may involve seeking foreign juries, it may involve seeking a change of venue. The exact form of relief we're requesting, I'm not prepared to say at this point."

Nackson most likely sealed his client's fate on this issue as soon as he uttered the words, "might involve a delay of the trials." From those words on, his argument of prejudice to his client fell on deaf ears.

"Yes, but, you see, I asked you the question are you ready to go ahead on the one case [meaning the murder trial]," Malech reasoned, "because putting cases off are not in the best interests of justice. I consider everything. So, what you're really saying is let's not go ahead with any trials. We'll try to go ahead with the one in April. You're saying that it looks like you can make it, but then again you're not sure. In any event, no matter what happens, never try the conspiracy case until you try the murder cases."

Again, Judge Malech made it official, ruling that there was no prejudice to Reldan in allowing the State its preferred order of trials: They would try the conspiracy case before the murder cases. Malech affirmed the January 9, 1978, trial date for the conspiracy indictment. Nackson would appeal the decision, even taking the matter to the New Jersey Supreme Court, but Malech's decision would hold. Appellate courts rarely disturb a trial court's housekeeping decisions. And, in a departure from his normal defense leanings, Judge Malech had handed the prosecution a clear advantage.

* * *

On January 5, 1978, four days before what the supposedly firm trial date for State vs. Robert R. Reldan and Albert H. Barber, attorneys in the case entered Judge Malech's chambers for a confidential, *in camera* discussion. Among them was a new face, Anthony G. Rathe, Esq., who sought court approval to be substituted as Reldan's attorney in all matters. Up to his old tricks, Reldan made the last-minute request to change lawyers in an attempt to delay the start of the scheduled trial. He'd tried that tactic, unsuccessfully, in the second Caplan rape trial, he was trying it now with the conspiracy trial, and he would try it again in the future.

While the Public Defender's office had assigned Joseph Nackson to the case, Reldan's family replaced him with Bergen County attorney Tony Rathe, who was tall and tan, matinee-idol handsome, and dressed to sartorial perfection. Apparently Aunt Lillian was back in the picture. Admitted to the bar in 1960, Rathe had extensive trial experience. Ironically, he was also the former law partner of Joseph Woodcock, who had been at the helm as Prosecutor when Reldan was indicted for the Heynes/Reeve murders. Reldan, not without some basis, claimed that Woodcock had been politically motivated, wanting to enhance his bid for governor by rushing to judgment and indicting him with insufficient evidence. Now, here was Reldan choosing Woodcock's former law partner to represent him in the same case. Reldan was shrewd. He understood that political clout could be valuable in the courtroom. Indeed, "who you know" often trumps "what you know."

In stark contrast to Frank Wagner, Tony Rathe's demeanor in front of a jury was polite, soft spoken, and non-confrontational. If the conspiracy trial ever got started, it was going to be interesting.

But the January 5 meeting did not start well for Rathe and Nackson. Judge Malech let loose with his favorite theme. "The ninth is just around the corner, and then comes these letters indicating change of counsel," Malech said. "Now, do you see why I say 'delay'? This is a favorite trick, if you will. I mean, I have to say this because of my experience as a judge. It's happened to me frequently . . . in important cases where the day of trial new counsel shows up and . . . the defendant insists he wants his own counsel, and he's entitled to him, but the court has some discretion there to forbid the delay in a trial." In the end, Malech gave his blessing for Rathe to take over Reldan's case, *"provided there is no delay."*

Tony Rathe advised Malech that, while he may need a *short* continuance to prepare his client's defense, he had hired Joe Nackson to assist him, thereby reducing the delay to a bare minimum. Rathe said he would only need 60 to 90 days to get ready, but Judge Malech was not so easily assuaged. Nackson and Rathe could go to Judge Galda or even Judge Trautwein—the County Assignment Judge and Galda's boss—Malech said, but he, himself, was not going to change the trial date of January 9, 1978. Nackson then interjected a new wrinkle.

"There is one additional thing that . . . needs to be said," Nackson announced. "I am certainly not going to indicate what they are . . . but . . . there are some not insubstantial differences between Mr. Reldan and myself with respect to the way the trial should be conducted, which would present a problem irrespective of the other problems we earlier raised. It's clear to me at this point that Mr. Reldan's interests and the interests of justice would best be served by having Mr. Rathe conduct the trial and not myself." *

Judge Malech didn't get the hint. He pressed for both Nackson and Ratheto be ready to try the conspiracy case on January 9—four days later. The alternative was that they could take their request for a delay to Judge Trautwein or Judge Galda.

Nackson pushed back. "Well, because of what happened," Nackson said, "I don't know if, at this juncture, I could represent him. You know, we're not talking of things in a vacuum, there have been developments in the case, certain things that he would like done . . . certain things . . . I don't think I would be willing to do, certain defenses I might not find acceptable to me or plausible to me that Mr. Reldan wants, that other counsel might advance."

Judge Malech stood firm and took a short recess to allow the attorneys to make their case for a delay to Judge Trautwein or Judge Galda. They went to Trautwein, who sent them to Galda, who sent them back to Malech. Galda wanted Malech to make the decision. With the responsibility back on him, Judge Malech saw a tactical retreat as the best course. He relented. The judge gave Tony Rathe the 90 days he said he needed to prepare. A peremptory date of April 3, 1978, was set for the conspiracy trial.

---

*An attorney cannot call a witness—even his own client—to testify under oath if the attorney knows that the witness is going to lie. In other words, if a criminal defendant discloses to his attorney that a, b, and c actually happened, and then tells his attorney that he is going to testify that x, y, and z happened, instead, the attorney cannot ethically call the witness. However, this presents an almost unsolvable dilemma for the attorney: In any criminal proceeding, a defendant has an absolute right to testify in his own behalf. What, then, can the attorney do? The attorney cannot perpetrate a fraud upon the court by allowing a client to testify falsely, but also can't blow the whistle on the client, either. The answer is simple, but not easily accomplished: The attorney must resign from the case. In so doing, the attorney cannot tell anyone why he or she is resigning, because that would violate the attorney-client privilege. The attorney has to take the hit—and that is exactly what Joe Nackson did, risking court sanction.

Wrapping it up, Malech delivered a parting shot. "If you die before [April 3], you will not be able to try it," he told Rathe. "You'll be excused, all right? . . . and if I die, I won't be here to try it."

"I hope it doesn't happen," Rathe said.

"Otherwise, we'll be here," Judge Malech admonished.

"I wish you good health, Judge," Rathe said.

"And the same to you."

No one died in the interim, and Indictment S-500-77, the matter of the State of New Jersey vs. Robert R. Reldan and Albert H. Barber finally went to trial on April 10, 1978, only one week past its peremptory date.

Chapter 16

I paint, I sculpt, I make furniture.

Jury selection consumed the entire first day, so it wasn't until Tuesday, April 11, 1978, that the actual trial began. Defendant Robert Reldan, almost 38 years old, no longer had the youthful, preppy appearance that had benefited him so well in previous trials. Still, his well-groomed good looks helped him, as did his business suit, crisp white shirt, and necktie. One observer would later say that Reldan looked like an insurance salesman—or co-counsel—seated there at the defense table.

Assistant Prosecutor Richard Galler initiated the action by delivering the State's opening statement. In every New Jersey criminal trial, the prosecution gives its opening statement first, followed by that of each defendant. (A defense attorney can defer his or her opening statement to the start of the defendant's case in chief, but no one ever does that, as the prevailing wisdom advises that it is best to get the defendant's version of facts planted in the minds of the jury early, before a barrage of State's evidence might close those minds.) At the end of the trial, the order of summations is reversed: Defense attorneys go first and the prosecution—which has the burden of proof—has the last word.

During his opening statement, Anthony Rathe dropped Robert Reldan's bombshell. Rathe explained to the jury that Reldan knew all along that Nick Gallo wasn't a hit man. *Everything* that had transpired, Rathe said—including the Gallo conversations, Reldan's letters to Barber, and the Williams brothers' cooperation with the police—was part of an elaborate hoax that Reldan had conceived as a way to get back at Bergen County prosecutors for the harassment and harm they had caused him in their phony murder investigation. Speaking on Reldan's behalf, his attorney contended that prosecutors were grasping at straws to catch him committing a crime—any crime—because they couldn't nail him on the murder charges. Intending to tell the hoax story to a newspaper reporter, Reldan was simply humoring the investigators, Rathe said, exploiting their inept methods and exposing their sleazy scheming.

Like all criminal defendants, Reldan had obtained the case discovery months before the trial date, including transcripts of the taped conversation with Gallo during the March 24 yard visit. The recording was devastating. It did not allow any plausible explanation other than that Reldan contracted with the putative hit man to do exactly what the indictment said he wanted to do: have someone rob and kill his aunt and her boyfriend. But, left to his own devices and with nothing but time on his hands, Reldan came up with what was, he thought, his only chance to beat the rap. After all, he was batting .667 in front of juries (two for three). He thought himself fully able to charm at least one juror to see things his way. Reldan believed that he could sell anything, including the idea that he was just foolin'. And why not? It had even worked with Aunt Lillian, who bought the hoax story. She was back in Bobby's corner.

When Anthony Rathe revealed Robert Reldan's preposterous strategy in his opening statement, Joe Nackson's reason for refusing to continue as Reldan's attorney of record became clear. Apparently, Rathe was willing to go along with the sham; he probably did not probe deeply into his client's story when he first heard the idea, for fear of having the same ethical problems that troubled Nackson. To his credit, Nackson didn't have the stomach for it.

The first State's witness was BCPO Investigator Ed Denning, who spent the rest of Tuesday, April 11, and all Wednesday morning testifying. In his direct examination by AP Galler, Denning detailed the investigative steps taken, including acquisition of the incriminating letters between Reldan and Barber. On cross-examination, both defense attorneys concentrated on Denning's dealings with the Williams brothers and their attempts to get a benefit for cooperating.

Through Denning, the attorneys were trying to damage the brothers' credibility, and they did an effective job of it, getting Denning to confirm that the BCPO went to bat for the Williamses by writing to the Camden County judge handling their case, praising their assistance against Reldan, and asking for a reduction in their sentences. Denning also admitted that his office was instrumental in getting both brothers transferred to the relatively relaxed, minimum-security environment at the Clinton Correctional facility for women. Rathe tried to impeach Denning, himself, on the question of why he had destroyed his investigative notes after completing his six-page formal report of the investigation. Rathe implied that, in preparing his final report, Denning might have inadvertently or purposely left out information that was important to the defense.

Ed Denning, who would rise to become deputy chief of investigators in the Bergen County Prosecutor's Office before his retirement in 1994, was, perhaps, the most respected BCPO investigator of his era. This respect derived from the highest professionalism in everything he did and an unflappable demeanor while doing battle on the witness stand. Rathe's attempt to cast aspersions on Denning's integrity would go nowhere with the jury. Denning also poked the first hole in Reldan's fairytale defense when he explained to the jury that it was highly improbable that Reldan had become aware of his meetings with the Williams brothers through the prison grapevine. Each such meeting had been encased in tight security.

Rathe engaged in one last area of inquiry, related to Denning's receipt of the letters exchanged between Reldan and Al Barber, a.k.a., the "Buzzard." Under questioning, the investigator acknowledged that he had relied on what Cliff Williams told him about his acquisition of the letters from Barber. Denning admitted that he had no independent knowledge regarding the supposed conversations between the Williams brothers and Reldan and Barber leading to the authorship of those letters. However, this line of questioning made little sense, since Rathe had made a point in his opening that the correspondence between Reldan and Barber was all part of Reldan's hoax.

As expected, Frank Wagner's cross-examination covered much the same ground as Rathe's, but more aggressively. Wagner went so far as to accuse Denning of deliberately putting pressure on Cliff Williams to manufacture evidence against the defendants. Denning did not take kindly to this denigration of his character. This type of cross-examination— seeking to misdirect the jury's attention by putting the conduct of the police on trial—is a common defense tactic in criminal cases. It often leads to acrimony in the courtroom.[*]

Wagner's cross, like Rathe's, did little damage to the State's case. His biggest point was to get Denning to admit that, up to Emily Williams's phone call to him on February 17, 1977, both of the brothers were likely involved in the conspiracy to rob and kill Reldan's aunt, but neither had been charged with the crime. With his client's interests foremost in his mind, Wagner also got Denning to agree that, absent the letters and the testimony of Cliff and Allison Williams—expected later in the trial—no evidence linked Barber to the conspiracy.

---

[*]Between Wagner and Denning, it ultimately led to this exchange:
    Wagner: "When you were told that Barber was planning to plot and kill Reldan's aunt—"
    Denning: "If you would calm down, I'll answer your question, if you would ask it in a proper manner."
    Wagner: "Well, I'm sorry if I . . . You think I didn't ask it in a proper manner?"
    Denning: Well, I don't enjoy being yelled at."
    Wagner: "Well, I don't enjoy yelling."
    Denning: "Then don't yell."
    Wagner: "I expect to get an answer when I ask a question."
    Denning: "Ask the question like a gentleman, and I'll answer it."
Ordinarily, trial judges step in to stop such exchanges. Malech said nothing.

Clifford and Allison Williams took center stage on the afternoon of Wednesday, April 12, through that Friday. To no one's surprise, the brothers' direct testimony was essentially consistent, as both described the job assignments that brought them in daily contact with Reldan and Barber (until Reldan's transfer to Trenton State) and their initial discussions with both defendants about a potentially lucrative B&E, which was the Williams brothers' specialty. Cliff Williams testified that it was Barber who first approached him about "a big job" involving Reldan, just a few days after he got to Rahway, but that Reldan joined in the conversation and planning soon thereafter. The conversations took a murderous bent after Reldan's indictment in the Heynes/Reeve case. Reldan asked the brothers' help in finding not just a robber but also someone who would kill his aunt and her companion as part of the job. In prison parlance, he wanted a man who was "heavy" enough to handle murder. After Reldan's removal to Trenton State Prison, he set up the system of communicating with the Williamses by letter or kite, going through Al Barber.

Assistant Prosecutor Galler knew that his star witnesses' criminal records and preferential treatment were fodder for cross-examination, so, on direct, he brought out as much as he could about those issues. Better that he reveal the Williamses' sordid past, than have the defense attorneys shock the jury with the revelations. Ordinarily, that's a good strategy. What Galler didn't bank on, however, was Judge Malech's propensity to allow defense lawyers the widest discretion in their cross examinations—wider than anything permitted in the criminal procedure rules. Prior *convictions* may be used to impeach the credibility of a witness, the theory being that, if the witness had no regard for the law and committed criminal acts, his regard for the oath to tell the truth was equally suspect. But prior *suspected* criminal conduct that was *not* the subject of a conviction, should not be used in this fashion. That was the rule—everywhere but in Judge Morris Malech's courtroom.

In his cross examination, unhindered by the rules of evidence, Tony Rathe delved into Cliff Williams's past crimes *and* his past suspected crimes. It was a departure from Rathe's usually mild-mannered treatment of witnesses, but no juror would object to his manhandling of the sleazy presence on the witness stand. Before the trial was over, a parade of such characters, each holding a bible in his hands and swearing to tell the truth, would taint the courtroom. It was as though a sewer line had erupted, spewing forth its offensive effluent in the hall of justice.

Rathe pounced. "The fact is, Mr. Williams, that in 1959 you and your brother were convicted of what was reputed to be the largest jewelry robbery in history," he said. "Isn't that a fact?"

"That's right, Sir," Williams admitted.

"And in '64," Rathe continued, "you were familiar with the Gamron jewelry case, were you not?"

"Yes, I was."

"That case was dismissed in 1966, was it not," Rathe persisted, "because a material witness disappeared?"

AP Galler objected to the question as improper, a dismissal of a case being inadmissible to impeach credibility. "I'm going to allow it," Judge Malech responded.

"That case was dismissed . . . because a material witness disappeared," Rathe charged. "Isn't that a fact?"

"I think so, yes," Williams admitted.

"In 1972, Sir, you were implicated in a $30,000 holdup by one Charles Borne," Rathe continued. "Were you not?

"Yes, I was."

"You know Charles Borne?"

"I met him once or twice," Williams affirmed.

"He was fatally wounded," Rathe said. "Was he not?"

"Yes, he was," Williams said.

Rathe continued. "He was prepared to testify in that matter in 1972, was he not?"

"I didn't know that for a fact, Sir."

"You know for a fact that he was fatally wounded?" Rathe asked.

"Yes, Sir," Williams admitted.

"And in April of 1973," Rathe said, shifting gears, "were you involved in a burglary in the home of Anna Boyce?"

"Yes, I was."

"And there was a co-conspirator," Rathe asked. "A Mr. Schaefer, is that right?"

"Yes, that's right."

"Now, at the time was this Mr. Schaefer, if you know, was he bargaining with federal authorities?" Rathe asked.

"I don't know that," Williams answered.

"But they found him with his head blown off, didn't they?" Rathe asked.

"Yes, they did."

"Now in that case . . . ." Rathe continued. "Do you recall a witness [by the name of Hansen] stating that Clifford Williams planted items in [his] parents' home in an effort to discredit [his] testimony?"

"Yes, I do," Williams admitted.

"Did you do that?" Rathe asked.

"Yes, I did."

Tony Rathe went on to establish that Jimmy Parcells, the hit man Cliff Williams had recommended to Al Barber for Reldan's job, had been Williams's co-defendant in the Anna Boyce robbery, showing that the Williams brothers were in fact closer to Parcells than Barber was. Further, in a disclosure that would have immense ramifications in the Reldan legal saga years later, Rathe determined that both Williams brothers were represented by a former assistant prosecutor named Larry McClure, who was, unbelievably, the law partner of Joseph Woodcock.

Both defense attorneys, to their professional credit, were well versed in the facts of the case and did a competent job in testing the credibility of the two Williams brothers as witnesses, aided by Judge Malech's extremely flexible rules for defense counsel. Despite these efforts, Clifford and Allison Williams stood up well in the face of the verbal assaults. They left the witness stand having done little or no damage to the State's case.

In the exchange involving his criminal history, Cliff was surprisingly frank, never arguing with the attorneys' characterizations of his slimy past. That sort of *honesty* scores points with jurors, even given its source. Jurors are more inclined to believe a witness who readily admits his shortcomings. Allison Williams displayed the same candor. Through both of their testimonies, the State was able to get the Reldan-to-Barber and Barber-to-Reldan letters—with all their incriminating statements—into evidence. Combined with the tape of the March 24, 1977, meeting between "Frank Parisi" and Robert Reldan, those letters would give the lie to Reldan's play-acting story—his claim of perpetrating a hoax to embarrass his BCPO foes.

Investigator Ken Nass testified briefly about the technical aspects of wiring Detective Nick Gallo for his undercover role at Trenton State Prison, both as to the failed procedure on March 8, 1977, and the successful one for the yard visit on March 24. There was not much use in cross-examining Nass on such matters, and neither defense attorney put any effort into doing so. Gallo followed Nass on the witness stand, testifying for the rest of the day on Friday, all day Monday, and half of Tuesday, April 18.

AP Galler's direct examination of Gallo on Friday afternoon focused on the March 8 window visit with Robert Reldan. The inaudible tape of that meeting was disallowed in evidence for obvious reasons, but Gallo was able to use the report of that discussion, which he had prepared from memory immediately after discovering that the taping system had failed. Gallo's report, itself, was not admissible, but he was able to refer to it to refresh his recollection throughout Galler's direct examination. Gallo's details—even without a tape to back them up—dealt a crushing blow to Reldan's manufactured defense.

When Nick Gallo described the moment in which he asked Reldan, on the prison phone, what he was supposed to do with the two people at the house he was going to rob, every eye in the courtroom was fixed on the veteran detective. Step by step, Gallo related how Reldan wrote something on a piece of paper, held the paper up to the window to show Gallo the words, "take out," and then he slowly drew his fingers across his throat in a cutting motion. Anyone observing the jury's reaction during Gallo's account of the particular episode and the look in Reldan's eyes had to know that the defendant's fate was sealed—then and there—as effectively as if Dandy Don Meredith were singing his *Monday Night Football* rendition of "The Party's Over" to seal the fate of that night's losing team.

On Monday, April 17, the jury heard the entire tape of the March 24 meeting between Gallo and Reldan. And they had in front of them, as an aid, the printed transcript of the conversation prepared by the BCPO. They would be able to hear the words being spoken and to read those words at the same time—a sure-fire way to insure that the information was emblazoned in their minds.

Tony Rathe delivered the only blow to Nick Gallo's solid performance on the witness stand. Since Lillian Booth was cooperating with her nephew's defense, Rathe knew that Gallo had insinuated himself into the wealthy victim's life much more than professional propriety should allow. He'd become friendly with Booth, socializing with her and her friends at parties, playing tennis and swimming at the Booth estate in Alpine, and soliciting Booth's help with a writing venture. Gallo had written a fictionalized version of an undercover case he had worked—not the Reldan case, but one strikingly similar—and asked for Booth's help in getting a movie producer to look at it. Booth still had strong contacts in the entertainment business, and she readily agreed to help the detective. Nothing ever came of it—the producer wasn't impressed by Gallo's creative efforts—and the matter was dropped, except that it made Gallo look unprofessional at the trial and gave the defense something to take pot shots at.

Nick Gallo fancied himself a Renaissance man, the resident creative type at the BCPO. When Rathe pressed him to reveal his varied creative talents, Gallo responded, a bit grandiosely, "I paint, I sculpt, I make furniture." Later, a former colleague of Gallo's would recall his penchant for "hobnobbing" with elite types in the arts, business, and government.

With his image slightly tarnished, perhaps, Gallo did his job well, and the jury knew it. Nothing could detract from the impact of the tape of that March 24 meeting. Assistant Prosecutor Galler was an astute prosecutor, and knew to end the trial on a high note. As soon as Gallo's testimony concluded, the prosecution rested.

It was the defense's turn to call witnesses and to do whatever they could to plant a seed of reasonable doubt in at least *one* juror's mind—just one. That was all that was necessary to get a hung jury. With the State's evidence as strong as it was, the two experienced defense attorneys had to have known that a not-guilty verdict would have been impossible; no way would *all* 12 jurors vote not guilty. With an acquittal out of the question, a mistrial was their only hope.

Frank Wagner initiated the defense on April 19, calling three fellow prisoners to testify on Al Barber's behalf. During the State's case in chief, Wagner had skillfully elicited testimony that the prosecution had offered Barber immunity if he agreed to testify against Reldan. Denning had arranged a call between Barber and Cliff Williams, and Williams related to Barber that he could get a free ride. Barber wouldn't do it. Even to benefit himself, he wouldn't violate the code and rat on his friend. That sense of honor had to resonate with jurors, Wagner thought, and he tried to impugn the Williams brothers further by calling witnesses who would disparage them.

Joel Sussman, Wagner's first inmate witness, testified that he knew Reldan, Barber, and the Williams brothers from Rahway State. Sussman had a prison job as the social worker for the wing where all of the men were housed, and he said he had numerous conversations with them. Sussman said the Williamses dealt drugs in prison, were known snitches, and did not have a good reputation for honesty. Cliff Williams had asked Sussman if he knew of anyone on the outside who might do a robbery for them. Sussman also relayed a lesson in prison sexual mores when he told jurors that, one day, he had walked in on the Williams brothers when they were performing oral sex on each other. Such testimony is clearly inadmissible, but Galler did not bother to object, nor did he cross-examine Sussman on the subject. It didn't matter and it served no purpose to highlight it for the jurors. It was what it was.

In his cross-examination, Galler used the typical means of attacking credibility: raising the witness's criminal record. But, then, the assistant prosecutor had a brilliant idea. He laid out a hypothetical idea that a prisoner, who was nearing his parole-eligibility date, might create a false plot in order to hoax the authorities. He asked Sussman if it sounded plausible that a prisoner, so close to freedom, might risk everything to play a trick. Sussman replied that it sounded crazy, that no inmate would ever do anything like that because it would kill his chances for parole. Defense counsel jumped up, strenuously objecting to the line of questioning. Judge Malech sustained the objection and told the jury to disregard Sussman's opinion on the subject, but jurors cannot *unhear* something that they have heard. Rather, the jurors noted the preposterous premise of Reldan's defense.

Wearing their orange prison jumpsuits, four more inmates testified for the defense. Like Sussman, all of them described Cliff and Allison Williams's bad reputations regarding truthfulness. One has to wonder at the jury's impression of all this. What reputation is a career criminal supposed to have for honesty? AP Galler cross-examined each inmate witness in turn, pointing out each man's deficient respect for law and order. Prior convictions of the defense witnesses ranged from B&Es and armed robberies to sexual assaults on minors. The combined effect of their testimony was negligible, by all accounts.

Tony Rathe attempted to support his client's hoax defense by calling inmate Joseph Louisa to testify. Louisa and Reldan had conversations preceding Reldan's meetings with his hit man—supposedly Jimmy Parcells. Louisa said he knew Parcells well and counseled Reldan to beware of a set-up. Parcells was on the lam for the big postal job he'd pulled off, and Louisa doubted he'd show up at a prison to case a new job. Louisa described Parcells for Reldan (confirming the description Barber had sent), adding that Parcells "walked with a limp." Louisa said he had given Reldan a foolproof way to test the expected visitor to make sure he was really Parcells. Louisa told Reldan to tell the guy that "Cowboy Joe says hello" and to see how he reacted to that. Joe Louisa's prison nickname was "Cowboy Joe," and he told Reldan that Parcells knew that. If the visitor acted like he didn't know what Reldan was talking about, it was a set-up and Reldan should be on his guard.

Louisa, who claimed to be friendly with the Williams brothers, said he got a letter from them in early February, 1977, asking if he knew Robert Reldan. The Williamses said they were "working some kind of deal with Bergen County" and they wanted Louisa to get friendly with Reldan and vouch for their trustworthiness. Louisa testified that he gave the letter to Reldan, but the letter would never be produced at trial as corroboration. Since such a letter would clearly prove Reldan's prior knowledge of the Williams brothers' duplicity—thereby supporting his hoax story—why didn't Reldan keep it and produce it at trial? Its absence from the defense exhibits left Louisa's testimony in that regard highly suspect. In his cross-examination of Joe Louisa, Galler emphasized this, thoroughly defusing any damage his testimony might have inflicted. It didn't help Louisa's credibility that he was serving time for committing sodomy on—and threatening to kill—a child under the age of 16.

Defendant Albert Barber began his testimony shortly after lunch on April 19, concluding at 4:00 PM that day. His defense came down to three assertions.

First, Barber said that he knew the Williams brothers had been professional thieves for more than 30 years, and he admired them for it, especially their sophistication when it came to stolen jewelry. Though he

147

listened when Cliff and Allison spoke about committing various high-profile jobs, they never spoke to him about plans to rob Reldan's aunt.

Second, Barber denied knowledge of Reldan discussing his aunt with the Williamses. The letters he sent to Reldan were done at Cliff's and Allison's behest; Barber claimed to have paid no attention to what he wrote. Similarly, he paid no attention to the letters Reldan wrote and simply turned them over to the Williamses. Nor did he place any importance, Barber said, on the letter from Reldan instructing him to disregard anything directed to Cliff and Allison. Although he said that Reldan gave him those instructions, he no longer had the letter and could not explain why he had not kept it, considering the fact that he had retained other correspondence.

Third, Barber tried to cover his bases by claiming that, even if his actions suggested that he had become involved in the plot against Lillian Booth, his involvement lacked criminal intent. The Williams brothers duped him, he said, because they knew him to be a good guy—unsuspicious and unquestioning by nature.

The problem with Barber's defense was its incredulity. Was it likely that Reldan—obsessed about secrecy and admittedly paranoid about police surveillance—would allow an uninvolved person to become privy to the criminal plot against his aunt? No. Furthermore, in formulating the conspiracy, why wouldn't the Williams brothers write directly to Reldan, rather than funneling incriminating evidence through Barber? There was no rational explanation. Barber even denied knowing that Reldan had a wealthy aunt. To the jury, that must have seemed highly improbable, especially since Reldan's need for money to pay for his defense in the murder cases, was the primary topic of conversation during the four days between Reldan's indictment on the Bergen murders and his transfer from Rahway to Trenton State Prison. How could anyone believe that Aunt Lillian's name and her great wealth did not come up in that context? Who was telling the truth on this point—Al Barber, or the Williams brothers?

Robert Reldan had no choice but to take the witness stand in his own defense. It was the only way he could hope to sell his story to the jury, or, more to the point, to sell it to at least *one* juror. When he took the stand, his criminal record would come out; Judge Malech had already ruled that seven of his prior convictions—including the rape of Bernice Caplan—could be used to impeach his credibility. In every court case, before jurors begin deliberations, the court always instructs the jury on the limited use of prior convictions. Jurors may use information about prior convictions to determine credibility, but may *not* use the information as evidence that the defendant is a bad person with a propensity to commit crime. That's the fiction. The reality is that, once a jury hears that a defendant, on trial for conspiring to murder his wealthy aunt, has a history of rape . . . well, game over.

Reldan started ranting about the Bergen County Prosecutor unfairly targeting him for the two murders. Jurors heard, from the defendant's own mouth, that he was a suspect in two brutal murders—murders they surely recalled due to the avalanche of publicity attending them less than two and a half years earlier. Reldan claimed that he was indicted for the murders on insufficient evidence because of Joe Woodcock's political ambitions. He said that investigators for the BCPO had harassed him and his family, trying to frame him. Attempting to set up the motivation behind his hoax defense, Reldan was attempting to convey his justification for wanting to embarrass the BCPO. Ready to blow the story wide open, he explained that he had been in touch with reporter Ed Flynn from *The Record* of Bergen County, but he was arrested for the phony conspiracy charge and then indicted in a rush, before he had the chance to give the story to Flynn.

Reldan confirmed the prior testimony about his introduction to the Williams brothers, but said "rockets went off" when they started to question him about the charges he might face in Bergen County. They seemed to have knowledge of the investigation, Reldan said, and suggested they had important connections in Bergen County and might be able to help him out. It seemed bizarre that Reldan, with his paranoia antennae usually at full deployment, would have accepted the offer of help from people of such short acquaintance. Reldan testified that his suspicions were magnified when the Williams brothers, themselves, raised the subject of robbing his wealthy aunt to get the funds necessary to persuade their Bergen County contacts to help Reldan with his problems there. Reldan said he distrusted the Williamses and avoided any discussions with them, especially when Barber was around. Barber talked too much, Reldan said.

When he was indicted for the murders, Reldan said Cliff Williams asked for information on his aunt so he could get the job done. Reldan claimed Williams was the one who suggested that no witnesses be left alive—that his aunt and her companion be murdered as part of the job. Also, Williams seemed to know that Reldan was being transferred to Trenton State before Reldan knew, and used that fact to try to get more information about the aunt. On January 24, when Reldan was shipped to Trenton State Prison without prior notification, he became convinced that the Williams brothers were working with Bergen prosecutors. This conclusion was affirmed, Reldan testified, when Joseph Louisa gave him the letter from the Williamses, in which they told Louisa they were working to set up Reldan.

Soon after being sentenced to Rahway for the burglary convictions, Reldan had created a notarized letter to forestall any idea that he would confide facts about his case to another prisoner. Yet, he couldn't produce the letter that Louisa said he got from the Williamses, proving that Reldan knew of their double-dealing beforehand. It was a serious hole in his defense, if, indeed, that defense ever had the slightest chance of succeeding.

Reldan testified that, after his conversations with Louisa, he understood that the BCPO would stop at nothing to implicate him in a conspiracy to murder his aunt, simply because they could not convict him for the murders of those two women. It would serve their dual purpose of blocking his possible parole for the burglaries and also saddle him with significant new prison time on a serious charge of conspiracy. He told the jury that his response to all this was to spend time in the prison law library "to see just how much I could do and how much I could say and how much I could get away with without actually being in the jackpot." That was when, he said, he formed the plan to pretend to go along with the police-orchestrated conspiracy. In carrying out the hoax, he hoped to put the BCPO "through as much trouble as they put me through. By the time they're finished checking out so much of the stuff I'm going to throw into this," Reldan said, "and some of the false leads I'm going to throw in and some of the baloney I'm going to feed them," he would feel that maybe he had evened the score.

Reldan said the last act of his hoax was the April 8 letter that he sent to AP Dennis Kohler, hoping to get a meeting with prosecutors. It was his intent, Reldan said, to contact reporter Ed Flynn afterwards and try to have an article published that would expose the scheme to frame him. He planned to give Flynn all of his advance knowledge of the prosecutors' plot and to establish with Flynn that anything he said to advance the trumped-up conspiracy he did solely to embarrass and humiliate the BCPO. Reldan claimed that the speedy indictment for conspiracy and "advocating" frustrated this demonstration of his innocence.

Reldan said he never told anyone, not even his lawyers, about the hoax he'd dreamed up. He was afraid that they would talk him out of it, or back out of representing him in the murder case. "What I was doing," Reldan said, explaining his reluctance to confide in the Williams and Connolly attorneys, "was perpetrating a fraud."

As the final piece of his direct examination, Rathe had Reldan look directly at Lillian Booth and Misha Dabich, who sat in the audience. Rathe asked his client if he meant to have the two people killed. Reldan, looking at his Aunt Lillian with as much sincerity as he could muster, denied having any such thoughts.

Prosecutors rarely get to cross-examine defendants with criminal records as extensive as Robert Reldan's. In such cases, the threat of exposing that record to the jury usually keeps the defendant off the witness stand, cloaked in the constitutional right of not having to testify. So, when Reldan took the stand in his own defense, AP Richard Galler had a rare opportunity, of which he took full advantage. He would use Reldan's criminal record against him, of course, but Galler first set about destroying the man's hoax defense.

Galler took Reldan through the taped conversation with Detective Nick Gallo on March 24, 1977, item by item, forcing the defendant to acknowledge that every bit of information he gave to the supposed hit man about his aunt's wealth, living habits, and residence were absolutely true. In the entire hour-long conversation between Reldan and Gallo, not one item of misinformation or misdirection gave credence to Reldan's claim that it was all a hoax. In questioning Reldan about the letters that went back and forth between him and Barber, Galler's attention to the details in those letters demonstrated the implausibility of both defendants' claims that Barber knew nothing about the conspiracy; in fact, the only logical conclusion was that Barber was a willing participant. Under direct examination by his own attorney, Reldan had complained that Barber "talked too much," which was the reason, he said, that he didn't confide in his friend about his conversations with the Williams brothers. But, if that were so, why even involve Barber as a letter-writing middleman? Why not communicate directly with Cliff or Allison Williams? Direct communications with the *known* police agents would have furthered—not hampered—Reldan's hoax scenario.

When questioned by his attorney, Tony Rathe, Reldan had emphatically stated his belief from the get-go that Gallo was an undercover cop. But, under cross examination, Galler was able to get Reldan to equivocate about whether or not he had pegged Frank Parisi as a plant. "I could have been wrong, you know," Reldan said. "I wanted as much proof as possible." When asked about Gallo's lack of a limp—the telltale sign that Joe Louisa had told him to look for—Reldan hedged about that, too. "Maybe he just might have had acupuncture," Reldan told Galler, "and was feeling good."

The point of Galler's questions was to show that, if Reldan had doubts about Frank Parisi's authenticity, why then would he have given Parisi all the *correct* details about his aunt—her wealth, her jewelry, where she kept it, the layout of her house, and how best to gain entry? Reldan tried to explain away the inconsistency, pointing out that he had told Parisi to wait a month before carrying out the hit. But that was a feeble excuse. It was unbelievable that he would endanger his aunt like that. The only reasonable inference was that he truly believed he was engaging a real hit man to rob and kill Lillian Booth.

Lastly, in a stunning development, Galler got Reldan to admit that it was he, not the Williams brothers, who first brought up the idea of converting what was originally just a robbery into a plan for killing, too. This was the opposite of what Reldan had testified to during his direct examination. When pressed for the reason why he added murder to the scheme, Reldan said, "I just decided to throw it in to juice up the plot"—in other words, to make things even more embarrassing for the prosecutors he hated.

Rathe would call both William and Marie Reldan, Robert's parents, to the witness stand to express their opinion that their son would never consider harming his beloved aunt, who had done so much for him. Opinions of that sort—going to the heart of the question before the jury—are clearly objectionable, but Judge Malech, true to form, allowed it. Attempting to bolster Reldan's alleged motivation in concocting the hoax scheme, the elder Reldans also supported their son's claim that BCPO investigators were harassing Reldan and his family.

Lillian Booth was the final defense witness. She told the jury that her nephew would never harbor any thought of harming her. They didn't believe her.

The defense rested after Lillian Booth's brief testimony, and all three attorneys then gave their summations to the jury. Frank Wagner went first, arguing passionately for his client, Al Barber. Tony Rathe delivered his summation, trying desperately to get the jury to disregard Reldan's criminal past and find some reasonable doubt as to his client's guilt—perhaps the most uphill battle Rathe would face in his legal career. AP Richard Galler spoke last, brilliantly. He knew that the tape of the March 24 yard visit was his strongest piece of evidence and that the jury would have that tape to review again during their deliberations.

"Listen to the tone," Galler urged the jurors. "Listen to the venomous anger as he talks about his Aunt Lil who was kind to him most of his life . . . . Listen to the way he talks about her, '*that bitch*.' Listen . . . to the hate in his voice and you'll see what he really meant, just by listening to his voice. You'll see that he meant to kill."

Following 11 days of testimony, summations by the three attorneys, and Judge Malech's charge on the law, the jury got the case of the State of New Jersey vs. Robert R. Reldan and Albert H. Barber shortly before 3:00 PM on April 25. They deliberated that afternoon until 4:30 PM, at which time the judge excused them for the day. They resumed deliberations the next morning at 9:00 AM. At 11:00 AM on April 26, 1978, the jury sent a note to Judge Malech. They had reached a verdict, having deliberated just three and a half hours in total. Both defendants were found guilty of all charges: Reldan on all five counts and Barber on the fifth count, the sole charge against him in the indictment. After ordering a presentence report to be prepared on each defendant, Judge Malech set June 26 as the sentencing date.

For his part in the conspiracy, Barber was sentenced to a term of two-to-three years in state prison. Then, Judge Morris Malech declared Robert Reldan to be a "habitual offender" under New Jersey law, which qualified him for enhanced punishment. In justifying the penalty he was about to impose—one firmly in keeping with his reputation as a tough sentencing judge—Malech said, "A careful examination of the presentence report and my observations made at the trial [convince me that] the defendant, Mr. Reldan, is a shrewd, calculating, and dangerous person to society." Malech sentenced Reldan to 20-to-25 years on each of the five counts in the indictment, all sentences to run concurrently. He then remanded Robert Reldan to Trenton State Prison to begin serving his sentence and to await his murder trial.

No one in the courtroom on June 26, 1978, would have believed that final justice for Susan Heynes and Susan Reeve would require three trials, consume millions in scarce public resources, and take 11 more years.

Chapter 17

His charm had already won him two hung juries.

Lillian Booth may have finally gotten the message. Twelve jurors—deliberating just three and a half hours, after 10 days of testimony—decided that nephew Robert Reldan conspired to murder her and Misha Dabich. To say it was an epiphany might be an understatement. The long-suffering aunt of perhaps the most ungrateful nephew in modern history closed her checkbook and departed the scene. Anthony Rathe, with little to work with, had done the best anyone could expect in the conspiracy case, but he wasn't about to undertake a month-long, double-murder trial for no compensation. Once again, Reldan was shopping for a new lawyer.

Frank Wagner's spirited defense of Albert Barber struck a responsive chord in Reldan. Abusing hostile witnesses, investigators, and prosecutors appealed to him. With no funds to hire a *name* defense lawyer (and his family's financial support denied him), Reldan had no choice but to declare himself indigent and accept representation by the Public Defender's Office. Wagner, a 57-year-old, veteran trial lawyer who liked doing battle in high-profile cases, readily agreed to handle Reldan's murder trial, personally. He would be the fourth lawyer—Edward Bennett Williams, Joseph Nackson, and Anthony Rathe having preceded him—to defend the murder case, but the first to have significant involvement. The others had done nothing but review discovery and think about a defense. Wagner now actually had to provide that defense.

The Williams and Connolly lawyers had fueled Reldan's obsession that the Bergen County Prosecutor's Office did not have the jurisdiction to try him for the Heynes and Reeve murders; indeed, according to the rationale he communicated to the Williams brothers, Reldan had sought to deny his old enemies the ability to prosecute him by dumping the women's bodies in Rockland County, New York, not far from the Jersey border. The fact that his Washington DC power-lawyers agreed with his assessment must have gone straight to Reldan's head; lack of jurisdiction became almost a mantra for him. Even if he and his lawyers were right, however, the question remained: What good would it have done him to prevail on that issue?

If Bergen prosecutors lacked jurisdiction, the Rockland County District Attorney's Office surely would have it. A successful motion to quash the Bergen County murder indictment for lack of jurisdiction would have simply transferred the matter to New York State, generating an indictment and prosecution there.

The motivation, then, for pursuing a jurisdictional dismissal of the charges had to have been strategic. A Rockland County jury might not be as invested, emotionally, in the outcome of the case, which involved two victims from across the border, in Bergen County. No jury is supposed to decide a case based on emotion, though it happened every day, and Reldan's defense lawyers knew that. But that seems like a false hope in this case. Any juror viewing the brutality of these murders had to feel sympathy for the victims, no matter where they resided. Reldan and his lawyers also may have believed that the Rockland County DA would not have been so personally committed to Reldan's demise. Without question, Reldan harbored a persecution complex when it came to the Bergen County Prosecutor's Office. He may have believed, correctly perhaps, that even if he couldn't beat the rap in New York, he still might have been able to engineer a better plea bargain with folks who didn't have it in for him.

Whatever the motivation, the first action Frank Wagner took on his new client's behalf was to file the much-awaited pretrial motion for dismissal of the murder indictment for lack of jurisdiction. Superior Court Judge Benedict Lucchi, sitting in Hackensack, heard the motion in mid-February, 1979. A new assistant prosecutor also took charge of the case, the third to appear for the State. AP Robert Leaman, 32, had a reputation as one of the Bergen office's top trial prosecutors, and his courtroom demeanor—portending the fireworks to come—was as feisty as Frank Wagner's.* Leaman's short, stocky stature contrasted sharply with the tall and slender appearance of his adversary, presenting a "Mutt and Jeff" look to observers.

The defense position on the jurisdictional issue was based on what Wagner said was a lack of proof that any crime had taken place in New Jersey. "I was not able to find any testimony or any evidence of any competent nature," Wagner argued to the court, "that would indicate that a crime against these two women was committed in this state or this County of Bergen." The defense attorney had done his homework and presented, methodically, his concept of the State's case. Susan Heynes disappeared from her home and turned up dead in New York State. There was no evidence of foul play in New Jersey, according to Wagner. She may very well have left the state voluntarily, only to lose her life in New York.

---

*Within two years, Leaman would become First Assistant Prosecutor, second in command to Prosecutor Roger W. Breslin, Jr., who succeeded Joseph Woodcock. Leaman earned the job through merit, as all of Breslin's appointments were earned. Woodcock had been a state senator before becoming Prosecutor and often allowed politics to enter into his decision-making. Not so with Roger Breslin, the scion of one of Bergen County's most respected legal families and a man whose integrity was never questioned.

Wagner's point was that no hard evidence pointed to a criminal act having been committed in New Jersey. Why, then, should New Jersey in general, or Bergen County, in particular, have jurisdiction over her murder? With Reeve, Wagner's task was harder; several witnesses had observed a young woman—likely Susan Reeve—in close proximity to a man—likely Robert Reldan—under sinister circumstances. Still, Wagner argued, there was no hard proof—only supposition—that Reeve left the state involuntarily.

Robert Leaman had a different take. The circumstances of each woman's disappearance, he said, suggested that neither left the state of her own volition. Heynes was a happily married woman, who was seen acting normally at 3:30 PM on the day she went missing. Her husband had communicated with her and was expecting her to be home when he arrived from work. Instead, the house was locked, and her house keys and car keys were left on the front seat of her car, which was still parked in the garage. Everything was normal, except she wasn't there. Admittedly, Susan Heynes could have left her home voluntarily, perhaps with a paramour or simply a friend, only to turn up dead in New York. Wagner might have had a point, except for the extreme similarity in the way both women were killed—strangulations, combining manual and ligature action by the killer and identical fractures of the hyoid bone—so rare as to constitute proof that the same person killed both women, as surely as if he had left his *signature* at the scene.

That identical MO tied the Heynes killing to the Reeve killing. Reeve's disappearance was a more provable abduction than Heynes's, given what witnesses reported. If Reeve had been forcibly abducted from New Jersey and killed by a certain person, and if Heynes had been killed by that same person, it stood to reason that Heynes, too, had been forcibly abducted.

The hair and scent evidence tied both women to Reldan's Opel wagon and Reeve to the vacant Booth house in Closter, thereby permitting an additional inference that at least an element of both crimes was committed in Bergen County, New Jersey. Leaman argued that the State's theory of the case rested on felony murder—that is, murder committed in conjunction with a companion crime, in this case, kidnapping. Because both kidnappings took place in Bergen County, an element of felony murder, therefore, also took place in Bergen County, giving the BCPO jurisdiction in the case.

Judge Lucchi denied the defense motion, citing in his reported decision the established legal principle that a state "has jurisdiction to try an offense where only part of that offense has been committed within its boundaries." All that was required in this particular case, Lucchi said, was that "a reasonable inference may be drawn placing New Jersey as the site of any criminal activity vis-à-vis the two murder victims." The State's kidnapping theory had held up.

Frank Wagner's next attempt to undermine the State's case was on the issue of *severance*, or, stated conversely, *joinder*. The State had elected to join the two murders together in one indictment and intended to try them together in the same court proceeding before the same jury. The defense, quite rightly, saw this as disadvantageous, as it would portray Reldan as not just a bad guy who had committed a murder, but as a *really* bad guy who had committed *two* murders. A living crime spree, in other words. Jurors, faced with evidence of two horrible crimes, would be less likely—if they had any such inclination at all—to give even the slightest benefit of doubt to such a personification of evil incarnate. If they found evidence in one murder sufficient to convict, they would likely convict for the second murder, too, no matter their view of the evidence for that crime.

The thrust of Wagner's argument, therefore, was that his client would be prejudiced by requiring him to defend two murders at once. There was also the problem of Reldan taking the stand to testify. Reldan claimed that he wanted to testify on the charge that he murdered Susan Heynes, where the evidence against him was weakest, but did not want to testify regarding the Reeve murder. If he took the stand in a double-murder trial, he could be cross-examined about both crimes, thereby prejudicing his ability to present his best defense to the Heynes murder.

There was a new judge assigned to the severance motion—James F. Madden, who would keep the Reldan case for remaining pretrial motions, right through the first murder trial. Known as Jimmy Madden throughout the Bergen County legal community, he had a gregarious nature. Of Italian-Irish extraction, his friendly, story-telling demeanor in chambers and during lunches with his colleagues stood in sharp contrast to his no-nonsense persona on the bench. He was a tolerant man, but when attorneys on either side pushed him too far with egregious conduct, he wouldn't hesitate to come down on them, even in front of a jury. He was a close friend of Criminal Assignment Judge Fred Galda and a nephew of Judge Joseph Marini, who presided at Robert Reldan's first jury trial—the attempted rape case involving the 14-year-old girl. (Though Reldan *won* that case in 1963 by getting a hung jury, it was later dismissed through a plea bargain.)

When a series of crimes is part of a continuing course of conduct, the State has a legitimate interest in trying all such crimes in one court proceeding. This is especially true when evidence concerning one crime would be admissible in the trial of another crime. Efficient use of court resources, a worthy policy goal, argues in favor of combining related crimes like this into one trial, and New Jersey evidence rules permit that, where no *undue* prejudice to the defendant results. Here, the method of strangulation in both murders was so strikingly similar as to warrant a reasonable inference that the same person killed both women. The characterization used in the law for this type of scenario is *signature*: The perpetrator commits multiple crimes—murder or any other serious offenses—in a distinctive way, which becomes a common denominator. On March 16, 1979, Judge Madden heard oral arguments on Frank Wagner's severance motion. Wagner and Leaman started bickering almost immediately, each complaining about actions of the other. Madden tolerated it a while, then roundly chastised both attorneys.

"Let's stick to the law and forget our difficulties as far as personalities are concerned," Madden said. "You're going to make it easier on me, on the jurors, and on yourselves, and the public will get a better impression of the legal system, if we all act as gentlemen and do not have any outbursts of emotion and take it nice and calm. Because the fact that I can scream louder than you can, or Leaman can scream louder than Wagner can, or Wagner can out-scream the both of us, is not going to help us reach a conclusion in this matter. All right?

"And I'll tell you quite frankly, it's my impression from sitting on the bench, histrionics by attorneys don't help jurors in any respect in reaching a conclusion, so let's proceed. Now, I try to be calm and cool and collected as far as this matter is concerned, but if you want me to act as a general and take over, I'm very capable of doing so and I will do so, and I want that understood right at this point, and from now on, from both of you. All right?"

Both attorneys agreed to behave but it would be a short-lived truce; the squabbling continued unabated, carrying through the first murder trial, which would last a month.*

---

*A typical exchange: Leaman is arguing his case for joinder, the primary point being the Medical Examiner's expected testimony about the similarity of the two strangulations, when Wagner interrupts.

Wagner: "He [Zugibe, the ME] is not even qualified for that, Judge. He's a doctor."

Judge Madden: "Go ahead. Let him—"

Wagner: "He's not even a forensic pathologist, for God's sake."

Leaman: "Your Honor, are we having a group discussion here, or can I proceed?"

Wagner: "You're—evidently, you're putting me to sleep."

Leaman: "You are, Mr. Wagner? You think we are somewhere other than a court of law?"

Judge Madden: "Please, let's not—"

Leaman: "Your Honor—"

Judge Madden: "Behave, will you?"

On March 23, 1979, a week after hearing oral arguments, Judge Madden denied Wagner's severance motion and ruled for the State, allowing joinder of the two murder charges in one trial. In a published decision, Madden concluded that "the evidence in one homicide would be admissible in the trial of the other, thereby rendering it unnecessary to sever on the theory that the jury would be improperly hearing other crimes evidence in a single trial." He also ruled that "the defendant will not be unduly prejudiced by a joinder of the two counts . . . ."

Frank Wagner vented frustration: "I think the prosecutor's insistence on a dual trial here indicates nothing more than a vengeance to try to convict," he said, "not for justice to be done." The redoubtable defense attorney need not have fretted; within two months, he would win Robert Reldan's biggest victory, to date.

* * *

When investigators applied for a warrant to search Robert Reldan's 1969 Opel Kadett station wagon, just hours after his October 31, 1975, arrest on the Norwood and Closter burglary charges, they went to the local municipal court judge. Local judges, a step below their Superior Court brethren, handle traffic and misdemeanor criminal offenses. They are also empowered to consider and issue arrest and search warrants, even for the most serious offenses otherwise beyond their jurisdiction. It's a dangerous game—going to a municipal court judge, who is presumably less trained and less experienced, for a search warrant involving a major case. Any challenge to the warrant would come before a Superior Court judge, who would have less compunction in overturning a lower court's decision than in ruling against a colleague at the same level.

Investigators wanted to search the Opel wagon for evidence regarding the Heynes and Reeve murders, for which Robert Reldan was now the prime suspect. His statement to Ed Denning and his record of assaults against women caused him to come under suspicion. Eileen Dalton had, by that time, picked Reldan out of a photo line-up, but other witnesses— notably, Raymond Lozier, Stephen Prato, the Fabrocinis, the Pittalugas, and, perhaps most important, employees in the fine jewelry department at Macy's Herald Square—had not yet made their information known to police. Denning and his BCPO superiors didn't believe they had sufficient probable cause to search the vehicle on the basis of the two murders; they may have been right, although "probable cause" is the threshold for such a search. It is a low hurdle that may have been reachable on the strength alone of Eileen Dalton's observations at the George Washington Bridge tollbooth. Dalton got her description of Reldan's height and weight wrong, but he was seated in a vehicle, which is a difficult circumstance in which to judge such things. She did, after all, pick him out of the photo line-up.

In any event, investigators didn't try to get authorization based on the murders; instead, they used the two burglaries as justification, without even mentioning the murders in the search warrant application. In executing the search warrant on November 1, 1975, BCPO investigators, FBI agents, and police practically tore the Opel wagon apart, ripping out flooring, vacuuming for trace evidence, collecting dirt samples from wheel wells—and sending everything to the FBI forensic laboratory in Washington DC. In short, they did everything they should have done in conducting a search for evidence in a murder case, all of which was extreme overkill for a search involving two non-descript burglaries.

Wagner meandered in his initial argument on the motion to suppress, but Judge Madden interrupted him and jumped to the point. "Isn't the pertinent question here," he asked, "whether or not the search warrant was issued as part of a pretext?"

AP Robert Leaman responded to that challenge by pointing out the legitimacy of the search on the basis of the burglaries and the theory that the State may use, to its own purposes, evidence of other crimes discovered during an otherwise legitimate search. Madden was ready for that argument and pulled out a law book. "I am quoting from the *Criminal Law Digest*, Mr. Leaman, page 489," Madden said. "'A search reasonable in its inception may nonetheless violate the Fourth Amendment by virtue of its intolerable intensity and scope . . . . Its scope and intensity must not be disproportionate to the circumstances giving rise to it. The notion that a search originally justified may be without limit is rejected.'"

Leaman stipulated that the search warrant was for the burglaries only, and Judge Madden granted Wagner a recess to review his arguments in light of that stipulation. Returning to the bench, Madden spoke first and left no doubt where he was heading.

"So that we may keep the arguments within reasonable limits," Madden said, "I would like to make a preliminary statement before I listen to counsel. Aren't we dealing here with a situation . . . where there are items seized beyond the scope of the warrant, and those items must therefore be suppressed? In other words, the warrant is conceded to be good, so everything within the scope of the warrant that is seized is good. However, Mr. Wagner contends that certain items seized . . . such as pieces of carpeting and vacuum sweepings, are beyond the scope of the warrant and must therefore be suppressed.

"What possible relevance to a break and entry charge and an attempted break and entry charge can such items as vacuum sweepings have? Why was the Federal Bureau of Investigation involved in a mere breaking and entry and attempted breaking and entry? Weren't they clearly looking for evidence in connection to a murder case or murder cases, and don't these actions go beyond the scope of the warrant issued? I think if we can keep ourselves within those parameters," Madden concluded, "we won't consume needless time and useless argument."

Thus bolstered by the court's statement, Frank Wagner blasted the prosecution's trashing of his client's rights in their "fishing expedition."

"They figured they had someone who was suspected of implication in some murders," Wagner said, "and without going the legal route by appearing before a magistrate to show their reasons so authorization could be given by an impartial person, [they committed] what would, in effect, be a violation of law . . . ."

The warrant application listed the items police were searching for—items usually associated with burglary, Wagner argued, and certainly nothing having to do with microscopic evidence that had to be gathered with vacuum sweepings and sifted through at the FBI lab.

Leaman followed the tried and true formula of a litigant who finds himself on the wrong side of the facts: He argued the law, ranging through the historical underpinnings of the Fourth Amendment, exclusionary rule, and right to privacy. It didn't work.

Judge Madden granted the defense motion to suppress all evidence collected as a result of the November 1 search of the Opel wagon, including the hair specimens that FBI lab technicians found to be similar to sample hairs taken from the two victims. Wagner pressed his advantage and sought to have the judge also rule that the scent evidence obtained through the use of Thomas McGinn's trained dogs also had to be suppressed, on the theory that it was the "fruit of the poisonous tree," a legal concept that excludes evidence piggy-backed on an illegal search. The dogs never would have been brought in, Wagner argued, without the intrusive, overreaching search of the vehicle in the first place. Leaman interjected. He couldn't presently locate Thomas McGinn, he said, so he had no intention of calling him and using the scent evidence, anyway. The assistant prosecutor may have been trying to forestall an expected adverse ruling, hoping to keep his options open for later in the trial, but Madden let the ax fall on that issue, too.

"No testimony is getting into this case concerning the use of the two German shepherds," Madden ruled, "and I'm not deciding the issue on its merits. That order will be fully enforced by me. That's understood, okay? That makes the motion moot."

Wagner incredulously said, "There is no dog scent going to be introduced in this case?"

"Right," Judge Madden affirmed.

Wagner continued, "On the trial of the indictment—"

"Definitely, right," Judge Madden said.

"Whether or not anything turns up later?" Wagner asked.

"Your Honor—" Leaman spoke up.

"Go ahead," said the judge. "What do you want to say?"

"Nothing, Sir," Leaman said.

"That's it, Judge Madden acknowledged. "Nothing concerning the dogs is getting into the case."

* * *

A few other motions went against the defense. The judge determined that Reldan's statement to Investigator Ed Denning on October 22, 1975, was voluntary and non-custodial. *Miranda* warnings were not required to be administered to Reldan before he was questioned about the Heynes and Reeve disappearances. It didn't matter whether he was a suspect or not, so long as he wasn't in custody and gave the statement without coercion. The judge would permit the State to play a tape of that interview for the jury, with certain non-admissible parts, like Reldan's talk of his counseling as a paroled sex offender, redacted to avoid prejudicing jurors.

If Reldan decided to take the witness stand in his defense, the State would be able to use seven prior convictions, including the Caplan rape conviction, to impeach his credibility. That ruling effectively kept Reldan off the witness stand in the murder case. If a jury became aware that the murder defendant before them, accused of abducting and killing two young women and raping at least one of them in the process, had a prior rape conviction . . . well, no limiting instruction by the court would be able to *unring* that bell after the jury heard it.

In a last-ditch effort to delay the trial, Frank Wagner went before Assignment Judge Theodore Trautwein to argue that press coverage of pretrial motions had reawakened public interest in the case, which had been dormant for 28 months. Wagner requested a stay due to adverse publicity, or a change of venue to another county. Judge Trautwein, as well acquainted with defense counsel delay tactics as Judge Malech had been in the earlier conspiracy trial, learned that Wagner was making the motion on the actual date for the start of the trial—May 21, 1979.

"This is an eleventh hour attempt," Trautwein said. "I want to know why you are doing it at this late moment." Wagner handed the court a collection of sensational newspaper accounts of the case that had appeared within the prior week in three different newspapers, but his efforts were to no avail. Trautwein denied the motion on the ground that it was premature. He said an extra-large jury pool had been summoned for the trial and he had every confidence that 16 fair-minded jurors could be selected—12 to ultimately decide the case and four alternates in case circumstances forced withdrawal of one or more jurors.*

Nothing now stood between Robert Reldan and his day in court. Arthur Reeve, father of Susan Reeve, would attend every day of the trial, as would Jonathan Heynes, husband of Susan Heynes. They would be daily reminders to the jury of the continuing human cost of Reldan's crimes, the aftermath of pain and sorrow that a murderer leaves behind for the living.

For his part, Robert Reldan had to have been optimistic about his chances. True, he had lost the jurisdictional and severance motions— setbacks, to be sure. But he had won the big one, his motion to suppress evidence. The judge had excluded from his trial the persuasive hair and scent-dog evidence that the prosecution could ill afford to lose in a largely circumstantial case. It was the biggest factor that Reldan had going for him—the biggest factor other than the way women were attracted to him. His charm, after all, had already won him two hung juries, and was about to win him his third.

---

*This was normal practice with any prominent case, especially one expected to last weeks. Over the course of a long trial, jurors fall by the wayside for many reasons: illness, inability to get along with fellow jurors, family emergency, stress of deciding a fellow human's fate, and so forth. Most trials, no matter what their length, start out with at least 14 jurors in the box. Trials that will last months often seat 16 jurors. If, through attrition for whatever reason, the number of jurors falls below 12 in any criminal trial, a mistrial will most likely be declared and the entire process started over again. In Reldan's second murder trial, which would take place later in 1979, just such an eventuality was barely avoided.

Robert Reldan's yearbook picture, Fort Lee High School, NJ, Class of 1958.
Photo by Irving Lloyd, Inc., Photographers, Teaneck, NJ.

Robert Reldan at 21 or 22, around the time of his first known New Jersey crime as an adult—the burglary of a Fort Lee residence and his attempted sexual assault on the 14-year-old girl living there. Courtesy of Bergen County Prosecutor's Office.

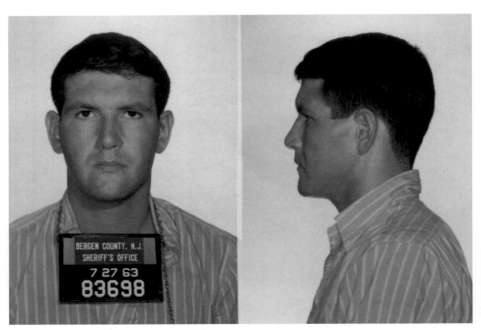

Reldan's mug shot after arrest in Closter on July 27, 1963, for carrying a concealed weapon in a motor vehicle. Courtesy of Bergen County Prosecutor's Office.

The VW convertible that Reldan used to follow Mrs. Caplan home. He parked it in front of her home, where both his victim and a passerby noticed it. Courtesy of Bergen County Prosecutor's Office.

The Heynes residence, viewed from the street looking toward the 2-car garage. Courtesy of Bergen County Prosecutor's Office.

MISSING PERSON

SUSAN HEYNES

MISSING SINCE OCTOBER 6, 1975
FROM 359 SCHRAALENBURGH ROAD
HAWORTH, NEW JERSEY

DESCRIPTION

Age 28 DOB 8-23-47
Wt. 110 lbs. Hgt. 5'6"
Brown Hair - Blue Eyes
Color White - British Accent
¼" scar right chin
Fair Complexion

CLOTHING

White Blouse, Blue Jeans,
Blue lace shoes,
Brown cardigan sweater
Brown woven purse -
Shoulder strap

MAY SEEK EMPLOYMENT AS NURSE

May also use maiden name -
SUSAN JOHNSTONE

ANY INFORMATION - NOTIFY

HAWORTH POLICE DEPT.
HAWORTH, N.J.

384 - 1900

Missing-person flyer distributed after Susan
Heynes's disappearance on October 6, 1975.
Courtesy of Bergen County Prosecutor's Office.

The Church of St. Mary the Virgin in Wolverton,
England, where Jonathan and Susan Heynes
were married in June 1975. The thirteenth century
landmark is situated in the heart of Shakespeare
country, not far from Stratford-upon-Avon. Five
months after the wedding, on a beautiful autumn
day, Susan Heynes's funeral would be conducted
in the same church.
Copyright © Robin Stott and licensed for reuse
under Creative Commons license:
(www.geograph.org.uk/reuse.php?id=1974186).

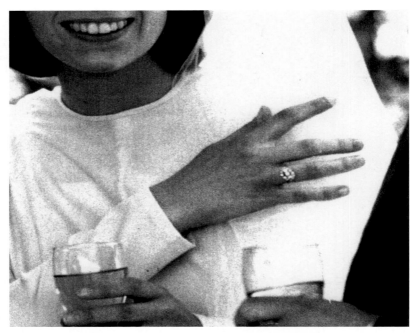

Susan Heynes on her wedding day in June 1975. The distinctive engagement ring on her right hand
would become crucial evidence against Reldan, although the ring, itself, was never recovered.
Courtesy of Bergen County Prosecutor's Office.

A sketch of Susan Heynes's engagement ring, which was made by the ring's maker, Saunders Jewellery, Ltd. Jonathan Heynes purchased the ring for his fiancée at Harrod's Department Store in London, England, in January 1975. This sketch was used at trial to prove that Reldan had possession of the ring soon after Susan Heynes's disappearance. Courtesy of Bergen County Prosecutor's Office.

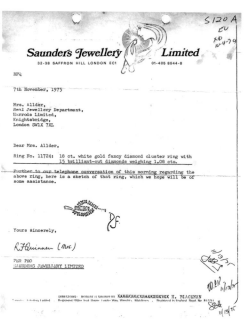

Saunders Jewellery Limited
32-38 SAFFRON HILL LONDON EC1   01-405 8644-8

7th November, 1975

Mrs. Allder,
Real Jewellery Department,
Harrods Limited,
Knightsbridge,
London SW1X 7XL

Dear Mrs. Allder,

Ring No. 11724: 18 ct. white gold fancy diamond cluster ring with
                 15 brilliant-cut diamonds weighing 1.08 cts.

Further to our telephone conversation of this morning regarding the
above ring, here is a sketch of that ring, which we hope will be of
some assistance.

Yours sincerely,

R.F.Quinnen (Mrs.)

Per Pro
SAUNDERS JEWELLERY LIMITED

View of the path to Lake DeForest in Valley Cottage, New York, where Reldan hid the body of Susan Heynes. Courtesy of Bergen County Prosecutor's Office.

Susan Heynes's body was found on October 27, 1975, by a Valley Cottage resident walking his dog. Twenty-year-old Matthew Shaindlin, pointing to the spot of his gruesome discovery. Courtesy of Bergen County Prosecutor's Office.

The vegetation-choked site where Susan Heynes's body was found. Courtesy of Bergen County Prosecutor's Office.

Susan Reeve, in a portrait taken shortly before her death. Courtesy of Mr. and Mrs. Arthur Reeve.

Anderson Avenue in Demarest, NJ, looking south toward its intersection with County Road. Witnesses last saw Susan Reeve walking north on Anderson Avenue. Courtesy of Bergen County Prosecutor's Office.

The intersection of Edward Street and Anderson Avenue, looking south toward County Road. Mary and Joseph Fabrocini left their home on Edward Street just before dusk on the evening of October 14, 1975, and began walking toward County Road on their way to an ice cream store. Susan Reeve crossed in front of them, from right to left, just after she alighted from the bus and began walking home. Courtesy of Bergen County Prosecutor's Office.

Robert Reldan's 1969 Opel Kadett wagon, after it was impounded by Closter, NJ, police on October 31, 1975, near a home Reldan had burglarized that same day. Reldan used the vehicle to abduct both Susan Heynes and Susan Reeve. Courtesy of Bergen County Prosecutor's Office.

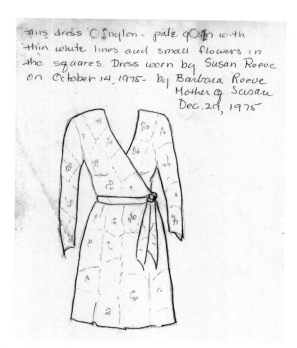

This dress Osnylon - pale green with thin white lines and small flowers in the squares. Dress worn by Susan Reeve on October 14, 1975 - by Barbara Reeve Mother of Susan Dec. 29, 1975

Sketch made by Barbara Reeve, Susan's mother, to show what she was wearing on the day she disappeared. Courtesy of Bergen County Prosecutor's Office.

Sketch made by Mary Fabrocini to show what a young woman was wearing on October 14, 1975—the day Mary saw her walking north on Anderson Avenue. Its close match to Barbara Reeve's sketch would become evidence at trial to prove Susan Reeve's path of travel on the day she disappeared. Courtesy of Bergen County Prosecutor's Office.

Entry to Tallman Mountain State Park in Rockland County, NY, where workmen discovered Susan Reeve's body on October 28, 1975. Courtesy of Bergen County Prosecutor's Office.

The swampy area where Reldan dumped Susan Reeve's body. Reldan had picnicked with a girlfriend less than 100 yards from this site two months earlier. Courtesy of Bergen County Prosecutor's Office.

Investigators retrieving evidence from the marshes where the Reeve body was discovered. Courtesy of Bergen County Prosecutor's Office.

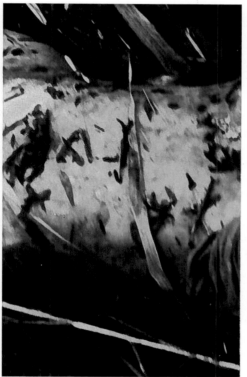

Photo of Susan Reeve's body showing embedded willow tree leaves. This key piece of evidence would prove that Reldan had moved the body after he became a suspect in the murders. Courtesy of Bergen County Prosecutor's Office.

Photo of Reldan taken at Closter police headquarters on October 31, 1975, after he turned himself in for a burglary he had committed that day. Authorities would hold him on $750,000 bail, an unheard of sum for burglary charges. By this time, he was already a suspect in the murders of Susan Heynes and Susan Reeve. Courtesy of Bergen County Prosecutor's Office.

The holding room from which Robert Reldan escaped during his second murder trial. He squeezed through the narrow window shown in the photo to the left of the open door. Courtesy of Bergen County Prosecutor's Office.

Hackensack, NJ, police officer questioning witnesses in the parking lot of an office building, where Reldan commandeered a car on October 15, 1979, to make good his escape during his second murder trial. Courtesy of *The Record* (Bergen Co., NJ)/NorthJersey.com, staff photographer Gordon Corbett.

The Cadillac Reldan commandeered during his escape, shown where it came to rest after Reldan ran it into a ditch in Tuxedo, NY, during a high-speed police chase. Courtesy of Bergen County Prosecutor's Office.

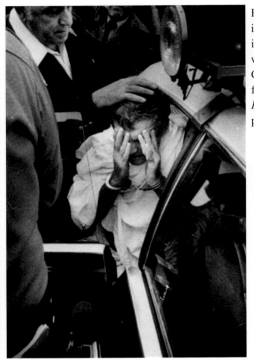

Reldan after being treated at Tuxedo Hospital in New York State on October 15, 1979, for minor injuries sustained in his escape. He was captured within an hour of his escape from the Bergen County courthouse and returned to that jurisdiction for the completion of his trial. Courtesy of *The Record* (Bergen Co., NJ)/NorthJersey.com, staff photographer Peter Monsees.

Robert Reldan addressing the court on February 7, 1986, during his third murder trial, in which he acted as his own attorney. Courtesy of *The Record* (Bergen Co., NJ)/ NorthJersey.com, staff photographer Ed Hill.

Robert Reldan, as he appeared at age 68 in 2009. Photo by the Bergen County Sheriff's Office.

Robert Reldan, about to be handcuffed and led from the courtroom on March 13, 1986, after a jury convicted him for the murders of Susan Heynes and Susan Reeve. Seated next to him is Frank Wagner, the public defender ordered by the court to provide Reldan with legal advice. Courtesy of *The Record* (Bergen Co., NJ)/NorthJersey.com, staff photographer Carmine Galasso.

Reldan addressing the court during his sentencing hearing on April 25, 1986. He would continue to proclaim his innocence and blame his convictions on an overzealous prosecutor's office. Courtesy of *The Record* (Bergen Co., NJ)/NorthJersey.com, staff photographer Danielle P. Richard.

Barbara and Arthur Reeve holding a photo of their daughter Susan, shortly after the Reeves won a $10 million judgment against Robert Reldan for causing Susan's death. Courtesy of *The Record* (Bergen Co., NJ)/NorthJersey.com, photo by Jake Roth, special to *The Record*.

Lillian Booth greeting a resident of the Actors Fund Home in Englewood, NJ, on April 23, 2003. Ms. Booth donated $2 million to the home, which was renamed in her honor. Courtesy of *The Record* (Bergen Co., NJ)/NorthJersey.com, staff photographer Danielle P. Richard.

Chapter 18

One juror, a woman, cast an unwavering 'not guilty' vote.

Frank Wagner interrupted Assistant Prosecutor Robert Leaman's opening statement 12 times, perpetuating the bad blood that had developed between the two lawyers during pretrial motions. The rancor would continue the entire trial, despite Judge Madden's best efforts to control it. The stakes are never higher than in a murder trial, and, once trial lawyers' passions are aroused, not even an embarrassing lecture from the judge may be enough to quell them.

Jury selection began on May 21, 1979, and took three days. With all 16 jurors seated by May 24, Wagner followed Leaman's opening with his own. Just minutes into his remarks, the defense attorney characterized the State's case as "hot air and a lot of wind and a lot of smoke." AP Leaman was on his feet immediately, objecting to Wagner's "argument," the type of rhetoric normally reserved for summations, not opening statements.

"I'm warming up to my opening remarks," Wagner said.

"Maybe you should cool down," Leaman retorted.

The attorneys had drawn battle lines days earlier, so Judge Madden addressed the jury after he upheld Leaman's objection. It was an unusual step. "I want everyone to understand," Madden said, "we're dealing here with a highly emotional situation, so that sometimes it is difficult for all of us to control our emotions to the fullest. However, if there are emotional incidents, I would say to the ladies and gentlemen of the jury at this time, it should not affect your deliberations, if we ever get to that stage of the case."

The judge was trying to defuse the situation as best he could, while at the same time advising the jury to disregard the antics of the attorneys and not let that interfere with their duty as jurors to give the defendant a fair trial. His aside—"if we ever get to that stage of the case"—was a bit of Madden's wry humor showing.

Wagner ignored the judge's admonition to refrain from argument and kept on his familiar course, calling the State's case, "nothing but a deck of cards that were stacked from the very beginning against Robert Reldan." Warming to his subject, Wagner gave the jury some advice. "What I'm saying and what I mean is this: That you shouldn't be taken in, like so many gullible sidewalk or carnival spectators who listen to the pitch of the pitchman, so to speak, puffing up their claims and making a lot of razzle-dazzle and allegations and statements to entice you into believing you're going to get something that they know they're not going to deliver." Wagner warned them "not to be fooled by the enormity or the immensity of this case in number of witnesses, the exhibits that you've been promised you'll see. It's a real production that's been made out of this case," he said, "because they have to do something . . . ."

In his opening, Leaman had referred to "circumstantial evidence" that he would present, but Wagner disparaged such promises as the State's efforts to manufacture something out of nothing: ". . . there are *coincidences* in this case," the defense attorney said, "but not *circumstances* upon which you can base a conviction."

Wagner wasn't about to let his client's good appearance escape the jury's attention. Reldan was no longer the clean-cut preppy of earlier trials—just 23 when he was tried for the attempted rape of Anna Maria Hernandez and 27 during the Caplan rape trials—but, at 38, he still imparted the image of a handsome, impeccably dressed man—a businessman, perhaps. At the conspiracy trial a year earlier, one observer said he looked like an "insurance salesman."

"Ask yourselves, as you hear the testimony about to unfold," Wagner implored the jurors, "is this a legitimate case against Robert Reldan? Is he or is he not a victim of coincidence, or is he, *as you look at him there* [Wagner pointed at his client], a murderer of two women?"

Wagner had already raised the issue of former Prosecutor Joseph Woodcock's motive in rushing to indict his client, and, now, just before ending his opening statement, he reminded jurors that "the charges against [Robert Reldan] arise not by reason of any real or believable evidence, or any reliable proofs, but because they exist only by reason of political expediency or political ambition . . . ."

Assistant Prosecutor Leaman called more than 60 witnesses to testify and marked for identification 165 exhibits—photos, diagrams, drawings, and physical items like the sandblasting mask—many of which would go into evidence for the jury to see and touch during deliberations. Orchestrating a prosecution of that magnitude is a tremendous task, with the need to schedule witnesses precisely to avoid courtroom downtime, interview witnesses again before they take the stand, prepare exhibits for introduction at the proper moment, and be prepared to deal with the inevitable glitches and surprises that occur in every major trial. Leaman had a pro, veteran BCPO investigator Al Cirello, to help with logistics.

The parade of witnesses included Jonathan Heynes and neighbor Dorothy Slater, both of whom established the 3:30 to 5:55 PM timeframe for Susan Heynes's abduction on October 6, 1975. The window was actually tighter, but the prosecution never refined it. Mrs. Slater saw Susan taking in clothing from the line at 3:30, and Jonathan said the laundry was neatly folded when he got home. Those facts taken together suggest that the earliest Susan could have been abducted was perhaps 3:35 or 3:40 PM. Also, Susan was going out to mail a package to her mother in England and had to have walked out the door well before the 5:00 PM closing time of most post offices. The only plausible explanation was that the abduction occurred between 3:35 PM and 4:30 PM. Because we know Reldan probably followed Susan Heynes home from her job interviews in Westwood, the abduction most likely took place closer to 3:35 or 3:40 PM. This *shortened* time frame would take on significance later.

Jonathan testified as to his observations that day and his wife's normal routine, revealing how far out of the ordinary her disappearance was.

Another set of witnesses—bus driver John O'Hanlon, the Fabrocinis, Stephen Prato, Raymond Lozier, Mark Pittaluga, and Arthur and Barbara Reeve—established Susan Reeve's actions from the time she alighted from the commuter bus in Demarest, at about 6:15 PM on October 14, 1975, to the time when she was abducted, less than 20 minutes later.

The circumstances drawing Robert Reldan into the Reeve disappearance on October 14 were deftly laid out, from Joseph Fabrocini's observation of the junk-filled, small station wagon abruptly turning in front of him to follow the route taken by the young woman seconds before, to the finding of the sandblasting mask and its irrefutable link to the defendant. Raymond Lozier's description of the abduction scene on Anderson Avenue and, later, his identification of the Opel wagon in the Closter impound garage further substantiated Reldan's involvement.

During Raymond Lozier's testimony, Wagner and Leaman clashed frequently, owing to that witness's particular importance. Finally, Judge Madden intervened, and the jury was present.

"Both of you are putting on a fine display," Madden said. "You know, we're trying a very serious matter here. Jurors are giving of their time. We have witnesses, such as Mr. Lozier, who are giving of their time, and we're not going to get anywhere if you two stand up and shout at each other. Now, I'm trying to be as fair as I can to both of you. Certainly I can come forward with some restraints, and if I have another outburst like this between you two gentlemen, I will."

Lozier was one of the State's biggest assets in the case and one of its biggest liabilities. As an eyewitness, he left a lot to be desired. Though he saw the vehicle, he'd gotten its color wrong, calling it variously "light-colored" and "dark brown." He made passing references to the possibility that a second man was present at the scene, but then stuck to the story of a single man and a single woman. During the investigative phase, the prosecution was so concerned about Lozier's ability to recall important details that they sent him to a hypnotist to see if that would help.* It didn't, and Wagner made the most of that failed attempt.

Leaman's direct examination of Lozier and Wagner's cross-examination took the whole afternoon of May 29, 1979, with the cross consuming most of that time. Wagner took advantage of Lozier's hazy memory to pick apart the man's testimony—item by item—but in recalling the cold, sinister-looking man standing next to the transfixed young woman, Lozier couldn't be shaken. The only avenue left open to Wagner in that regard was to plant a seed of doubt in the jury's mind: Perhaps the man Lozier saw wasn't Robert Reldan.

Wagner knew, from reading police reports he had received in discovery, that investigators had shown Lozier a photo line-up, including Reldan's picture, and that he'd failed to pick out Reldan. This failure to identify Susan Reeve's presumed abductor was significant, because Lozier had said that he'd made eye contact with the man and described his sinister stare. Near the close of testimony for the day, Wagner exploited his advantage on this issue.

"Have you ever identified a person you saw standing next to a girl that day?" Wagner asked.

"My identification was not very strong," Lozier said. "I was shown some photographs of a number of different men. I identified one as a probable—only as a probable. There was considerable hesitation in my mind about the photograph."

Wagner pressed on, violating the most sacrosanct axiom of the trial lawyer: Never ask a question you don't know the answer to. He decided to risk it and see if Lozier could make an in-court identification of Robert Reldan, seated right there at the defense table. He had one thing going for him, besides Lozier's poor performance as a witness. During direct examination, the prosecutor had not asked Lozier to make the identification. Presumably, if Leaman had any confidence that Lozier would correctly point to Robert Reldan, he would have asked him to do it.

"Today," Wagner asked, "did you ever see this man next to that car at that time and place?"

"I would not convict a man—" Lozier said.

Wagner interrupted. "On your testimony?"

Lozier continued. "—on my—"

It was Leaman's turn to interrupt. "Objection!"

Judge Madden intervened. "Just answer the question," he said.

---

*Using a qualified hypnotist to facilitate a witness's recollection had recently been approved by the New Jersey Supreme Court, provided that reliable procedures were followed.

"On my memory of what that man looked like at that time," Lozier said.

"Thank you," Wagner said.

That exchange ended the defense's day on a high note. Wagner had effectively dealt with one of the State's most important witnesses, if not neutralizing his testimony, at least showing the holes permeating it—like a sieve. Lozier would be back on the stand the following morning, May 30, when Robert Leaman would get his chance to rehabilitate him.

Then, a most curious thing happened.

Al Cirello sat down with Raymond Lozier after the day's testimony, and Lozier told the investigator that Frank Wagner's fellow attorney looked a lot like the man he'd seen standing next to the car on October 14, 1975—the one who was seemingly in control of the young woman.

"What do you mean?" Cirello asked. "Wagner doesn't have another attorney working the case with him."

"Sure he does," Lozier responded. "The guy in the suit sitting next to Wagner."

Lozier was referring to Reldan, of course. He'd mistaken the well-attired defendant, listening intently to the proceedings and studiously taking notes, for co-counsel in the case. He had felt afraid to make a fool of himself by pointing out the resemblance in open court. Wagner had already created too many embarrassing moments for him that day.

Al Cirello hustled Raymond Lozier off to AP Leaman's office to apprise the prosecutor of the development and to see if there was a way to work it into Lozier's testimony the next day, when he would be back on the witness stand for re-direct examination.

On May 30, Wagner wanted to make a few more points on cross, before Leaman got another chance with the witness on re-direct. He showed Lozier a sketch he'd made of the October 14 scene, while being interviewed by investigators weeks afterwards. It depicted the vehicle differently from the way Lozier described it during testimony on May 29—mistakes Lozier now freely admitted, in a peculiar way.

"I was having a difficult time trying to recall what that particular vehicle looked like and my fingers seemed to tell me the situation," Lozier said. "My hands seemed to know more than my head."

Finally, Lozier's death by a thousand cross-examination cuts ended, and it was the assistant prosecutor's chance to salvage something on re-direct. He went for it.

"Mr. Lozier, you were asked one other question yesterday," Leaman said. "I don't believe you answered definitively. Do you have an impression of the man you saw on October 14, 1975?"

"Yes, Sir," Lozier said. "Fades with time, but I have an impression of the man."

The question and answer suggested stagecraft, a rehearsal of the moment.

"Would you look around the courtroom, please?" Leaman said. "Is there anybody in this courtroom that resembles the man that you saw on October 14, 1975, standing next to the car?"

Catching the drift, Frank Wagner jumped to his feet.

"Now, Judge, this is really going too far," Wagner objected.

"I agree," said Judge Madden.

"No," Leaman said. "I'd like to approach the bench."

Wagner protested. "He's already said—"

Leaman persisted. "No, Sir. I'd like to approach the bench."

Wagner said, "—he couldn't—"

"I'd like to approach the bench," Leaman continued.

"I thought there was testimony that he said he could not identify him," said the judge.

"That's correct," Wagner agreed.

"No, Sir," Leaman insisted. "That is not what he said. I offer you a transcript of that question yesterday." Having anticipated the objection, Leaman arranged for an overnight transcript of the prior day's testimony on this subject.

"*I can remember what's going on in this trial,*" Judge Madden stated. "*I don't need a transcript. I can recall vividly what his 10 or 12 words were concerning Mr. Wagner's—one of Mr. Wagner's last questions yesterday afternoon. I'll sustain the objection.*" (Emphasis added.)

Leaman then blundered: He pressed the judge on the issue, hoping he could somehow get him to reverse himself and allow Lozier's identification of Reldan into the record. Not only did Leaman fail miserably, he brought greater attention to his witness's deficiencies by allowing the judge, himself, to comment on them openly. When jurors hear the judge—the 800-pound gorilla in the courtroom—criticize an element of proof, they take special notice.

"Your Honor, most respectfully," Leaman persisted, "I do not believe that he . . . answered that question definitively."

"He answered the question yesterday," said the judge. "And I'm not going to allow you to get into a contest with Mr. Wagner."

"Most respectfully, I ask Your Honor if you would like to review the transcript," Leaman continued. "He did not answer the question, Sir. He did not. I would like to hear his answer, Your Honor, if you would—"

"I'll sustain the objection," Judge Madden repeated. "It would be highly prejudicial to the defendant's case at this time. We went through this matter already. He was asked a question and he . . . gave an answer at that time."

Leaman, ignoring the judge's growing ire, spoke to his witness. "Can you describe for us, Mr. Lozier, [your] impression of the man you saw standing by the car?"

"Now, again," Wagner said. "Objection."

"I'm going to sustain the objection," Judge Madden said again. "We've gone through this on two or three occasions before."

"Your Honor, I don't want to prejudice the defendant," Leaman tried. "The State has a right to a fair trial also." Another blunder by Leaman—suggesting the judge wasn't being fair.

"He's already given his impression as to the description of the individual on at least two or three prior occasions on direct examination," Judge Madden said. "It's not proper re-direct."

"Your Honor, Sir," Leaman continued. "I must submit that he did not answer that question and that I have a right to ask him now if there's anyone in this courtroom that resembles the man that he saw next to that car."

The assistant prosecutor was ignoring the old saw, "If you find yourself in a hole, stop digging."

Judge Madden ostensibly relented, but not really, saying "Let me look at the transcript then."

The judge glanced at the document perfunctorily, an expression of disdain on his face. Then, handing the transcript to his bailiff, he said, "I'll sustain the objection. Give this back."

Leaman finally got the message, at least temporarily, and asked no further questions. But his failed attempt to get the in-court identification gave Wagner another opportunity—which he took—to continue discrediting Lozier on re-cross.

Wagner questioned the witness. "Now, did you ever tell anyone that the car you saw was a light car in the first interview?" Wagner, of course, knew all about Lozier's equivocating on the vehicle's color.

"Apparently, I did," Lozier said. "I do not recall it as such."

"Then," Wagner said, "you changed it from a light car in your second interview to a brown or a dark brown car, right?"

"Yes," Lozier admitted.

Wagner took the opening. "Then, in the third or the fourth or the fifth or the sixth or the eighth or the ninth or the tenth interview, it becomes the *red* car in your mind?

"I don't remember 10 interviews," Lozier said.

During another 15 or 20 minutes of re-cross-examination, Wagner scored points on Raymond Lozier's faulty memory. If Lozier's time on the witness stand had been a boxing match, the referee would have signaled a TKO and stopped it. Leaman made a feeble attempt at rehabilitation when it came his turn again, but, by the time Lozier departed the stand just before a break on May 30, the State's case was very much in jeopardy.

After the jury left the courtroom on break, Leaman took his final shot at the in-court identification issue. He read into the record from the same transcript that the judge had earlier reviewed and rejected. The attorneys squabbled some more, before Madden finally ended the discussion.

"He could not identify," Judge Madden said. "I'm not going to handle a homicide [trial] and then let some witness come up here after a day and a half of testimony and then say someone in the courtroom resembles someone that he looked at and saw perhaps five to 20 seconds at the most. This matter is too serious for that type of testimony. I don't think he can make an identification. He didn't make one on direct examination and I will not allow testimony along the lines that someone resembles someone that was next to a motor vehicle."

The rest of May 30 went almost as bad for Leaman. Stephen Prato took the witness stand. Prato was the young man who had seen a suspicious-looking male trailing a young woman on Anderson Avenue that October 14, just before sunset. He had undergone direct examination by Leaman, then cross-examination by Wagner. Leaman was questioning Prato on re-direct about details of questionable relevancy, when Judge Madden—still chaffing at the assistant prosecutor's over-the-top persistence on the Lozier in-court identification issue—finally blew his stack.

"How much longer are you going to be?" Madden asked Leaman. "I mean, we've been going over something here for a long, long time and I haven't interjected myself at all, but the young man has described something that he saw. Now, we've been in Englewood Hospital [Prato was on his way there when he made his observations] for the last 15 minutes and I think it's making a bad impression on me listening to this because I don't know what it has to do with the case and the jurors. I don't know what we're talking about."

"Your Honor—" Leaman tried to explain.

"The young man could have testified in this case . . . from two to five minutes," the judge argued. "He drove by a spot from 15 to 30 seconds, at the most. We've had him going up and down Anderson Avenue five times, what he saw in the rearview mirror, what he's doing in Englewood hospital, and we've wasted an awful lot of time in this case with the last 15 witnesses I've heard. From now on, I'm going to interject myself in this case, and we're going to move it."

Leaman tried to speak. "Your honor, I—"

"If you want to finish with this witness," Judge Madden said, "we can finish, and the jurors can get to lunch. I've laid the law down."

"I have no further questions," Leaman said.

"We've been through this on direct and cross-examination again, said Judge Madden. "I don't like to interject myself in the case at all but we've been listening to too much direct examination and too much cross-examination that has nothing to do with the issues in this case. Now, you are finished with this witness. He can go home. If not, we will finish with him and the jurors will go to lunch. Are you finished with him?"

"Yes, Sir," said Leaman, learning to stop digging his hole.

Judge Madden looked at Wagner. "How about you?"

"I have nothing," the defense attorney said.

"Step down," said Judge Madden. "Thank you, Mr. Prato."

* * *

AP Robert Leaman would have better days before the trial's end. Not surprisingly, Denning was his usual strong presence on the witness stand. The modified tape of his interview with Reldan was played for the jury, followed by witnesses to disprove Reldan's manufactured alibis for the relevant dates and times. Reldan's familiarity with the Lake DeForest and Tallman Mountain State Park sites was revealed to the jury. Cliff and Allison Williams both testified, but Wagner's withering cross-examination of the brothers may have neutralized the value of Reldan's admissions to them. Not only were their criminal records laid bare, but the fact that both were out of prison—thanks in part to their cooperation with the prosecution—had to have been an affront to juror sensibilities. Cliff was in a halfway house, an intermediary step before parole, but Allison was already on the street, perhaps casing their next jewelry heist.

Melvin Norman, the jewelry buyer at Macy's, held up well on the witness stand and established a clear link between Robert Reldan and Susan Heynes's engagement ring. It was damning evidence. Who but her killer could have pried that ring off of her finger? Reldan's action in retrieving the ring from Macy's the day after his interview with Denning was tantamount to an admission of guilt. Wagner tried to exploit weaknesses in the way Norman had handled the transaction with Reldan—the sloppy recordkeeping—but it did not negate the underlying fact: Defendant Robert Reldan was in possession of Susan Heynes's engagement ring (and trying to profit from it) 15 days after her abduction and murder.

Dr. Frederick Zugibe, the Rockland County Medical Examiner, was unshakable in his testimony. It would be difficult for any cross-examiner to attack the forensic conclusions of the man who had written the book on forensic pathology, and who had conducted more than 5,000 autopsies. Wagner tried, but did not succeed. Zugibe's conclusions about the two murders—the rare combination of manual and ligature strangulation used in both instances, the fractures of the hyoid bone in identical ways, the willow leaves, *rigor mortis*, lividity evidence showing that Susan Reeve's body had been moved after death (after Reldan's BCPO interview), and the evidence of Susan Reeve's rape—built a strong case against the defendant. Any reasonable person had to see that the accumulation of circumstantial evidence was no unlucky combination of coincidences, no politically inspired frame-up.

After the State rested its case, Frank Wagner also rested for the defense, without calling a single witness. It was preordained that Reldan, himself, would not take the stand—his criminal record, especially the Caplan rape, would have torpedoed his case for sure. Since Reldan did not testify, Wagner was able to keep from the jury most of his client's criminal past, the only hint of which was his prison sentence for the two burglaries, which brought him in contact with the Williams brothers. Wagner had also tried to use that information as a reason for the prosecution to try to frame his client for the murders. He was an available scapegoat, as Wagner put it.

However, it was surprising that the defense did not call any witnesses. Judy Reldan, for example, did not testify for her husband or attempt to provide him with an alibi. By the time of the trial, she had bailed out of her marriage and was not even considering the idea of perjuring herself in his defense. Wagner had no experts to cast doubt on Zugibe's testimony, which the defense attorney surely recognized as a serious obstacle. Given Wagner's experience, it is hard to believe that he would let pass an opportunity to challenge the ME's conclusions. The only possible explanation was that he couldn't find a pathology expert who disagreed with Zugibe. In the end, Frank Wagner decided to rely on his cross-examination of the State's witnesses to create the reasonable doubt he needed to either win for the defense or, more likely, hang the jury and get a mistrial.

Wagner and Leaman delivered their summations on Wednesday, June 13, 1979. Both men finished well. Assistant Prosecutor Leaman, recognizing that the strength of his case was in the aggregate and not in any individual element, urged jurors to remember the big picture when they began their deliberations. In his opening statement four weeks earlier, he had likened the State's case to a jigsaw puzzle, whose picture did not reveal itself until all of its pieces were in place. Now, he said, those pieces showed the picture of a guilty Robert Reldan.

"I am not asking you to convict this man based on a single piece of evidence," Leaman said, "but on the totality of the evidence. I'm not asking you to convict this man based on Raymond Lozier's observation, Stephen Prato, or the finding of a mask on Anderson Avenue. I'm asking you to put all these things together and see if, in fact, it comports with common sense, if it makes sense to you."

Leaman continued in this vein, holding each piece of the puzzle up for the jury to see—the testimony of each important witness—and then carefully placing that piece into the whole to reveal the picture that he had crafted. When he finished his summation, Leaman felt good about the job he'd done, but he was experienced enough to know that it hadn't been a perfect performance on his part. Still, he trusted this jury to do the right thing. He was sure they would do the right thing.

After the lunch recess on Wednesday, Judge Madden charged the jury, designated the alternates, and sent the remaining 12 men and women into the jury room to deliberate.

The jurors deliberated the rest of Wednesday, all day Thursday, all day Friday, and part of the day Saturday, June 19, 1979. That day, they informed the judge that they were hopelessly deadlocked and would not be able to reach a verdict. Judge Madden had already employed the *deadlock* charge, coaxing them to try again, to no avail. Finally, there was nothing left for him to do but thank them for their service. He declared a mistrial.

Robert Reldan hugged a beaming Frank Wagner and turned, smiling, to his family in the row behind him. He had *won* again.

* * *

For the rest of the weekend, Robert Leaman had to have been upset by the unsatisfactory result, after spending months preparing for and conducting the trial. When the case went to the jury, he'd felt good about it. The defense had presented no evidence, and the State's witnesses, he believed, had established a strong, if circumstantial, case. They had stood up well, with a few exceptions, to Frank Wagner's cross-examination— even the Williams brothers, with all their baggage.

What, then, had been the hang up? How had Robert Reldan managed to frustrate justice once again, hoodwinking a third jury in his long criminal career? Was there something Leaman missed in the State's proofs? A gap left unfilled? He wondered what the final vote had been. How many votes to convict? How many to acquit?

On Monday, June 18, BCPO Detective John David sought out his colleague, Al Cirello, as soon as he arrived for work. Together, they went to Leaman's office and related a story that brought relief to the troubled assistant prosecutor.

John David's daughter, Bernadette, had been a juror in the Reldan trial. Her affiliation with the Bergen County Prosecutor's Office had been fully disclosed during jury selection and would have allowed Frank Wagner to get her excused from the panel for cause. It is extremely rare for a defense attorney to allow a potential juror with police or prosecution connections to remain; a "for-cause" challenge is usually automatic in such instances, and Leaman had been astonished when Wagner did not take the opportunity to scratch someone who might clearly be prosecution-leaning. Whatever his reasons, Wagner did not reveal them.

It may have been Bernadette David's race; she was black. The conventional wisdom among defense attorneys at the time was that black jurors were less trusting of police and more receptive to the idea that police might lie and frame an innocent defendant. New Jersey would soon be embroiled in a federal lawsuit against its state police for racial profiling—pulling over black drivers to search for drugs with no probable cause to suspect them, other than their race. Wagner may have thought the benefits of Ms. David's race outweighed the detriment of her having a father in the BCPO. He was wrong about that—Bernadette voted guilty. And she also reported to her father—after the trial was over, so she violated no law—exactly what went on in the jury room during deliberations. It was an eye-opener, a look behind the curtain of Robert Reldan's history of success in jury trials.

Ten of the jurors had voted to convict Reldan of both murders. One juror was undecided. And one juror, a woman, cast an unwavering "not guilty" vote. She had become, in Bernadette's opinion, so enamored of the handsome and smiling defendant in the dock that she refused to consider the inculpatory evidence against him. No amount of persuasion by other jurors could shake her. The undecided juror, also a woman, had become friendly with the "not guilty" holdout during deliberations, and, together, they formed an alliance. Bernadette believed the undecided female juror would have gone along with the majority, if her friend had done so.

But that didn't happen. Reldan's power to charm this particular juror could not be broken. The only option, Bernadette said, was to advise the judge that they were deadlocked.

Leaman's initial anger toward the recalcitrant juror was short lived. In fact, Bernadette's information came as good news. The State's case against Reldan was basically sound—ten jurors were ready to convict him. One dysfunctional juror, refusing to abide by her oath, had scuttled his case and doubled his workload by necessitating a re-trial. Leaman was disappointed in that outcome, but felt more confident than ever in his ultimate victory over Reldan.

For the re-trial, Leaman would be able to use Raymond Lozier's in-court identification of Reldan as the last person to be seen with Susan Reeve alive. He would bring that out on direct examination, and there was no way any judge could block him. It would be a devastating addition to the State's case—devastating to Robert Reldan. The assistant prosecutor had another strategy change in mind; in the second trial, he planned to call two witnesses whom he had not used in the first trial. It would take a special ruling by the judge, but if Leaman was successful, then Reldan was as good as convicted—a dead cold cinch.

Assistant Prosecutor Leaman would do his best to ensure an early date for the re-trial. He requested the first available date in September 1979, in fact, after the summer slack off. Within weeks, he was notified that a mid-September date had been set down by the Assignment Judge. Judge Paul Huot would preside at the new trial. Evidently, Judge James Madden had enough, and asked *not* to be reassigned. Given his difficulty controlling the attorneys the first time around, Madden's opt-out surprised no one. Leaman directed Al Cirello to contact all witnesses and ensure their availability for the new date. He also arranged for witnesses to get transcripts of their testimony in the just-completed trial—a prudent step to avert inconsistent testimony in Reldan II.

The thought of a Reldan III never entered Robert Leaman's mind.

Chapter 19

A 'be careful what you wish for' scenario that could backfire.

Less than a month after the hung jury in Reldan I, Judge Paul Huot held an in-chambers conference with attorneys Wagner and Leaman on July 3, 1979, to discuss how the second trial, now set for mid-September, would unfold. Huot was a former Democratic mayor of Ramsey, a Republican stronghold in northwestern Bergen County. His success in politics demonstrated his ability to get along with people, no matter what their views or ideology. In legal circles, he was known as a highly competent judge who kept his cool. Given the obstreperous behavior of both attorneys in the first trial, Huot may very well have been handpicked by Criminal Assignment Judge Fred Galda to handle the second trial for that very reason—his even-tempered demeanor and calming influence. But his patience would be tested in Reldan II.

Judge Huot would rule, as Judge Madden did, in favor of the prosecution on the issue of Reldan's seven prior convictions. They would be admissible to attack the defendant's credibility, should he take the witness stand. Huot also agreed that Reldan's October 22, 1975, statement to Investigator Ed Denning could be used against him. Leaman didn't say so at the time, but he'd changed strategy on the issue for the second trial. He had decided *not* to use Reldan's taped statement.

In the first trial, Leaman played the tape for the jury while Denning was on the stand, then called witnesses to show that Reldan had lied about his whereabouts at the relevant times on October 6 and 14, 1975—the respective dates of Susan Heynes's and Susan Reeve's disappearances. But proof that Reldan had manufactured his alibis wasn't 100% certain. What if Orbit Inn bartenders were mistaken, and Reldan was in the bar but had slipped their notice? What if the guy who steam-cleaned the Opel's engine was off by an hour in his recollection of the time? The strategy of using the tape, Leaman concluded, was a mistake; it gave Wagner an opportunity to argue that Reldan had already fully cooperated with investigators and supplied detailed information about his activities on those days. If Reldan wanted an alibi, Leaman decided, he'd have to provide it himself, which meant taking the stand and relinquishing the cloak of secrecy about his crime-ridden past.

During the pretrial conference, the assistant prosecutor said that he had a lead on locating Thomas McGinn, the dog trainer who had gone missing for the first trial. When Leaman couldn't find him, McGinn was never called to testify about his dogs tracking the scent of both women in Reldan's Opel wagon and the scent of Susan Reeve in Lillian Booth's Closter house, to which Reldan had access. Judge Madden had precluded Leaman from using McGinn's testimony, primarily because of late notice to the defense of his intentions. There was also a question of McGinn's dog searches being tainted by the improperly obtained warrant to search Reldan's vehicle. Leaman had then dropped the matter because he couldn't find McGinn and, therefore, wouldn't be using him. But, with locating McGinn a possibility in the re-trial, Leaman wanted to open the door to calling him as a witness.

Frank Wagner objected to the damaging evidence coming in for Reldan II. He argued that it should be suppressed, just as the hair evidence had been. Huot reserved on the issue and said that he would hear arguments from both sides when the prosecution located McGinn and decided to use him. Huot gave Leaman until July 20 to find McGinn and inform Wagner of his intentions. The matter became moot when the State never did track down the dog trainer's whereabouts or, if it did, decided not to use him for undisclosed reasons. There was an indication that McGinn had run into trouble of his own—serious enough to affect his credibility—but no proof of that was ever produced. In any event, the scent evidence discovered by smell experts Veed and Drux, decisive as it might have been, would never be used against Robert Reldan in any of his murder trials.

But Leaman dropped another bombshell during the pretrial conference. He advised the court and Wagner that a "Rule 55" hearing might be required, in that he might call two witnesses to testify about Reldan's previous criminal behavior. In a trial, prior criminal conduct is not admissible to show that a defendant has a propensity to commit crime, or that he is an evil person or of bad character and that he should, therefore, be found guilty for that reason alone. However, prior conduct *is* admissible if it is needed to prove some other fact, such as identity, motive, absence of mistake, state of mind, and various other elements often at issue in a criminal trial. In the meeting, Leaman did not disclose which witnesses he intended to call for this purpose, but Wagner had to know he meant Bernice Caplan and Blanche Mate. Both had been incapacitated by Reldan's use of chokeholds. If Leaman could get that evidence into the Reldan II trial through a creative interpretation of Rule 55, not even the most infatuated female juror would fall prey to Robert Reldan's charm.

Judge Huot said he would hold a hearing, outside the presence of the jury, when Leaman decided to call these two special witnesses. The purpose of the hearing would be to determine if the probative value of the testimony was outweighed by its prejudicial effect on the jury, an exceedingly fine line for a judge to walk. Other crimes are *always* prejudicial; the trick is to decide whether the importance of the proofs involved was worth the certain prejudicial effect. Rule 55 decisions are the stuff of conviction reversals. For a prosecutor to introduce such evidence was a dangerous strategy, a "be careful what you wish for" scenario that could backfire.

Leaman intimated that he had yet to decide about calling the Rule 55 witnesses, but that may have been gamesmanship. He had all but committed to bringing them into the case. He intended to shut every possible door to a second Reldan *victory*.

Huot, like all judges, wanted to avoid surprises during the trial. Surprises made for bad decisions, while a bit of forewarning, as a courtesy, allowed a judge to anticipate legal questions and to be prepared. With that purpose, Huot probed Wagner on special defenses he might employ.

"Obviously, I can't require you to tell me," the judge said, "but if you will, just for my own preparation, [what is the] general nature of the defense? Lack of knowledge, lack of intent, alibi, lack of mental responsibility, entrapment, self-defense, insanity, general denial?"

"Innocent," Wagner said.

* * *

After a week of jury selection, Reldan II commenced on September 19, 1979, with opening statements—first by Assistant Prosecutor Leaman, then by defense counsel Wagner. The trial would develop, at least initially, much the way it did in Reldan I. The State would again call 60 witnesses and mark 165 evidence exhibits. And the same bickering and animosity would surface between the two attorneys, though not as pronounced as it had been in the first trial. Perhaps Leaman and Wagner had learned how costly such conduct can be in front of a jury. Judge Huot would still be cast into the role of peacekeeper, but as things unfolded during the month-long second trial, battling lawyers would be the least of his problems.

AP Leaman was mindful of Reldan's role-playing in court—his special knack of appearing to be an innocent victim, himself, unfairly accused. In the first trial, Leaman had ignored the look of the well-dressed businessman or co-counsel or insurance salesman sitting next to Frank Wagner, but he wouldn't make that mistake twice.

"You will see that a much different picture of Robert Reldan emerges," Leaman said in his opening statement, "than this man sitting here now, this man in the courtroom. The picture that you will have at the end of this case is of a cunning, clever, cool, calculating murderer. And it will be your job, you have taken an oath as jurors . . . to evaluate the evidence and decide the case on the evidence . . . not on sympathy, emotion or passion, not on some concept in your own mind of what a murderer looks like."

Leaman also laid the groundwork in his opening to support first-degree convictions for both murders. He knew the rape evidence would get him over that threshold for Reeve, but he needed to prove an added felony in the Heynes case, and kidnapping was the only possibility. Leaman emphasized the circumstances of the two disappearances and the only logical conclusion the jury could draw—that *both* women were kidnapped. He knew his factual basis was weaker for Heynes, but hoped he might be able to piggyback on the strength of the Reeve abduction.

As before, Jonathan Heynes was the State's first witness, and his testimony was in line with what he had said in the first trial. On cross-examination, Frank Wagner focused on the one chink in this witness's otherwise unassailable testimony. Heynes had made a mistake in a written description, which he'd given to police soon after the disappearance, of Susan's engagement ring. And, of course, Wagner knew about that from reading the discovery reports.

"And, did you not also tell [police]," Wagner questioned him, "that there was a white-gold engagement ring, cluster-type, with a large diamond in the center and 15 small diamond chips around it? Didn't you tell them that?"

"From what you've shown me," Heynes admitted, "unfortunately I said there was one [diamond] in the center and not three in the center [as was the case]."

"Unfortunately is right," Wagner charged. "You said it was one, right? That's all I am trying to find out—if you did or did not say it was one [diamond]."

"I don't recollect saying," Heynes said, "but I wrote it down on that paper."

Jonathan Heynes tried to explain that he was under stress when he gave the information about his wife's ring, which accounted for his error. He said the sketch supplied by the ring's manufacturer in England, with its depiction of three center diamonds, was correct. The jury surely understood the emotions that could cause such a mistake, under the circumstances of a missing spouse, but Wagner had accomplished what he'd wanted, planting a seed of doubt—maybe the ring Reldan had unquestionably sold to Macy's wasn't, in fact, Susan Heynes's ring.

On September 24, 1979, Raymond Lozier took the stand, and he was grilled that entire day, to the exclusion of all other witnesses. The jury already knew that the witness was key to the State's case. In his opening, Wagner had given them a preview of the man's poor memory and the State's failed attempt to prop him up with hypnotism. Wagner interrupted

Leaman's direct examination 40 times, but Lozier was a more confident witness in the second trial and performed well. Either he got over his nervousness, or Leaman did a better job of preparing him.

AP Leaman had Lozier describe what he saw while driving south on Anderson Avenue in Demarest the evening Susan Reeve was abducted—namely, the sinister-looking man standing next to the small station wagon, apparently in control of the young woman.

"I was preparing to, tentatively to turn behind the car to come up alongside," Lozier said. "The scene disturbed me." Lozier did not stop to investigate, perhaps deterred by the threatening look Reldan had given him as he drove by at a slow speed.

"Now, Mr. Lozier," Leaman asked, "is the man that you saw on the evening of October 14, 1975, in this courtroom today?"

"Yes, Sir," Lozier answered.

"Would you look around and tell me if you see him?" Leaman asked.

"I do," Lozier testified.

Leaman asked, "Would you point him out please?"

Lozier indicated Reldan and said, "Sitting there at the end of the table."

Leaman, milking the moment for all it was worth, probed further. "What man, Mr. Lozier?"

"With the red tie and yellow shirt looking at me the way he did that same night," Lozier said.

"I'm sorry?" Leaman asked.

"He's looking at me almost the way he looked at me that night across the car," Lozier said.

Apparently, Lozier's identification threw Reldan off his usually calm demeanor, causing him to glare menacingly at the witness—something the jury may not have picked up until Lozier pointed it out. It was an objectionable comment, but Wagner remained silent, even as Leaman asked if Lozier was sure of his identification and Lozier said, "There is no question about it."

Frank Wagner did his best to shake Lozier's testimony, pointing out his uncertainty as to the identity of the man when confronted with a photo array four years earlier, much closer in time to the actual event. The exchange between witness and defense lawyer became heated, causing Leaman to object and Judge Huot to intervene.

"I don't have anything in the record, Mr. Wagner, to indicate that Mr. Lozier is hard of hearing," Huot said. "No one on the jury or the court is, so it is not necessary to yell."

Evidence of Lozier's better preparation for the second trial got to Wagner. He wasn't scoring as many points, and it frustrated him. He challenged Lozier, demanding to know what Leaman had coached him to say. Lozier's response was pure poetry to a prosecutor's ears.

"My instructions were to tell the truth," Lozier said, "and to show you courtesy."

Near the end of Raymond Lozier's testimony, Judge Huot had to intervene again because of inappropriate behavior—not by Frank Wagner, but by Wagner's client. The judge stopped the proceedings and sent the jury out of the courtroom, without explanation. Then, he turned to Wagner and issued a warning.

"Mr. Wagner, I know that you know better, so will you please convey to your client that he is to sit there impassive, and I'm tired of the faces being made and the motions he is going through," Judge Huot said. "If he wants to testify, he'll have that opportunity. But, he can't try to testify by his actions and faces when someone else is testifying."

Wagner said that he wasn't aware his client was doing that, but Huot wasn't impressed.

"Well, I am [aware]," the judge said, "and I'm telling you. Aside from the fact that it is discourteous, it is an attempt to influence this jury with his facial expressions and emotions, and I will not tolerate it any further."

When Raymond Lozier left the stand late that afternoon, the State's case was in a far better posture than it had been at the same point in the first trial. Leaman had gone to great lengths to protect his witness during Wagner's cross-examination, interrupting the defense attorney 70 times. Robert Reldan had to sense that things were not going well. They didn't get any better the next day.

On September 25, Reldan, wearing a grey suit, light-blue shirt, and dark tie, sat impassively and listened, as the parade of damaging witnesses continued. Mark Pittaluga testified about finding the sandblasting mask, which linked Reldan, incontrovertibly, to Anderson Avenue near the time of the Reeve abduction. Robert Conklin and Michael Bettmann testified about their discovery of Susan Reeve's body, just as Mathew Shaindlin had done with respect to Susan Heynes's body. Detectives from Closter, Demarest, and Palisades Interstate police added the information compiled by their departments during the investigation.

The court did not hear testimony on September 26, but was back in full swing the following day, which was devoted in its entirety to Dr. Frederick Zugibe, the Rockland County Chief Medical Examiner. Dr. Zugibe did not disappoint, but was as strong in his testimony as he had been in the first trial. One new piece of information came to light on cross-examination. The ME estimated that Susan Reeve's death had occurred within eight hours of her rape. In other words, she could have been raped and still have been kept alive by Robert Reldan for as long as eight hours before he killed her. If that were so, it supports the theory that Reldan had a "safe house," a place where he took both women to rape and terrorize them before he killed them. He could not have kept her alive so long in the woods where he initially dumped her body, before moving it to Tallman Mountain State Park.

Allison Williams would not be called to testify in Reldan II but Clifford Williams took center stage on September 28. His testimony consumed most of the day. Again, he held up well despite his shocking criminal history. Judge Huot was not one to ignore the rules of evidence in favor of either party, so Williams's alleged involvement in the mysterious deaths of witnesses against him did not come out. Later that day, Roberta Gimbel, who lived in Arizona and went by her married name of Davis, testified about her dates with Reldan near the two sites where the bodies were found. After her testimony, Leaman asked the court to have the jury taken to both sites—Lake DeForest in Valley Cottage and Tallman Mountain State Park—so they could see for themselves the places where the defendant had allegedly put the two bodies. Judge Huot ruled that transporting the jurors on such a trip was not a prudent use of the court's time, especially when the sites may have changed in the intervening four years. He denied the application and adjourned the trial until October 2.

With the way things were going, Reldan's only solace may have been a newly acquired friend. Sherry Ann Stevens had been a spectator every day of the second trial. Court personnel couldn't help but notice the striking blonde, primarily because of the heavy makeup and strong perfume she wore. "It was enough to knock you out," one officer later said. She was a dental hygienist who lived with her mother in a second-floor apartment in Hasbrouck Heights, New Jersey. At times, she affected a British accent and used the more British-sounding Townsend as her surname. Claiming to be a fashion model, she often dressed the part.

Ms. Stevens had become infatuated with Robert Reldan. Part of the way through the trial, Reldan noticed her staring at him in a supportive and sympathetic way. He responded in kind with friendly glances of his own, and then he asked his attorney to request permission for him to speak with the woman during trial recesses, under the supervision of a Sheriff's officer. Judge Huot granted the request, and Reldan and Stevens huddled each chance they got, within sight of the officer but not necessarily within his hearing.

Robert Reldan had his latest female conquest, one he would try to put to good use later.

Chapter 20

Does anyone besides me know how dangerous this fucking guy is?

Near the end of September, 1979, Deputy Attorney General Charles Buckley was prosecuting a state grand jury indictment, across the third floor Rotunda from Judge Huot's courtroom. Though the Division of Criminal Justice had nothing to do with the prosecution of Reldan, Buckley had lived in northern Bergen County at the time of the murders and maintained an interest in the Reldan investigation. On breaks in his case, Buckley occasionally dropped by to observe the progress of Reldan's second murder trial.

On one such visit, Buckley ran into an old friend, Detective Nick Gallo. Buckley knew Gallo from the early 1970s, when they had served together in the Bergen County Prosecutor's Office. When Buckley came in, the detective was standing in the rear of Judge Huot's amphitheater-like courtroom, muttering to himself. The trial was in recess and the two men had a chance to talk, but Buckley could see that his former colleague was close to the boiling point.

"Nick, how are you doing?" Buckley said in greeting. "You here to watch your favorite playmate?" Gallo's successful role in the undercover sting that resulted in Reldan's conviction for conspiracy to murder his aunt was, by then, famous within the law enforcement community, and Buckley didn't miss a chance to tease his friend about it.

But Gallo was in no mood for kidding.

"What the fuck is going on?" Gallo said, pointing toward the well of the courtroom where Robert Reldan was happily engaged in conversation with a well-dressed blonde, seated in the spectator section, no more than three feet from the defendant. A seemingly disinterested Sheriff's officer sat nearby.

"Does anyone in this courthouse besides me know how dangerous this fucking guy is?" Gallo said. "She shouldn't be allowed to get so close to a guy doing as much time as Reldan is."

Gallo told Buckley that he had complained to Prosecutor Roger Breslin about Reldan having permission to converse with the woman during trial recesses. Breslin commiserated with his detective, but said he could take no action. Courthouse security was the Bergen County Sheriff's responsibility, and the prosecutor felt that he couldn't get involved. "I can't tell the Sheriff how to do his job," Breslin had told Gallo.

As Buckley and Gallo walked from the courtroom, the detective continued to vent. "Amazing," he said, shaking his head. "They just don't know who they're dealing with."

Buckley watched as his friend took the stairs to the BCPO spaces a floor below. "Just wait," the detective said in a parting, over-the-shoulder comment. "Something's gonna happen."

* * *

The court sat just half the day on October 2, 1979. The main testimony came from John Truncali, owner of Closter Jewelry and a regular buyer of used goods from Robert Reldan. Reldan had shown him a woman's engagement ring shortly after Susan Heynes's disappearance, and Truncali offered him $50 for it. Reldan rejected that amount as too low and later told Truncali he got $100 for the ring in New York City. Truncali had just a cursory look at the ring, without a loupe, but testified that it had a design similar to the Saunders Jewellery sketch of the Heynes ring. Charles Wolthoff, a contractor Reldan often worked with, would testify that Reldan tried to sell him a similar ring; afterward, Reldan also told Wolthoff that he sold the ring in New York.

The most startling revelation on October 2 took place outside the courtroom. Robert Leaman had the afternoon free and took advantage of the respite to contact upcoming witnesses and review their expected testimony in advance of scheduled court appearances. He phoned Chief James DiLuzio of the Closter Police Department to review Raymond Lozier's observation of Reldan's Opel station wagon when it was impounded in Closter; Lozier had gone to the Closter police station in December 1975 to get fingerprinted for his job and recognized the Opel as the vehicle he saw on Anderson Avenue on October 14. DiLuzio, a detective captain at the time when Lozier came to view the Opel, was to testify about how the vehicle was stored. As far as Leaman knew, DiLuzio's only contribution would be to corroborate Lozier's testimony.

After discussing with Leaman the circumstances of Lozier's identification of the vehicle, DiLuzio dropped a bombshell on the assistant prosecutor. He told Leaman that he had seen Reldan's red Opel station wagon on October 6, 1975, in the driveway of Susan Heynes's residence at 359 Schraalenburgh Road in Haworth.

Leaman was aghast. A senior police officer, in possession of perhaps the most damning evidence possible in a major homicide case, and keeping silent about it for four years? Leaman felt that the matter had to be handled by someone more senior in the BCPO hierarchy. He contacted First Assistant Prosecutor Raymond Flood, and made arrangements for DiLuzio to come in for an interview that afternoon. DiLuzio showed up at 5:02 PM and was ushered into a private interview room, where Investigator Ed Denning awaited. It would be a formal statement, under oath. A verbatim transcript was made by a BCPO stenographer.

Denning began the interrogation, with Flood, second in command of the BCPO, joining soon after its start. As DiLuzio related his story, it had to have been difficult for Denning and Flood, two dedicated law enforcement professionals, to keep their anger in check.

"What prompted you," Denning asked, "to tell Mr. Leaman about an observation you made on October 6, 1975?"

"I had been giving quite a bit of thought very recently and in the past that I may hold the key to the case involving Robert Reldan," DiLuzio said. "I explained to Mr. Leaman that the day Mrs. Heynes was reported missing in Haworth, I had occasion to be on Schraalenburgh Road and observed a car parked in the driveway of the Heynes residence."

Chief DiLuzio explained that when he was a captain in the Closter Police Department, in charge of the detective bureau, he was also operating a contracting business on the side. He had permission to operate that business part time, but he was not supposed to do so while on duty as a police officer. On October 6, 1975, his contracting company was patching Schraalenburgh Road, between Durie Avenue in Closter and Prospect Avenue in Haworth. DiLuzio lived on Durie Avenue and had gone home for lunch that day, a permissible break from duty. After lunch, DiLuzio said, he drove south on Schraalenburgh Road to inspect work his paving crew had done. His drive took him past the Heynes residence, which was the third house in Haworth from the Closter line, on the east side of the roadway.

Denning asked DiLuzio to describe the Heynes house.

"I would classify the house as a colonial-type house," DiLuzio said. "L-shaped, with the garage on the left or the northern end of the house. Two-car garage. Front door faces the driveway."

Denning asked what exactly DiLuzio saw on October 6, 1975, when he drove past 359 Schraalenburgh Road and looked up the driveway toward the house.

"The driveway is approximately in the middle of the property," DiLuzio said. "To the right is a lawn and heavily shrubbed. Looking at the driveway, you would be looking at the front door of the garage, a little jug off to the left or the north side of the driveway. That's a turn-around. On October 6, at approximately between 1:00 and 2:00 PM in the afternoon, I had observed a small compact station wagon parked in the driveway. The front of the car would be facing north and backed up to the dogleg of the house so the passenger side of the wagon would be approximately in front of the step of the house. Passenger side would be adjacent to the front door of the house."

"So then, would this car be almost parallel to Schraalenburgh Road?" Denning asked.

"Yes," DiLuzio confirmed. "It would be parallel to the road."

"What color was that car?" Denning asked.

"It was a reddish color," DiLuzio replied.

"Is there anything else you can recall about the car?" Denning asked.

"It was a compact, red, two-door sedan," DiLuzio stated. "Had roof rack on it, chrome roof racks."

Denning asked the detective how fast he was going when he passed the Heynes house, and DiLuzio said, "15 or 20 miles per hour." He was traveling slowly because he was inspecting the work his crew had done.

"When did you first become aware that Mrs. Heynes was in fact missing?" Denning asked.

"Probably a day or two later," DiLuzio said. "When I saw the missing-person's report at headquarters." DiLuzio was in charge of Closter's detective bureau and should have been acutely aware of a possible abduction from a home less than 200 yards from his town's border.

"At that time, did you realize that you observed this red compact in the Heynes driveway?" Denning asked.

"I put no significance to it at the time," DiLuzio said. "To me, it was just a car that probably belonged in the house."

"Did you realize what I'm getting at?" Denning pressed. "Did you realize that was, in fact, the Heynes house?"

DiLuzio replied, "Not when I first read the report, no."

"When do you recall first being aware that that was the Heynes house?" Denning continued.

"Probably a week or two later," DiLuzio said.

Denning then asked DiLuzio when he first realized that the car he saw in the driveway was Robert Reldan's vehicle, impounded in the Closter police garage on October 31, 1975. DiLuzio said he was involved in the search for Reldan that day (Reldan had fled on foot, after the Leeds burglary in Closter, leaving the Opel behind) and saw the car when he returned to headquarters about 5:00 PM, after Reldan turned himself in.

"When I observed the car," DiLuzio said. "Something in the back of my head said, 'Where did you see that car before?' I didn't . . . still it didn't register."

By the time Reldan's vehicle was impounded, Susan Heynes's body had been discovered and identified. DiLuzio, as the senior detective in Closter, had to have known that fact. He also had to have known, living just blocks from the Heynes residence and traveling Schraalenburgh Road every day of his working life, exactly where Susan Heynes lived and how significant it was for Reldan's Opel wagon to have been in her driveway on the date she went missing.

Denning continued, "Did you make any connection at all at that time between the Heynes murder case and Robert Reldan's Opel station wagon in the municipal garage?"

"No."

"How long was Robert Reldan's car kept in your municipal garage?" Denning asked.

"Approximately October 31," said DiLuzio, "to sometime in March, when it was turned over to his wife in '76."

"During that time," Denning said, "how many times would you estimate that you saw that car?"

"Every day." DiLuzio said. When he grasped where Denning was heading, he added, ". . . subconsciously, something kept saying to me, that played a part someplace in something I was doing. I couldn't pin it down." He said the first time he linked Reldan's car with the Heynes murder case was in late 1977 or early 1978 (two years later!), when his review of another murder case triggered the connection. And, even then, DiLuzio said nothing. Denning drove the point home.

"Now after making that determination in your own mind," Denning said, "why didn't you come forward with the information at that time?"

"I think I have to give you three reasons, Eddie," DiLuzio said. "Number one, I've got a lot of self pride and I've always considered myself an excellent police officer. I think I probably felt why wasn't I smart enough to come up and put these pieces together. They were right there in front of me. Why didn't I key them together? And make the connections. *Secondly, I really had no business being on Schraalenburgh Road that day checking on work that a corporation of mine was doing.* [Emphasis added: Finally, we get to the real reason.] I think the main consideration, am I exactly sure of what I'm saying to you was fact and would it look like to the prosecutor that I was trying to put the blame on somebody three years after the fact that I didn't recall at the time. Giving it very much soul searching, especially after the acquittal of the first trial—"

"You're talking about the first murder trial, the hung jury case?" Denning clarified.

"Right," DiLuzio said. "Then, I think it came to me that I really held the key to the conviction of Mr. Reldan."

In DiLuzio's rambling answer to the crucial question—why didn't he come forward after making the connection between Reldan's car and the Heynes abduction and murder?—we see, perhaps, the worst dereliction of duty a police officer could ever perpetrate. As captain of detectives, DiLuzio was a rising star in the Closter Police Department, with a clear shot at becoming chief one day. He was permitted to operate a side business while captain, provided he did not engage in that business while on duty, and, yet, on October 6, 1975, that is exactly what he did, and he *didn't* do it between 1:00 and 2:00 PM, just as he was leaving home after lunch.

DiLuzio's fudging of this time frame was a deliberate attempt to minimize his violation of the policy regarding his side business, established by the chief and town fathers. By fixing his sighting of Reldan's vehicle to just after his legitimate lunch break, DiLuzio was mitigating his abuse of the privilege he had been granted. He had to have seen Reldan's car in the driveway of the Heynes home between 3:35 and 4:40 PM, when he had no right to be in Haworth inspecting his company's work. It is irrefutable that Mrs. Slater's conversation with Susan Heynes took place at 3:30 PM. Heynes was alive and well at that time. In fact, DiLuzio had to have spotted Reldan's Opel near the very moment when Reldan was occupied in subduing his victim and/or placing her in his vehicle. Reldan would not have spent a minute longer than necessary in that driveway. Is it possible that DiLuzio saw a struggle take place, and still kept silent to protect his job prospects? One has to shudder at the idea that a sworn police officer would be so callous, but who knows?

In 1977, DiLuzio became deputy chief and heir apparent to the top job, but the town council required him to give up his side business. In the interview, DiLuzio boasted to Denning about his "impeccable record" as a police officer. If he had come forward in late 1975 or early 1976, when he should have made the connection between Reldan's vehicle and the Heynes murder, his violation of the stricture against performing side work while on duty would have come to light, to the detriment of his clean record and, perhaps, his chance to become chief.

Keeping quiet about what he saw on October 6, 1975—what he knew to be "the key to the conviction of Mr. Reldan"— DiLuzio got the promotion and became deputy chief in 1977. On April 1, 1978, DiLuzio was rewarded again for his silence. On that date, he made chief. And, still, he kept silent. It wasn't until the 1979 hung jury that DiLuzio's crisis of conscience became a factor. Still, he waited four months before coming forward, finally realizing that his placing personal interest ahead of duty might become a double-murderer's ticket to freedom.

Perhaps Chief James DiLuzio of the Closter Police Department deserved credit for doing the right thing on October 2, 1979, but, by that time, it was too late for his information to be of any benefit to the prosecution of Robert Reldan. Reldan's second trial was well underway, and the prosecution had provided nothing pertaining to DiLuzio's observation to the defense in discovery; it is doubtful that the judge would have allowed the testimony at such a late date. Indeed, using DiLuzio's testimony about seeing Reldan's car in the driveway of the Heynes residence on October 6, 1975 would have played right into the defense's conspiracy theory of the case—that the State was out to get Reldan and would stop at nothing to achieve a conviction. After a hung jury in Reldan I, the State, all of a sudden, calls a surprise witness with an astounding— perhaps preposterous—revelation? Wagner would have had a field day with that scenario.

DiLuzio could have been charged with and prosecuted for official misconduct, a second-degree crime; at the very least, he should have been required to resign his office. Instead, Chief James DiLuzio served out his career and retired with honor, his impeccable record intact. He now lives in Florida, collecting a lifetime pension and benefits.

* * *

As the trial reached its fifth and final week, three separate dramas played out. They would rock the courthouse, the Bergen County Sheriff's Department, the Bergen County Prosecutor's Office (including Detective Nick Gallo, who became so angry he put his fist through a glass door), and everyone else involved in Robert Reldan's second murder trial.

Chapter 21

If you convict this bum, there will be another $900 to follow.

On Tuesday, October 10, 1979, shortly after 10:00 AM, Judge Paul Huot called both attorneys into his chambers, along with the defendant. Defense counsel Frank Wagner and Assistant Prosecutor Robert Leaman had barely settled into their chairs when the judge, his face contracted with concern, said, "We have a problem." He was holding an envelope by its corner, using a handkerchief to avoid touching the paper with his fingers.

"I have here an envelope addressed to [juror] Sharron Suffern . . . postmarked from Hackensack, New Jersey, October 9, 1979," Huot began, his tone somber. "And in the envelope I have a blank sheet of paper, and another sheet of paper in which there is one hundred dollars—ten $10 bills—and on the second sheet of paper, typewritten, it says, 'If you convict this bum there will be another nine hundred dollars to follow. You will only be doing what is right.'"

Judge Huot explained that the juror had shown up for court that morning with the letter. Obviously nervous about it, she asked a court official for permission to speak with the judge—something that couldn't be permitted without further inquiry. She told the official her reason for the unusual request and turned the letter over for the judge to inspect it before she was brought into chambers to see him. After examining the envelope's contents, Huot summoned the two attorneys and Reldan, wanting them to be present for the interview with Mrs. Suffern. A court reporter was also there to record the discussion, word for word.

As soon as she was brought into the judge's chambers, Sharron Suffern, still visibly upset, told how she got the letter. Her husband Larry, a mailman in their hometown of Englewood, was at work sorting that morning's mail when he came upon a letter for her. The way it was addressed seemed unusual, so he called his wife at home and asked permission to open it. When he read the contents to her, Mrs. Suffern told her husband she would stop at the post office and get it from him on her way to the courthouse for the trial. She had the presence of mind to take a larger envelope, in which she deposited the letter and its contents to preserve any fingerprints.

Huot asked Mrs. Suffern who had handled the letter, besides her husband, and she mentioned the names of the court administrator, his clerk, and the assignment judge—all of whom got involved before the letter found its way to Huot, the person it should have come to first. Huot then asked perhaps the most important question: Who else *knew* about the letter, besides herself and her husband? She gave the hoped for answer: no one. Relieved that none of the other jurors in the case had been tainted by the knowledge, Judge Huot ordered Sharron Suffern to remain silent about the letter and its contents and to wait in a separate room, apart from other jurors, until he could discuss how to proceed with the attorneys and defendant.

The court was operating in a vacuum. It was probably a situation of first impression in the Bergen County courthouse, if not the entire state. Huot had never heard of anything like that happening before, and it was certainly not something covered in his legal or judicial training. The integrity of a month-long trial hinged on how he dealt with the issue. He had to determine if any other jurors got the same letter and $100 down payment on a promised $1,000 bribe, but the very act of asking jurors about it would produce the contamination he was trying to avoid.

If there was one thing operating in the court's favor, it was that Larry Suffern was a mailman, who had intercepted the bribery letter and handed it over to his wife before the normal mail-delivery time. If other jurors had similar letters about to be delivered to their homes later in the day, they may not yet know about them, since they all had to be in court by 9:00 o'clock that October 10 morning. Huot cautiously asked Wagner and his client how they thought he should proceed: Did they want him to poll the jurors individually to see if any of them got the letter and were remaining silent about it?

Jury tampering is a rare occurrence, but, when it is discovered, the most likely outcome is a mistrial—something Judge Huot and the prosecutor wanted to avoid, considering the resources already expended on the case. The judge was trying to get Wagner's advice on the procedures he should follow to insure a fair trial, but the defense attorney was reluctant to offer any suggestion, perhaps mindful of the advantage the odd incident presented. A mistake by the judge in handling the problem would give Wagner an issue on appeal, one sufficient to overturn an adverse verdict. Defense attorneys *like* appealable issues.

If the judge were to question other jurors to see who may have received a similar letter, the trial would probably be compromised because of the distraction represented by the attempted tampering. If the judge treated Mrs. Suffern's letter as a singular occurrence, without inquiring into the extent of the tampering, an appeals court would certainly void a guilty verdict and force a retrial. In effect, Huot was damned if he did question each juror—and damned if he didn't.

Judge Huot turned to Wagner. "I feel that, in that area [polling the jurors], I have to be guided by what you and Mr. Reldan want," he said.

"I don't have any ideas," Reldan said, nodding toward Wagner. "It's up to him."

"This is—what happens to this juror now?" Wagner asked.

"Obviously, this juror should be excused, I think," said Judge Huot.

Leaman finally said, "Yes."

"I understand that, Judge," said Wagner. "But, I mean, this jury was selected, you know, with some sort of care or concern over the particular jurors that were selected to sit in on the case, and now we're going to lose a juror through no fault of ours and—" Wagner was already laying the premise for an appeal, no matter what the judge decided to do, but Reldan interrupted.

"Plus, the guy in the hospital," Reldan added. The mother of juror number 13, Lewis Blanda, had called earlier that morning to say her son had been taken to the hospital.

The trial had started with 16 jurors in the box. With Blanda and Suffern eliminated, that still left 14 jurors—12 who would decide the case and two alternates. Wagner and Reldan were angling for the judge to declare an immediate mistrial, but Huot stopped that idea cold.

"I don't know of any decision or statute that justifies a mistrial when you still have 12 left," Huot said. "I don't think I have any authority to do that."

The judge then gave Wagner an opportunity to confer with his client privately. In a short while, Wagner and Reldan came back into chambers.

Wagner nodded at his client. "He said that of all the jurors, she [Mrs. Suffern] has been one that's at least acknowledged his presence or said 'Hello' to him."

"Not 'Hello,'" Reldan said. "But 'Good Morning,' when she comes in, in the morning." Reldan had discovered his *charm* target, apparently. "And all of a sudden," he continued, "now she's going to be off the case."

Judge Huot reiterated that he did not have the authority to declare a mistrial when there were still 12 jurors to decide the case, even if one of the lost jurors had been civil toward Reldan. If he was wrong about that, Huot said, the defense had an issue for appeal. The more important question was whether or not the other jurors should be polled.

"Judge," Leaman spoke up, "I would think that you could inquire of the other jurors without specifically asking them if they received—"

"Who is going to admit if they—"Wagner said. "Oh, my God!"

"If they haven't come forward already—" Reldan said.

"Just think of this," Wagner pointed out. "If you inquire and somebody has received something and hasn't told you or then tells you—"

"Of course, you know, if it were done yesterday as it appears [from the October 9 postmark], the others would probably not have received it yet," the judge reasoned. "She just happened to get it because her husband is in the post office. The others may be receiving it today, and an inquiry at least would put them on notice that, if they get one, if they had any thoughts of not telling us, they then will tell us tomorrow."

Huot continued trying to elicit from the defense their preferred manner of proceeding: Did Wagner and his client want him to make an inquiry of each juror or not? He emphasized that he was not going to give the prosecutor an option on that issue, but would leave it to the defense. Wagner asked how he would go about it.

"The initial inquiry, I think, would be, 'Has anyone contacted you in any way, verbally or in writing, in connection with this case?'" Judge Huot proposed. "If I got a 'no' answer, I would probably drop it then, and if I got a 'yes' answer, then I would be more specific with respect to what we have here. That would be the only way I could see of not opening the door and letting the rest of them know what happened, and still it would infer to them, I suppose, that someone had been contacted and would probably infer that it was either Mr. Blanda or Mrs. Suffern, since both of them are not here."

It was clear from the discussion that Frank Wagner was not going to be helpful. Huot understood it was to the defense's advantage *not* to cooperate, but gave Wagner time, again, to confer privately with Reldan. Before leaving the room, Reldan asked the judge to read back the typewritten note one more time, and Huot accommodated him.

"If you convict this bum there will be another nine hundred dollars to follow," Huot read from the letter. "You will only be doing what is right."

"Thank you," said Reldan.

While Reldan and Wagner were out of the room discussing their strategy, Judge Huot arranged to have the Suffern letter delivered to the Prosecutor's Office for fingerprint analysis. A half-hour elapsed before both attorneys and Reldan returned to the judge's chambers. Wagner gave Judge Huot his client's decision.

"We feel that the other jurors should be interrogated, perhaps tomorrow, though, rather than now," said Wagner. "It's so the letter would have time to be transmitted, since this juror received it only because her husband is a mailman; otherwise, she wouldn't have received it yet. And then we would determine what the next step would be."

It seems clear that Wagner and his client were trying to manipulate the outcome. If the court waited for the other jurors to receive their mail, without disrupting the transmittal of the bribery letter to jurors, then more jurors besides Mrs. Suffern could become tainted and have to be dismissed. With only two alternates left, the inevitable result would be a mistrial—exactly the best result Robert Reldan could hope for, given the way the trial was going so far.

Fortunately, Judge Huot had given the problem more thought. In the process, he came up with a plan to save the day.

"Because of our concern that other jurors may receive a similar-type letter today," explained Judge Huot, "I thought about ordering either Sheriff's or Prosecutor's detectives to accompany each juror home to check the mail when it is delivered to their home. And, that way, if anybody gets one, we avoid the fingerprints of different people and maybe have a better opportunity of finding a print of who may have sent it. We will also know whether anybody else did or did not receive [the letter] without having to rely on their statement."

Assistant Prosecutor Leaman immediately voiced support for Huot's suggestion, even though the judge had previously said he would give the prosecution no input. The risk of a mistrial loomed large in the assistant prosecutor's thinking, causing him to suggest that, even after jurors were escorted home to have their mail checked, the entire jury should be sequestered for the balance of the trial. Sequestration—completely cutting off the jury from the outside world, isolating them from family and friends, newspapers and other media, and any other potential source of unauthorized information—is an extreme imposition on any group of citizens serving on a jury, especially for the duration of a lengthy murder trial. But, here, the trial was in its closing stages, and an order to sequester the jury for the few remaining days was likely the only way to insulate them from learning about the attempt to influence their deliberations.

Judge Huot liked the idea of sequestration and gave Wagner a chance to discuss it privately with Reldan. After a few minutes, they were back and agreed that sequestration was the only viable option. "Well," Wagner said, "I had requested that in the beginning, Judge." Wagner asked if Sharron Suffern, with whom Reldan felt a connection, still had to be excused. Huot said he saw no alternative but to excuse Mrs. Suffern. The judge then released the attorneys and Reldan, to reconvene at 1:30 PM, when they would discuss next steps.

Judge Huot remained busy during the lunch break. When he, the attorneys, and Reldan met again that afternoon, it was in the investigations division of the Sheriff's Department. Again, their discussion took place on the record. Assembled in the room were 20 deputies, and the judge was about to set down procedures to be followed to insure that the jurors were kept separated from their mail and any other potentially compromising scenario.

Huot announced that he had decided to sequester the 14 remaining jurors for the duration of the trial. He then instructed the officers to escort the jurors home, individually, with one officer assigned to each juror. The officers would allow the jurors to pack a bag with things they would need for their stay in the hotel during sequestration. While at each juror's home, the assigned officer would inspect the mail that had arrived that day, preferably without the juror knowing about it. If need be, they could ask a spouse to look at the mail, again without giving a reason.

"What I'm looking for," Huot told the group, "is a plain envelope addressed to the juror, postmarked Hackensack, October 9. There will be no return address and it will be a cheap-type envelope that you can pick up in the five- and ten-cents store. If you find such an envelope, ask the spouse for permission to take it, but I want it brought back unopened."

An officer asked if the envelope would be handwritten or typewritten, and Huot answered. He fielded other questions and clarified his instructions. The letters were to be seized with the permission of a spouse or other occupant of the house but without the juror's knowledge.

Huot then required all Sheriff's officers assigned to take an oath, before departing to get ready. "I ask that you swear that the juror committed to your care will be transported from the courthouse to his home and returned," the judge said. "And that you will not permit him to speak to anyone concerning the case, make any communication to his family other than to explain that he is being sequestered, and that you do not permit him to read any newspaper articles, listen to any radio or television reports concerning this case, and that you not discuss with him anything that I have told you or that is transpiring in this case."

The judge, attorneys, and Reldan reassembled in the closed courtroom, where Huot reaffirmed his decision to excuse Sharron Suffern, juror number 16. Wagner objected, preserving his client's right to appeal on that issue. Huot then called in Mrs. Suffern. He thanked her for her forthrightness and explained why he had to excuse her. After Suffern left the courtroom, the remaining jurors were brought in so that the judge could discuss the sequestration decision and what it entailed, without giving the explicit reason for it. They were then allowed to collect their coats and, later, were dispatched, one at a time, with their assigned officers.

While the jurors were out of the room, Reldan's defense counsel again moved for a mistrial. He did not anticipate that he would get one, but wanted to preserve the record for appeal. He set forth the grounds of the bribery attempt, and added a new angle—the problems jurors were having with one particular member of their group.

Earlier in the case, juror number 14 had been the subject of complaints from the other jurors. They said that she distracted others in the jury room by playing loud music and she wasn't paying attention while witnesses were testifying. At the time of the initial complaint about the juror, Huot gave both attorneys the option of having her excused, but both sides had to agree. Leaman was willing but Wagner demurred. After the bribery letter, Wagner had a change of heart, seeing it as an opportunity to get rid of one more juror—whittling down their numbers and increasing his client's chances for a mistrial. Wagner asked that juror number 14 be excused. If it happened, this excusal would have reduced the number of jurors to 13, since Suffern had been excused and Blanda was still missing and presumed ill. But Leaman interjected, telling Judge Huot that he, too, had changed his mind. He would not consent to the removal of juror 14. Since the attorneys again did not agree on the subject, Huot refused to excuse her. Wagner accused Leaman of "playing games."

"That may be, but who started playing the games?" Judge Huot pointed out. "You, or the prosecution? I don't know, but if that's the way you want to try a case, then you get stuck with the results. You had an opportunity [to remove juror number 14] when the prosecution was willing. You chose not to accept it at that time. Now you have changed your mind and he has changed his mind."

Wagner intimated that it was his client—not him—who had made the decision to keep juror number 14 (a woman—presumably another Reldan charm target).

But Judge Huot wasn't sympathetic. "If the defendant wishes to give orders to his attorney, then he also has to accept the responsibility for his actions," the judge retorted. "He can't blame you for something if he is the one who insisted on it." Huot turned to Reldan and said, "You know, you either have an attorney, and you follow his advice, or you have an attorney who is a puppet to do what you want him to do, [in which case] you have no right to complain about the results."

Late in the day, at 4:55 PM, the jurors were all back in the courtroom, with their packed bags. They were ready to go to a nearby hotel that would be their home for the next few days. Among their number was juror number 13, Lewis Blanda, who apparently had recovered from his illness, as he was back, ready to serve. Since no testimony had been taken in the interim, Huot welcomed him back, happy that jury strength was now back to 15. Mrs. Suffern was the only one removed.

Before excusing the jury for the night, Judge Huot told them again not to speculate as to the reason for their sequestration. He also reminded them of their obligation not to discuss the case until they began deliberations at the conclusion of the trial. He suggested that they speculate, instead, on who would win that night's baseball game—the first game in what would become a memorable World Series between the Pittsburgh

Pirates and the Baltimore Orioles.* (Huot was a Pittsburgh native.) The judge also gave them the next morning off. They would be brought back to court for an afternoon session beginning at 1:30 on October 11. Judge Huot planned on questioning each juror individually that afternoon, on the record in chambers with just the attorneys and defendant present, to make sure none of them had heard about or seen an attempted bribery letter.

After the jury departed, Judge Huot informed the attorneys and the defendant that—without the jurors becoming aware—Sheriff's officers had recovered two more letters, both unopened. One letter was at the home of juror Julius Muscari, the other at the home of juror Peter Carson. Huot said the assigned officers would return to the homes of the remaining jurors the next day to see if any similar letter arrived after a day's delay. If so, it would be seized, like the others, with the permission of a responsible adult at the juror's home. If the officers could not obtain permission, the judge would sign a warrant for the seizure.

* * *

The second tsunami-like force to sweep over Reldan II took shape slowly, even before Mrs. Suffern blew the whistle on the attempted jury tampering. AP Leaman had alerted the court and the defense of his intention to call two special witnesses under the authority of New Jersey Evidence Rule 55—the "other crimes" rule. He supplied the judge and Wagner with his legal brief on October 4, and, with the jury absent, Huot heard testimony from the witnesses—Bernice Caplan and Blanche Mate—on October 9 so he could determine for himself if Reldan's offenses against the two women qualified for admission in the current trial under Rule 55. In attacking both women, Reldan employed chokeholds, first using the crook of his left arm around Caplan's throat to incapacitate her and then applying his hand to that purpose, and using his left hand on Mate's throat. The State had already established, through Dr. Zugibe's testimony regarding the fractured hyoid bones, that both murder victims were strangled manually, as well as with a ligature.

No state allows a defendant's prior crimes to be used at trial to show that the defendant is a bad person and, therefore, probably guilty. However, under Rule 55, the State *can* introduce evidence regarding other crimes in order to prove some other issue in the case, including but not limited to identity, motive, common scheme or plan, *modus operandi*, or

---

*Pittsburgh would become the first team to come back from a 3-1 deficit to win the series in seven games.

absence of mistake. Before Rule 55 evidence can be admitted, though, a trial judge must conduct a hearing to determine the basis for allowing it in and, more importantly, to determine whether its probative value outweighs its almost certain prejudice to the defendant. Once the evidence is allowed, the judge must give a limiting instruction to the jury, insuring that jurors consider the evidence only for the specific purpose it is being admitted, *not* to show a defendant's propensity to commit such crimes. But, when jurors hear other crimes evidence, it is impossible for it *not* to have a prejudicial effect.

In his legal brief, AP Leaman contended that Reldan's assaults on Caplan and Mate were admissible in the murder trial on three grounds: first, to show "intent"; second, to show "design, common scheme or plan"; and, third, to show "identity and *modus operandi*."

Judge Huot denied the State's Rule 55 application on the basis of "intent," stating that the intent to commit murder or rape "is inferable from the commission of the act and need not be further established by the State" unless a defendant were alleging mistake or accident—two defenses not present in the Reldan case. Reldan was denying any involvement at all. Huot also found the State's second reason for using Caplan's rape and Mate's assault to be inappropriate.

"This court cannot see a logical connection between the [Caplan] event in 1967, the [Mate] event in 1971, and the events in 1975 as being any type of plan or design," Huot said. "The earlier acts established that the defendant has assaulted women, but that does not establish that he has a 'design, common scheme or plan' to assault women."

Judge Huot saw too much dissimilarity among the four separate crimes to establish that the *modus operandi*, or MO, was the same for each. That left one final peg on which the State could hang its Rule 55 hat: identity. And, on that, the State prevailed.

"The use of force to the throat of a person is rare in any type of crime," Huot said. "Because of that, it is concluded that such method is unique and tantamount to a signature, so that it qualified under the exception contained in Rule 55 as probative of the issue of identity only. The testimony of Mrs. Caplan and Ms. Mate will be allowed, limited solely to that issue, and the jury will be so advised."

With that ruling, the stage was set for the most dramatic day of testimony in Reldan II.

* * *

On the morning of October 11, Judge Huot informed the attorneys and defendant that Lewis Blanda, juror number 13, may not have been totally honest with the court regarding the bribery letter. Blanda was the juror who had been hospitalized, and, even though he was not present in court on October 10, Huot sent an officer to his home to see if one of the letters had been delivered. When the officer arrived at the home, he found Blanda there, resting on a couch. He'd been treated and released from the hospital for an undisclosed ailment.

The officer asked Blanda's mother about the mail that day, and she said that only a dentist's bill had been received. Blanda was brought back to court and sequestered with the rest of the jurors, but he hadn't had time to pack enough clothing. So, later that night, October 10, an officer went back to the residence to get more clothing for him. At that time, Mrs. Blanda turned over to the officer a bribery letter, which had been opened. The family told the officer that Lewis Blanda had, indeed, read the letter before he was brought back to court that day. They said they were frightened and didn't know what to do—that was why they lied about it to the officer initially.

At 10:30 that night, Judge Huot received a telephone call with the information. He waited until the morning to discuss it with the attorneys and the defendant. The letter that Lewis Blanda had received and read was delivered to the court that morning. It was identical to the other bribery letters.

The two Sheriff's officers assigned to Blanda testified about what they saw and what they were told at his residence—both initially and on the return trip, when they acquired the letter. Lewis Blanda was then brought into court and put under oath. When the judge questioned Blanda, he admitted receiving and reading the letter. He offered no reason for failing to bring the letter to the court's attention, and denied discussing the letter or its contents with any other juror at the sequestration hotel. Blanda said the only people he discussed the letter with were his family. Once the officers discovered the letter, Blanda was sent home from the hotel on the judge's orders. The judge also called Blanda's family members into court and questioned them. All of their stories matched.

Leaman argued that Blanda had to be removed from the jury, based on his having read the bribery letter. Wagner used the occasion to renew his motion for a mistrial, which the court promptly denied. Huot ended up dismissing Lewis Blanda. He had kept silent about the letter, Huot said, and couldn't be trusted to serve impartially.

After the lunch break on October 11, Judge Huot ordered remaining the jurors to be brought to chambers, where, in the presence of the attorneys and Reldan, he questioned each juror, individually, about any "communications" made to them or by them about the trial. That process resulted in the excusal of two more jurors. One was the juror about whom complaints had been received earlier; she was dismissed because she overheard a co-worker talking about the case and said it might influence her deliberations. The second juror had spent time with both Blanda and Mrs. Suffern, and the judge felt that he knew more about the bribery letter than he was admitting.

In total, five bribery letters were recovered but only two jurors—Suffern and Blanda—had actually read the letters. Sheriff's officers seized the other three without the jurors' awareness. The court was ready to resume hearing testimony on October 12, but with the dismissal of four jurors, the panel was down to the minimum of 12 members. If any problems arose with one more juror, the judge would have to declare a mistrial.

* * *

Who could have been behind this harebrained scheme to bribe jurors? Three decades later, the mystery remains, but, even with few facts at hand, one can deduce the likely culprit.

First, consider the whole idea—the absurd premise on which the plot was based. To achieve the avowed goal, 12 jurors had to vote *guilty*, but, whoever sent the letters only sent five of them. Those five jurors, assuming they accepted the bribe, wouldn't have known who else also might have been on the take. The plan would hinge on all of them keeping silent about the bribe, but persuading up to 11 others to support a guilty verdict. If any one of the bribed jurors didn't go along with the scheme, and informed authorities about it, the plot would fail. The chances such a scheme could succeed were absolutely zero, yet whoever concocted it invested $500—not a sum a disinterested party would throw away on a whim.

Would family members of the victims undertake something so utterly impractical and so blatantly illegal? Arthur Reeve was a prominent attorney and former judge, so it is not likely that he would be a party to something like that. Jonathan Heynes had been so nervous while taking a polygraph exam he had to lie on the floor in the midst of it to calm himself. Not the stuff of a criminal. Both families had already been through one mistrial and would not have welcomed a third trial after the ill-conceived bribery attempt was uncovered, as any observer had to know it would be.

On the other hand, what if the scheme was not harebrained, but brilliant? What if the object was *not* to engineer a guilty verdict, but to facilitate a mistrial?

Newspapers don't report juror names and addresses. To protect jurors' privacy and to prevent intimidation, such information is withheld, and the only people with access to it are court personnel and the attorneys involved in jury selection. And one other person: the defendant, who has the names and addresses of jurors so that he can assist his lawyer in choosing the panel that will decide his fate.

Robert Reldan, the only one with a motive to tamper with the jury, was the probable mastermind behind this made-to-order bribery incident. Why did he target just five jurors? Sixteen served on the jury panel, including the four alternates. Dismiss five jurors—whether they accepted the bribe or not—and how many are left? Eleven, which is one juror short of the minimum. The letters were a near-guaranteed way to trigger a mistrial. Reldan was not only brilliant in his conception of this plan, but also economical. All he needed was the disqualification of five jurors, and all he spent was $500 to accomplish it. It was a bargain if the scheme accomplished its goal—getting him out of a trial that was not going well.

It would have succeeded, but for one chance occurrence that Reldan could not have anticipated: Mailman Larry Suffern intercepted his wife's letter and gave it to her ahead of the normal delivery process. Had he not done that, *five* letters would have been waiting for jurors when they got home from court on October 10 or 11. And five jurors would have read those letters, so the only remedy would have been their dismissal from service and the declaration of a mistrial.

Reldan couldn't have sent the letters himself, of course, but he easily could have enlisted a confederate to do that for him. It's not likely that any Reldan family member would take part in such a plan. They had been through hell with Bobby over his 20-year criminal career, and they had never engaged in any illegal activities. But Reldan had the power to gain cooperation from someone else—a compliant woman, perhaps, someone with whom Reldan had been permitted to huddle with in secret conversations during trial recesses, someone with no compunction against breaking the law to help her fantasy lover escape justice, someone like Sherry Ann Stevens—a.k.a. Sherry Townsend—the sometime dental hygienist, wannabe fashion model, and everyday Reldan II spectator, whose infatuation with Robert Reldan knew no bounds.

Chapter 22
He looked like an attorney, or one of our clients.

The jury had not heard testimony in one week. The last witness to appear was BCPO Investigator Ed Denning, who testified on October 5, a Friday, to the fact of his interview with Reldan on October 22, 1975. But Denning did not testify as to Reldan's offered alibis for the two relevant dates. Following his revised strategy for the second trial, Leaman decided not to offer the October 22 interview tape into evidence.

Denning also testified about taking Roberta Gimbel to the Tallman Mountain State Park site, where she had picnicked with Reldan in August 1975. He had measured the distance between that spot and the location where Susan Reeve's body was found. It was less than 100 yards.

The court did not sit that weekend, and the following Monday, October 8, was a religious holiday. Jurors were also excused from attendance on Tuesday, when Judge Huot conducted the Rule 55 hearing, taking testimony from Bernice Caplan and Blanche Mate outside the presence of the jury.

The jury waited in the jury room, their private enclave where they pass brief moments and interminable periods, waiting for the judge and lawyers to settle legal issues out of earshot of the jury.

Before jurors were even brought back in, Reldan's counsel, Frank Wagner, tried to head off the cavalry charge that he saw heading straight for his client. He offered to stipulate for the record, in front of the jurors, exactly what the State hoped to accomplish by the testimony of Bernice Caplan and Blanche Mate. He was even willing to allow Leaman to craft the stipulation language—anything to avoid having the two female victims tell their stories in person.

"Sir, on behalf of the defendant," Wagner said to the court, "I wish to make this request now, that the court accept the stipulation that Robert Reldan was, in fact, on two prior occasions the offender against two women, setting forth whatever details the prosecutor wishes to set forth in regard to the rape and the assault with intent to rob."

Leaman was quick to refuse the offer of any such stipulation, knowing that no words read to the jury could have the same effect as Caplan and Mate, themselves, testifying about their ordeals at the hand of Robert Reldan.

Wagner countered, accusing the State of refusing the defendant's offer of proof solely to prejudice the jury against him. Of course, Wagner was right, if by 'prejudice' he meant presenting proofs in the most graphic detail possible. Judge Huot had already decided that the jury could hear the Rule 55 evidence because the probative value outweighed the prejudicial effect on juror sensibilities. Leaman was not about to give up that advantage. Before allowing Leaman to call his first witness, however, the judge tried to prepare the jury for what they were about to hear.

"Now, you're going to hear testimony with respect to some prior conduct of Mr. Reldan," Huot explained. "Just because he may have done something in the past does not mean that he did something again. You may not consider it on the theory that, well, somebody did something bad so, therefore, they have to be bad all the time. It's strictly prohibited. "I'm letting you hear some testimony to help you, if it does," Judge Huot continued. "You have to evaluate it along with everything else. But, if it helps you in any way in arriving at the identity of the perpetrator of these two events [the murders], then of course it may be used by you."

Back when lawyers wrote evidence rules and the words judges use to explain those rules to lay persons, it probably would have been just as effective if those rules and explanations were crafted in ancient Latin or Greek. No matter how conscientious a judge tries to be, the average lay person cannot comprehend the limited purposes of Rule 55 evidence (and other esoteric legal concepts, with which jurors must grapple).. Once jurors learned how Reldan had attacked the two women—from the victims themselves—there was no way that they could realistically limit their consideration of that evidence to a narrow legal premise. All instructions by the court to that effect would be meaningless.

Bernice Caplan was called to the witness stand first. After covering the preliminaries—where she lived, how long she had lived there, and so forth—Leaman asked about what occurred on April 27, 1967.

Mrs. Caplan described how Robert Reldan came to her door that day, using the ruse of a mistaken delivery address to gain entry. Asked if she saw the man in the courtroom, she pointed to Reldan, sitting at his attorney's side at the defense table. Reinforcing the in-court identification, Leaman asked her to describe what the man was wearing, as if the jury might have taken Frank Wagner for the perpetrator.

"Light brown suit, dark tie, and pale blue shirt," Caplan responded, describing the well-turned-out defendant's attire. The jury would soon be acquainted with a Robert Reldan who was different from the pleasant-looking man they had been observing for the last four weeks of the trial, the one whom some jurors would acknowledge with a polite nod, "Good Morning," or another greeting—as one human being to another.

Caplan was asked to demonstrate, utilizing a BCPO detective as a prop, the chokehold that Reldan had used to subdue her. She stood and placed her left arm around the man's neck, locking it in the crook of her arm. "The center of his elbow was in the middle of my throat," she said.

"What happened next?" Leaman asked.

A hush fell over the courtroom. "He pulled me back to the wall between the den and the bathroom, and he began to molest me sexually," said Bernice Caplan. "And at that time, he kept tightening his grip on my neck. And I said, 'You're choking me.' And he said, 'If you scream, I'm going to kill you. If you scream, I'm going to kill you.' He kept punching me in the back with his right hand."

"Did he say anything else to you?" Leaman asked.

Mrs. Caplan answered, "He said, 'I have a gun in my pocket.' He said, 'I'll kill you if you scream.' "

"Did you have any other conversation with him while he was doing this?" Leaman asked.

"I just said, 'Why are you doing this?'" she said. "And he said, 'I'm crazy, don't you know.' "

"You said he molested you," Leaman confirmed. "I'm afraid you will have to describe for us exactly what happened."

"Do I have to say that again?" asked Mrs. Caplan.

"As best you can," Leaman said. "Mrs. Caplan, please."

"All right," Mrs. Caplan replied. "I'll tell you."

And then, Bernice Caplan, rape victim, was forced to retell the details, just as she had done for the first rape trial in which Reldan got a hung jury, for the second rape trial in which Reldan was convicted, and now, 12 years later, for a murder trial. She did so with emotion, a victim's pain etched on her face for all to see. When she was finished, Leaman thanked her, saying he had no further questions. Wagner knew better than to conduct a cross-examination. What happened next took everyone by surprise.

As she was leaving the witness stand, Bernice Caplan stumbled in a near faint, saved at the last moment from collapsing to the floor by a court officer standing nearby. This occurred directly in front of the jurors. Caplan's husband, a spectator, rushed forward to take his stricken wife from the officer, place her in his arms, and lead her out of the courtroom. As Mr. Caplan passed the defense table, he turned toward Reldan and muttered something, his face contorted in rage. Months later, when Frank Wagner filed his appeal in the case, he would claim that Mr. Caplan said to his client, within earshot of the jury, "If I could get my hands on you, you son-of-a-bitch, I'd kill you."

Judge Huot ordered the jury from the courtroom as soon as he saw what was happening, but the damage had been done. AP Leaman got what he wanted—the live testimony of a prior Robert Reldan victim—but there could not have been a better example of overkill. Had it really been necessary to stage this event in front of the jury, to put this victim through the wringer for a third time in public? Or would a stipulation, with as much detail as Leaman thought necessary, have sufficed? Those questions would be answered in due course, by a higher authority.

The testimony of Blanche Mate, coming on the heels of Bernice Caplan's testimony and dramatic exit from the courtroom, was almost anticlimactic. The jury was brought back into the courtroom barely two minutes after the shocking scene they had just witnessed, only to hear another story of the defendant's brutality. The combined effect was as lethal to Reldan's defense as a Rocky Marciano one-two punch.

Again, Leaman covered the preliminaries and then he asked his witness what happened after she drove into her garage.

"I drove my car into the garage and," said Blanche Mate, "the door of the car opened on the driver's side and a knife was at my throat."

"What happened when you found the knife at your throat?" Leaman asked.

"I was terrified," Mate said.

Leaman asked Blanche Mate to identify her attacker in the courtroom, if she could. As Bernice Caplan had done, Mate pointed to Robert Reldan and described what he was wearing. Leaman asked what happened next, after she found the knife at her throat.

"I asked him what he wanted," she said. "He said my money. I told him to take everything. My purse was on my arm, right next to him. There was a pause and he didn't take anything. The only thing he did was put out the headlights of my car, and then I felt I knew what he wanted."

Wagner objected immediately to Blanche Mate's speculation about what Reldan wanted (if such a visceral reaction could be termed speculation). The judge sustained the objection and directed the jury to disregard what Mate had said in that regard. But the jurors would forget Blanche Mate's fear that she was about to be raped by Robert Reldan as quickly as they could forget Notre Dame's cathedral bells, if Quasimodo had just rung them directly overhead.

Ms. Mate also demonstrated how Reldan had grasped her throat in a chokehold, attempting to gain control over her and keep her quiet. She described her struggle with Reldan and how she managed to escape through the passenger-side door.

"What did you do after getting out of the car?" asked the prosecutor.

"I got outside," she said. "I stood in the middle of the driveway and started screaming."

"And did you see what Mr. Reldan did?" asked Leaman.

"Yes."

"What did he do?" he asked.

"I'll never forget," said the witness.

Mate proceeded to describe how Reldan had calmly walked up the driveway and, when he got to the end, turned around and stared at her, before moving off to the main thoroughfare. She ran to a neighbor's door and asked them to summon the police. Later, officers brought Reldan back to her apartment, in custody, and she identified him as her attacker.

Wagner did not cross-examine. As any good trial lawyer knows, you do not ask a damaging witness to repeat her story and inflict the damage a second time, unless it is absolutely necessary to correct something important—something *really* important.

Before Blanche Mate was out the door of the courtroom, Robert Leaman was on his feet. "Your Honor, the State of New Jersey rests its case against Robert Reldan," he said.

Wagner rested for the defense, too, not calling a single witness in Reldan II—the same strategy he had followed in the first trial. But, here, Wagner's sense of his client's probable fate had to have been far different from his feelings at the close of Reldan I. He was too savvy to place false hope on another hung jury. The testimony of Bernice Caplan and Blanche Mate had settled that. As the trial ended, it was clear that Reldan's only chance lay in the appellate process, and Wagner knew that he had plenty of ammunition in that regard.

Reldan appeared downcast. He had sat through two full trials and listened to more than 60 witnesses testify against him, twice, each supplying links in the powerful case that the State had managed to present, especially in the second trial. He had to know that his luck was about to run out.

After both sides rested, Judge Huot advised the jury that the evidence phase was over, but that their sequestration would have to continue; it was too late, he said, to have the attorneys present their summations. With the weekend upon them, Huot had decided to delay the attorneys' summations until Monday, October 15, after which he would charge the jury and direct them to begin deliberations. He excused jurors for the weekend, sending them back to their hotel and directing them not to read anything about the case or discuss it amongst themselves. Before they left the courtroom, Judge Huot gave one final instruction.

"Again, I remind you, please do not speculate about anything," Huot said, "or any of the delays, or what may have occasioned them or the fact that some of you are still here and some of you are not. But enjoy your weekend, and you can look forward to being home shortly."

Judge Huot couldn't have known it at the time, but the delays in Reldan II were far from over. In fact, the most startling event in the trial was still to come . . . and would propel the Robert Reldan murder case, once more, to the brink of disaster.

* * *

The Bergen County Sheriff's Office (BCSO) had two primary functions in the criminal justice system. It operated the county jail, which housed prisoners serving short sentences for minor offenses until they had done their time; it also temporarily housed more dangerous inmates who were doing time in state prison, but who were required to appear for trial or other proceedings in the county courthouse. The BCSO was also responsible for courthouse security, which included moving prisoners from the main jail to the adjacent courthouse and back again when court ended for the day.

During the 1970s, the BCSO was having difficulty fulfilling those two missions. Two of its officers had been shot—one fatally—by prisoners who were attempting to escape. The department had been the subject of a grand jury investigation in 1975 and 1976, after allegations of criminal activity and mismanagement at the jail. New Jersey grand juries are empowered to consider not only criminal conduct on the part of individuals, but also malfeasance on the part of government institutions and agencies. When they find such deficiencies, they hand up a "presentment," a public declaration by an independent, quasi-judicial body that a governmental agency is not properly performing its duties. It does not have the force of law, but does carry weight.

In its January 1976 presentment against the BCSO, the grand jury recommended that all officers assigned to the jail be required to complete the state's Corrections Officer Training Program, as well as in-service training. It urged that written guidelines be developed so that all officers would know their specific duties and responsibilities. Lastly, the grand jury detailed a need for frequent surprise searches of the entire jail—including physical pat-downs of all jail inmates whenever their location within the prison system changed—for weapons and other contraband.

Despite the warnings, the BCSO had done little to remedy the shortcomings that everyone acknowledged were still rampant in 1979. In the three and a half years between the presentment and Reldan's second murder trial, two more county jail prisoners had actually escaped. Few, if any, of the grand jury recommendations had been implemented. The

BCSO was understaffed, and political interference impeded Sheriff Joseph Job's ability to hire permanent officers who were properly trained. He resorted to temporary, inexperienced personnel under the auspices of the federally funded "Comprehensive Employment Act," or CETA. The new hires did not have formal training as corrections officers, except for on-the-job training they received from superior officers. It was a hit-or-miss proposition that depended on the inclination of those in command.

Shortly before 8:00 AM on October 15, 1979, Officer Daniel Artymiak, a CETA hire with less than eight months on the job, reported for duty at the jail's second-floor lock-up. The more experienced officer assigned to that duty station had called in sick, so Artymiak became primarily responsible for the 39 inmates housed in the main jail on that date. His most immediate task was to ensure that prisoners scheduled for court appearances that morning were ready. As the officer reached Robert Reldan's cell, Reldan said he wanted to take a shower prior to going to court. Artymiak unlocked the cell and, pressed with getting so many prisoners ready, allowed Reldan to go to the shower room unescorted. About 15 minutes later, Reldan returned with just a towel wrapped around him and requested permission to get dressed for court.

For the sake of convenience, since he was going to court almost daily, Reldan's trial clothes were kept in the second floor security cage, which also contained the riot gear that officers might need for a jail disturbance—nightsticks and tear gas canisters, in particular. Prisoners were not allowed access to the security cage, but Artymiak, under pressure that morning, allowed Reldan to enter the cage unaccompanied, to retrieve his trial clothes. Then, without frisking Reldan or patting down his clothing, Artymiak took him back to his cell so Reldan could get dressed for court.

Just before 9:00 AM, Judge Huot's clerk sent word that the judge wanted Reldan brought to the holding room, as the trial would be getting underway. Again, without patting down the prisoner, Artymiak took him to another part of the jail, where Officer Joseph Vuocolo, another CETA hire, awaited. Vuocolo handcuffed Reldan, but also neglected to do a pat down. Questioned later about his procedures that day, Vuocolo said, according to an investigative report, that he "didn't frisk any prisoners, didn't know he was supposed to, and that he had never been told to search or frisk prisoners in his custody."

Officer Vuocolo escorted the handcuffed Reldan on an elevator ride to the courthouse's second floor, where he turned him over to two longtime Sheriff's officers, Lieutenant Floyd Dempsey and Officer Hendrik VanDerWerf. Neither of those officers bothered to frisk Reldan, either. They took him down a long corridor to the older part of the courthouse, known as the Rotunda, and then they went up an elevator to the third floor, and then to a holding room, just off Judge Huot's courtroom. The holding room had two windows facing out onto Court Street, on the north side of the courthouse. The windows normally had bars on the outside, but the bars had been removed a few days earlier, to facilitate cleaning the building's exterior. After uncuffing Reldan, Lieutenant Dempsey left the room to take care of a problem with one of the jurors, leaving VanDerWerf alone with the prisoner. VanDerWerf had previously locked up his weapon in the adjoining clerk's office, so he was not armed—fortunately, as things turned out.

To wash up and comb his hair, Reldan was allowed to use the bathroom in the rear of the holding room, with the door left open so VanDerWerf could keep an eye on him. Upon leaving the bathroom, Reldan strolled to one of the windows and stood there, gazing out at passing cars. Directly observing his prisoner, VanDerWerf had his back to the closed door of the holding room. Suddenly, Reldan spun around and sprayed a chemical substance into the officer's eyes, temporarily blinding him. VanDerWerf slumped to the floor, his back to the door. He immediately began banging on the floor and door, shouting for help.

Within seconds, Sheriff's Officer Patrick Kiernan—who was Judge Huot's court aide—and Lieutenant Dempsey responded to VanDerWerf's calls. They had to force the holding room door to get their fellow officer's body out of the way so that they could gain entry. Once inside, they found VanDerWerf on the floor, writhing in pain, and the window was cranked partially open. They checked the bathroom. Reldan was gone. The time was approximately 9:10 AM.

Reldan had managed to squeeze through the window's narrow opening. In a spectacular jump from the third floor of the courthouse, he avoided an iron railing six feet out from the building and landed in a clump of bushes some 35 feet below, sustaining minor cuts and bruises and spraining his back. He limped along Court Street for half a block before he crossed an intersection and then spotted a late-model, blue Cadillac being parked in the rear of a law office on Essex Street. Attorney Carmine Grimaldi, the driver, was just arriving for work.

Hurrying as fast as he could toward Grimaldi, Reldan yelled to the attorney that he had just been involved in an auto accident and needed help. Reldan's habit of using a pretense to get within striking distance of his victims seemed instinctive. As Grimaldi turned in response to the calls, Reldan raised his right hand and sprayed tear gas in the man's eyes, causing him to fall to the ground in pain with his legs splayed under his own car. People came running out of the building in response to the 59-year-old attorney's cries for help, including Grimaldi's nephew, William Grimaldi, also an attorney working in the same building. William later told a *Record* reporter that Reldan, dressed for court in a blue business suit, "looked like an attorney or one of [our] clients." As Reldan reached down, grabbed the stricken man's car keys, jumped into the Cadillac, and started it, the younger Grimaldi thought that Reldan was rendering assistance to his uncle. Only after Reldan snarled at them to pull the fallen attorney from under the car did William Grimaldi realize that he was the attacker, not a Good Samaritan. As soon as the nephew pulled Carmine Grimaldi free of the car, Reldan gunned the engine and raced out of the parking lot, heading west on Essex Street, a main thoroughfare that was normally crowded with cars and pedestrians at that hour.

Barreling through red lights, weaving in and out of traffic, and often driving on the wrong side of the road, Reldan managed to reach State Route 17, about a mile and a half from the courthouse, without crashing or injuring any bystanders. He sped north on 17 toward New York State.

Not hearing sirens or seeing other signs of pursuit, Reldan forced himself to slow a little and at least give the appearance of a driver going with the flow of traffic—not an escapee on the lam. He realized that he might need money, so he pulled into The Fashion Center, a Paramus shopping mall fronting on Route 17, to see what opportunity might present itself.

At 9:30 AM, Patricia Grabinski, a bank employee, was walking to work on the left sidewalk of the mall's service roadway. She was carrying a pocketbook and an umbrella on her forearm, closest to the road. She heard the car approach from behind and turned to see a blue car rushing toward her, driving on the wrong side of the road. In a flash, an arm stuck out of the car and swiped the pocketbook and umbrella from her grasp, as the car sped toward Route 17 northbound.

Reldan had what he hoped would be cash for gas and food. The problem was that his robbery alerted authorities to his route. Paramus police had just received a bulletin about the escape. Seeing the likely connection between the Grabinski robbery and the courthouse escape, they advised the Sheriff's department about the incident at the shopping center. The BCSO transmitted an alarm to all area police agencies at 9:45 AM, alerting them to Reldan's probable escape route: Route 17 northbound through Waldwick, Ramsey, Mahwah, and, eventually, into Rockland County in New York State.

On orders from their headquarters, Patrolmen Patrick Reynar and Vincent D'Andrea of the Sloatsburg, New York, police department positioned their patrol cars at the intersection of Route 17 and Sterling Mine Road, about 16 miles north of The Fashion Center. Within five minutes, the officers saw a Cadillac approaching from the south. The car matched the description they'd been given. As the car neared, it accelerated onto Sterling Mine Road, and then it headed back toward Ringwood, New Jersey. A high-speed chase ensued. Police from the towns of Tuxedo and Ramapo joined the Sloatsburg officers in the pursuit. But, near an intersection with Route 84 in Tuxedo, Reldan lost control of the Cadillac and the car spun into a ditch on the right side of the road. Police pulled up behind the vehicle and shouted to the driver to get out with his hands up.

Reldan did not comply with the order. Instead, he revved the car's engine, trying to extricate the vehicle from the ditch. A Ramapo officer drove around the Cadillac, blocking it from forward movement. Finally, Reldan obeyed orders and turned off the engine.

Weapons drawn, police approached the fugitive, who was holding the tear gas canister in his hand. They yanked him from the car. The serial number on the canister would correspond to those from the batch stored in the second floor security cage of the Bergen County jail. The time was 10:15.

Robert Reldan had known freedom for one hour.

* * *

Summoned to Judge Huot's chambers along with Wagner soon after the escape, AP Leaman was prepared for the crisis. Quoting legal precedent that dealt with cases in which a defendant had voluntarily absented himself during trial, Leaman argued that the trial should continue without the defendant. He also noted that case law gave the prosecution the right to a powerful jury instruction—namely, that the defendant's flight was due to "consciousness of guilt." Ready to proceed, Leaman asked for permission to reopen the State's case so that he could present testimony relative to the escape.

Judge Huot, taking a more cautious approach, wanted to find out more before reaching a decision, but, without the jury present, he allowed Leaman to present evidence on the escape.

The Sheriff's officers who were responsible for guarding Reldan were called in to explain, under oath, what had happened. Lieutenant Floyd Dempsey, employed by the BCSO for 28 years, was in charge of the Reldan detail, which had assumed control over the prisoner when he was transferred from Trenton State Prison to the county jail for trial. Dempsey explained how he and Officer Hendrik VanDerWerf, a 12-year BCSO veteran, picked up Reldan at the jail elevator and took him to a holding room, next to Huot's courtroom.

It was normal procedure to guard an incarcerated defendant in a side room until the judge and lawyers were present in court. Already dressed for trial, the defendant would have his shackles removed, preparatory to being escorted into the courtroom. The defendant would be seated next to his attorney, with no outward sign that he was a prisoner by the time when the jury was brought in. The only clue was that Sheriff's officers hovered nearby.

Initially, Officer VanDerWerf had his gun with him in the holding room, until Dempsey directed him to take it to the clerk's office, next door, and lock it up. Dempsey said that he was called away to attend to a problem with one of the jurors, leaving VanDerWerf alone with Reldan, when Reldan overpowered VanDerWerf with the tear gas. VanDerWerf testified that the first thing he noticed when Reldan turned was his eyes, which were "beady," the officer said, to the point of being strangely inhuman.

Judge Huot and the lawyers absorbed the information that the Sheriff's officers presented. The judge was determined to complete the long, stressful trial without allowing Reldan's escape to get in the way. He took under advisement whether to permit Leaman to reopen the State's case and argue that the escape, which the sequestered jury presumably knew nothing about, was a sign of guilt. Huot was reluctant to complicate further an already complicated case.

* * *

When captured, Reldan complained of leg pain so he was taken to Tuxedo Memorial Hospital for an examination, including x-rays. Doctors could find nothing seriously wrong with him, from the courthouse leap or the car crash, so they treated his cuts and bruises. Reldan requested a wheelchair, which he received. Then, Reldan was brought before a New York magistrate, where he formally waived his right to an extradition hearing and voluntarily agreed to be returned to New Jersey. Frank Wagner had phoned him and advised that the trial would proceed, with or without him. By late afternoon on October 15, Reldan was back in his cell at the Bergen County jail.

Chapter 23

I couldn't stand by and watch them lie me into prison.

Judge Huot entered the courtroom on October 16, prepared to begin the final phase of Reldan II—summations by both attorneys. Huot had considered the assistant prosecutor's motion to reopen the State's case for evidence pertaining to the escape. He was ready to rule against it.

"Because the case is concluded and because prior crimes evidence was allowed," Huot said from the bench, "the court finds that the inference of consciousness of guilt is not as strong an inference as it would be had there been flight from the scene of the crime or flight after apprehension or even flight during the early stages of the trial. The State's application to reopen is denied, and the court will not charge [the jury] with respect to flight."

That accomplished, Judge Huot turned to Reldan, seated before him in a wheelchair. Still steaming after the defendant's escape, Huot delivered an ultimatum.

"Now, obviously," Judge Huot began, "I had not originally anticipated Mr. Reldan's presence here [accomplished only because he was captured and waived extradition], and I would have advised the jury that his absence was voluntary. I find today, however, he has arrived in court in a wheelchair. The jury may not be permitted to speculate on the cause of his injury. I am not going to permit any attempt at seeking of sympathy . . . Therefore . . . the jury is going to be advised as to the necessity for that wheelchair."

Wagner sounded duly concerned. "Sir, I don't understand . . . going to be advised as to what?"

"Why he is in a wheelchair," the judge stated.

"What does that mean?" Wagner asked, "'Why he is in a wheelchair . . .'"

"That he was injured through his own actions and not because some authority may have hurt him or because he may be using it to secure sympathy," Judge Huot explained. "I have been advised by the doctors in Rockland County and in Bergen County that there is nothing wrong with him, that he doesn't need a wheelchair. If he wants it, he may have it, but he is not going to use it to try to gain sympathy. Bring the jury down."

"Excuse me," Wagner said. "Mr. Reldan says he needs this for transportation, not for sitting."

"Whatever reason he may think he needs it," Judge Huot said, "the jury will be advised that he is in it because of his own voluntary actions and not because of some other reason."

Wagner conferred with Reldan, and then advised the court that his client was "perfectly willing to sit in a regular chair because he is not going to be walking around the courtroom." Huot relented. He conditionally agreed not to say anything to the jury about Reldan's incapacity, real or imagined. However, mindful of Reldan's earlier use of facial expressions and body language during trial to testify without taking the stand, the judge admonished both defense lawyer and defendant.

"Let me advise you, Mr. Wagner, and you can warn your client, any overt action by him to indicate pain or discomfort while we proceed with the summations and charge will lead to an instruction to the jury as to how he acquired his injuries," the judge said. "If he gives any indication, they will be told. If he sits there and behaves himself as if nothing occurred, then nothing else will be said about it. So, the key is in his hands. How he uses it is up to him."

Wagner acknowledged the warning, Reldan changed seats, and the wheelchair was removed from the courtroom. Judge Huot welcomed the jury back and instructed them, once again, not to speculate as to the cause for the many delays in the case. Sequestered throughout, the jury presumably had no knowledge of Reldan's escape and capture, though the story was plastered across the front pages of that morning's newspapers, complete with a diagram of his leap from the county courthouse window, maps of his escape route—by foot and stolen car—and photos of a hospital-gowned Reldan being transported by police after his capture.

Wagner gave a strong summation in a cause that he had to know was lost. He covered potential weak spots in the State's case in detail, his command of one month's testimony impressive. During the defense attorney's summation, tempers flared again between Wagner and Leaman, as Wagner occasionally veered over the line of what was proper and what was not. Lawyers are given leeway during summation, which is, after all, final *argument*, a last chance to influence the jury. Leaman objected repeatedly and the court mostly overruled his objections. At one point, Judge Huot commanded the assistant prosecutor to "sit down."

Because Wagner's summation lasted more than an hour, the judge decided to break the jury for lunch before proceeding with Leaman's final argument. It was a welcome respite, however brief, for 12 jurors, who had to have been mentally, emotionally, and physically exhausted after the mystifying events of the preceding week.

Leaman began his summation with a personal attack on Frank Wagner.

In that great legal drama *Witness for the Prosecution*—a smash on London and Broadway stages before becoming a 1957 movie starring Charles Laughton, Marlene Dietrich, and Tyrone Power—a murder trial was contested no less vigorously than the two Reldan murder trials. But, in that British courtroom, barristers politely saluted their opponents whenever points were scored, or engaged in delightful banter that challenged each others' minds, not their patience. In the American system, at least as manifested in Reldan I and II, points scored were acknowledged with figurative bludgeons, not rapier wit or gentlemanly salutes.

"I say to you quite candidly," Leaman told the jury, "that what occurred this morning was a travesty. He [Wagner] took each piece of evidence and twisted it and distorted it based upon his recollection and tried to convince you that it points to something other than what it obviously does, the logical and reasonable inferences that flow from the evidence. Intentionally or not, he tried to deceive you, mislead you, and I know you will not fall into that trap."

Wagner was on his feet objecting, and Judge Huot sustained the objection. Attacking a lawyer's arguments is permissible; attacking a lawyer personally, by attributing a motive to deceive, is not.

During his lengthy summation, AP Leaman made one costly error. Trying to establish a basis for the jury to find that Susan Heynes was kidnapped from her home—a necessary element to raise her murder to a crime of the first degree—Leaman threw in an inapt, offhanded comment that scuttled the kidnapping premise. It was his bad luck that Judge Huot caught it. The judge would comment on it later, treating it as a significant admission by the State.

"She [Susan Heynes] did not leave that house willingly on the evening or afternoon of October the 6, 1975," Leaman said, "and *that* you can infer from the evidence. She left against her will, I submit to you, by force, apparently surprised either in the driveway of her home or in the garage area of her home somewhere near the car. She either left that house against her will on that day *or she died in that very garage*. [Emphasis added.] She may have died in the course of a robbery, or she may have died during the course of a sexual assault. We just don't know and never will. But we do know that was the last time Mrs. Heynes was seen alive."

The State had produced no evidence related to the robbery of Susan Heynes while she was alive. None of the jewelry she kept in her home was missing. Her engagement ring was taken, but it may very well have been removed after her death, which would not have been sufficient to satisfy the felony requirement for first-degree murder. Because the victim's body was ravaged by animals, no scientific evidence of sexual assault existed. The only possible additional felony in the Heynes case was kidnapping, provable by inference, and Leaman gave that away by suggesting—in his summation—that she could have been killed on the spot, in her garage. Haworth Patrolman Pizza had observed no evidence of a struggle in that cramped space. But for Leaman's statement that the murder *could have* occurred there, the clear inference had been that she was abducted from her property and murdered elsewhere.

Aside from that one slip, however damaging, Leaman's summation pulled together the State's case. Addressing every piece of circumstantial evidence, the assistant prosecutor likened the various elements of his case to strands in a rope, each successive fiber adding to the overall strength of the whole, but no single fiber able to break it. He argued, powerfully, that if the jury found one or two weaknesses in the State's case—for instance, Raymond Lozier's spotty memory or Clifford Williams's sordid criminal career—the strength of the whole was still sufficient to carry the jury beyond any reasonable doubt.

Leaman finished his summation as he finished the testimony phase of the trial—with reference to the same two defense-crushing witnesses, Bernice Caplan and Blanche Mate. It is unlikely the jurors needed any reminder of the impact the two women had made just four days earlier.

Given the length of the two summations, Judge Huot decided to wait until October 17 to charge the jury. On that next morning, the judge's charge lasted two hours. He pointedly did not charge kidnapping as a felony addition to the Heynes murder. Directly after his charge, the judge momentarily excused the jury to give the attorneys a chance to take exception to anything he had said. Leaman was quick to request an amendment to the charge to allow the jury's consideration of kidnapping for the requisite felony element to the Heynes murder, but Huot refused, citing Leaman's speculation that Susan Heynes may have been killed in her garage.

With the jury down to just 12 members, there was no need to select alternates by lot. All remaining jurors began deliberations at 11:25 AM. Almost immediately, the first jury question came back—a request to have Clifford Williams's testimony read back to them. During the afternoon, the jury asked to hear again testimony of two other witnesses (bus driver O'Hanlon and a bus passenger), and the court complied. Each time, the court reporter read the testimony verbatim from his notes, with the jury in the box and the judge, lawyers, and defendant present.

Shortly after 6:00 PM, Judge Huot was informed that the jury had reached a verdict. The jury had been out less than seven hours, including a lunch break. AP Leaman had to be ecstatic when he got the news, which could only mean one thing—a conviction. No jury could have found Reldan *not guilty* so quickly, not after the evidence the State had amassed against him. The players were summoned to the courtroom and, at 6:37 PM on October 17, 1979—four years after the disappearances of Susan Heynes and Susan Reeve—jury foreman James Hodges read the verdict. On Count One of the indictment, murder of Susan Heynes, "Guilty," but only in the second degree. The jury failed to find evidence of an accompanying felony. On Count Two of the indictment, murder of Susan Reeve, "Guilty of first-degree murder." Jurors had accepted Dr. Zugibe's testimony that the victim had been raped before she was killed. They also may have found that she was kidnapped, the evidence clearly pointing to that felony, too.

Judge Huot thanked the jury for their service. Intending to apprise the jurors of the reasons for all the interruptions to the trial, the judge temporarily excused them. With the jury out, Huot sentenced Reldan to a mandatory life sentence on the first-degree conviction and, for the second-degree conviction, ordered a presentencing report.

Reldan was taken away to begin serving his life sentence, which was to run consecutively to all other sentences that he was then serving, including the one for attempted murder of his aunt, Lillian Booth, and her male companion, Misha Dabich.

Before dismissing the jury, Judge Huot called them back into the courtroom. To satisfy their curiosity about the summary removal of four of their members, he produced an unopened letter that had been delivered to one of the jurors still serving. The judge got the juror's permission to open it, and then he did so. Showing the contents—ten $10 bills—Judge Huot then read the bribery note. He also disclosed what jurors would soon learn from relatives and friends after returning home—that Reldan had tried to escape on Monday and had been captured and returned to Bergen County that same day. The 12 men and women left the courthouse that evening with the sense that they had fulfilled an important civic duty, that they had put away a dangerous killer for the rest of his life.

* * *

Two days after his conviction and life sentence, Robert Reldan wrote a letter from Trenton State Prison to Sheriff's Officer Hendrik VanDerWerf.

"I am writing to tell you that I hope you are as well as can be expected under the circumstances," Reldan said in his letter. "I am not so much sorry for what happened, because I couldn't stand by and watch them lie me into prison, but I am very sorry it had to happen to you. I would have wished it could have been another officer on duty, perhaps one that was not as nice to me as you were, and as I said, I'm sorry I had to take advantage and I really hope you're O.K., but I could not pick the time to go. I hope you can understand and know it was nothing personal and I hope you do not get into any trouble because it was no fault of yours, and I will say so if you need me to. Same for Lt. Dempsey. Guess that is all. Sincerely, Robert R. Reldan."

* * *

After the presentence report was compiled, all parties reassembled in Judge Huot's courtroom in January, 1980, for two purposes. Frank Wagner had filed a motion for the court to set aside the jury verdict as being against the weight of evidence. That motion is routinely filed after every criminal trial that results in a conviction, and is denied 99.99% of the time. Huot denied Wagner's motion, without even allowing the prosecutor to comment. There was no question in his mind that Reldan's guilt was fairly proven.

All that remained was for Judge Huot to impose sentence for the second-degree murder of Susan Heynes. Wagner made an emotional plea for leniency, actually breaking down in tears at one point. "Bob Reldan, whatever he is, presents an enigma to society," Wagner said. "The people that dealt with him—particularly his father, mother, and sister—they don't know the Robert Reldan in this [presentence] report," Wagner said, pointing to the report on the table before him. Reldan, as if to console his attorney, reached out and touched his arm.

Leaman made a counter-plea for the maximum sentence allowable by law for second-degree murder: 30 years in prison. The court needed no prodding from the State to do its duty, under the circumstances.

"These are always difficult decisions, recognizing the background of a young man who initially had everything going for him," Huot said. "Good student, good athlete, wealthy family—all the grand things that could have been accomplished for society had he been channeled and directed the proper way. Unfortunately, because of that background and intelligence, that polish that was achieved, when channeled and directed toward evil, was able to accomplish greater evil."

Required by law to state fully the basis for his sentence, Judge Huot was clear and concise. While Reldan's family and lawyer may have thought him worthy of sympathy, the only sympathy warranted was for the victims and their families. Huot also dismissed the notion that he had to be severe in his sentencing to deter others from committing similar crimes. "People who commit the type of crime with which we are presently faced rarely consider punishment," Huot said, "rarely if ever consider that they would be caught." The judge faced just one consideration—"the protection of society."

"The crimes were particularly brutal, but the callousness with which the bodies were disposed of made them even more heinous," Judge Huot said. "There is little likelihood that anyone, whether it be in Bergen County, New Jersey, or in the United States, would be safe if Mr. Reldan were on the streets. And, I fulfill my duty for the rest of the citizens to see to it that their safety is protected, that must be my first concern."

Judge Huot sentenced Robert Reldan to a term of 30 years for murdering Susan Heynes, consecutive to the life sentence he had already imposed for the first-degree murder of Susan Reeve and consecutive to every other sentence Reldan still had to serve.

"It is unfortunate to admit that we are in a society incapable of solving someone's problems or protecting ourselves except by incarcerating that person for the rest of his life," Huot said in closing. "But there are no other solutions. I arrive at this conclusion regretfully, but Mr. Reldan may not be permitted to be free again."

* * *

On April 8, 1980, a Bergen County grand jury indicted Robert Reldan for his October 15, 1979, escape, plus the other crimes he committed during that escape: aggravated assaults on Officer VanDerWerf and attorney Carmine Grimaldi, theft of Grimaldi's vehicle, and robbery of Patricia Grabinski. Reldan pleaded "not guilty" to the charges and went to trial before Judge Alfred Schiaffo in Hackensack later that year. Again, Frank Wagner defended him. The trial lasted four days, and Reldan was convicted on all counts. Judge Schiaffo later sentenced him to a concurrent term of 15 years for those crimes, but that sentence was to run consecutive to all other sentences Reldan was serving.

* * *

One postscript to the events of October 15, 1979, is worth noting. Upon learning of Reldan's escape that morning, an enraged Detective Nick Gallo, seeing his worst fears and predictions come true, smashed his fist through the glass window in an entryway door to the Bergen County Prosecutor's Office. In an internal, non-criminal proceeding, Prosecutor Roger Breslin brought Gallo up on charges. Despite Gallo's claim at the hearing that the broken window was an unintended accident, he was convicted and subjected to departmental discipline.

After a 25-year career in law enforcement, Nick Gallo retired in the 1990s. He died in 2005, remembered by former colleagues as a unique brand of Renaissance man.

Chapter 24

She had a loaded shotgun, 20 inches long, and sawed off at both ends.

Department of Corrections Sergeant Michael Voight was upbeat, despite the fact that he was still working at 3:15 PM on Easter Sunday, April 19, 1981. In 45 minutes, he would be off-duty, free to go home for a holiday dinner with his family. Voight had enjoyed the past several months of his current assignment to the security ward, on the third floor at St. Francis Hospital in Trenton, just six blocks from the state prison. Inmates who were not treatable at the prison infirmary were housed in the St. Francis security ward while undergoing specialized medical care.

Under him, Voight had two corrections officers, a force he deemed sufficient to maintain order at the hospital facility with fewer problems. The hospitalized inmates' physical limitations lessened security risks, and the accommodations and chow were much better than at the prison. No inmate wanted to lose those perks by being branded a troublemaker and sent back to the general prison population.

A call from Lieutenant Carter at the prison interrupted Sergeant Voight's musings. Carter, the officer in charge of uniformed personnel for that shift, had a request of his subordinate. Inmate Robert Reldan, whom Voight remembered as a bad actor when he was working inside the prison, was being escorted over to the hospital emergency room, and Carter wanted Voight to do a security sweep of the area before Reldan arrived.

Reldan claimed to have injured his right rib cage the day before, while working in the prison yard, and was complaining that his pain had worsened. The duty nurse who examined him was skeptical, but no technicians or doctors were working in the infirmary on Easter Sunday, so she requested that they get Reldan to the emergency room at St. Francis for x-rays.

I'd be skeptical about that guy, too, Voight thought, remembering reports of his escape when he was on trial in Bergen County. Lieutenant Carter told Sergeant Voight that he had called an ambulance service to transport Reldan the short distance to the hospital, but the rig hadn't arrived yet. He said that Reldan would be handcuffed and that two officers in a marked patrol vehicle would follow the ambulance to the hospital emergency room.

Voight assured the lieutenant that he would have a look around. Before heading to the emergency room, he grabbed a radio transmitter from the charging deck and told the other two security-ward officers where he was going and for what purpose. He walked to the service elevator and pressed the button for the first floor. Only when the elevator started its descent did he realize that he'd forgotten his service revolver. He didn't bother to go back for it.

Arriving at the first floor, in the midst of the emergency-room bustle, Voight turned right and moved down a hallway that led to the ramps where ambulances delivered patients. He made eye contact with a woman who appeared to be loitering in that area, a place where non-hospital personnel were rarely seen. Voight recognized the woman at once: She'd been a frequent visitor to Reldan when Voight was stationed inside the prison, and she was memorable during those Sunday contact visits for the sexy outfits she always wore. But, in the ambulance loading area, Voight noticed that the woman seemed like she was trying to make herself indistinguishable, wearing a kerchief to cover her blonde hair and large, dark sunglasses. She appeared almost dowdy, wearing jeans under an overcoat—not really appropriate for the April weather—and she was carrying a large, plastic shopping bag.

Despite the woman's attempts at concealing her identity, Voight was sure he recognized her. Nevertheless, he walked past her without acknowledgement, thinking about what action he should, or could, take. He couldn't just arrest her on the spot. Although her presence was suspicious, with Reldan on his way over to the hospital, she hadn't done anything wrong as far as he could see. But, given Reldan's history, it couldn't be mere coincidence that she was hanging out at the very time when her boyfriend was scheduled to arrive for treatment. Voight knew he had to do something, and quickly. But the question remained: *What* should he do?

Voight continued down the hallway and saw a uniformed City of Trenton police officer about to enter the coffee shop. *This might be the answer*, he thought. Voight ducked into a side corridor, out of the woman's view, and radioed the security ward, getting one of the two officers he had left there. He instructed the officer to call Lieutenant Carter to see if he could hold up Reldan's transport. If it was too late to stop it, Carter should send back-up right away. Voight also told the security ward officer to get his gun from the locked desk, where he'd put it, and to come running, arming himself and bringing Voight's gun, too.

Voight then entered the coffee shop and spoke to the Trenton officer, apprising him of the situation and asking for assistance. Patrolman Thomas Keegan, a seven-year police veteran, readily agreed to help. Together, they went back out to the emergency room area to look for the woman, but she was not where Voight had spotted her. Retracing their steps back toward the coffee shop, they entered the hospital's lobby. There she was, sitting alone, with the shopping bag between her legs.

The two officers walked toward the woman, with the intention of talking to her. As they approached, Patrolman Keegan saw her look up at them and then quickly lower her head. His suspicions aroused, Keegan decided not to question her in the lobby; instead, he asked her to accompany them to a place where they could talk privately. He did not mention the reason for his request, but she went along voluntarily, holding her shopping bag with both hands. They directed the woman to a small office, off the hallway leading away from the lobby. Just then, Officer Wagner from the security ward arrived, armed and carrying Voight's gun.

Since the hospital was Trenton's jurisdiction—not the State Corrections Department's— Keegan naturally took control of the situation. He followed the woman into the office, with Sergeant Voight remaining in the doorway and Officer Wagner taking up a post in the hall. Keegan asked the woman why she was in the hospital at that particular time, but she remained silent and unresponsive. When the officer said he wanted to look inside her shopping bag, he saw a look of panic come over her face. She clutched both handles of the bag in her hands.

Fearing for his safety, Keegan lunged at the bag, attempting to wrest it from the woman's grasp. In defense, she brought the bag closer to her body. On a second attempt, Keegan gained control of the bag, tearing it in the process and revealing loose clothing inside as well as a protruding piece of wood, which appeared to be the stock or butt of a weapon. Taking the object from the bag, Keegan held in his hands a loaded shotgun, about 20 inches long and sawed off at both ends. He immediately unloaded the weapon and advised the woman that she was under arrest. She resisted briefly, before he was able to handcuff her. Inspecting the contents of the bag, the patrol officer found a box containing 22 Remington "Shur-shot" 20-gauge shotgun shells.

The arrested woman was taken to Trenton police headquarters, where she was identified as 29-year-old Sherry Ann Stevens of Hasbrouck Heights, New Jersey.

Eight minutes after Stevens was removed from the hospital, Robert Reldan arrived by ambulance, with two corrections officers accompanying him. Almost simultaneously, the back-up squad that SergeantVoight had requested also arrived. As soon as Voight briefed them, the scene commander ordered Reldan to be removed from the ambulance, placed in a corrections department vehicle, and returned under heavy guard to the prison.

Formal charges of attempted escape were not initially lodged against Reldan. It was not necessary, given his incarceration. But, on June 16, 1981, two weeks after Reldan's forty-first birthday, a Mercer County grand jury returned a nine-count indictment against both Sherry Ann Stevens and Robert R. Reldan on assorted conspiracy, escape, and weapons charges. At their subsequent arraignments, both defendants entered not-guilty pleas, followed by a defense motion to suppress evidence that Patrolman Keegan had seized, but the hearing judge concluded that the warrantless search of Ms. Stevens's shopping bag was justified by exigent circumstances.

On October 27, 1981, Sherry Ann Stevens pleaded guilty to two counts of the indictment—conspiracy to commit an escape and possession of a weapon for an unlawful purpose. She was sentenced to five years imprisonment, with three years of parole ineligibility.

Robert Reldan pleaded guilty that same day to the same two charges and was sentenced, pursuant to a plea bargain, to 15 years, with 7½ years of parole ineligibility. The sentence was to run consecutive to all other sentences Reldan was then serving. Other charges were dropped. Reldan would later successfully appeal the length of the sentence, on the ground that a statute used to fix that term did not apply to him, since it was enacted after he committed the offenses. But, when the matter was remanded for a new sentence, the prosecutor argued for the imposition of habitual offender status against Reldan, and he was resentenced to exactly the same 15 years as before. Later, the new sentence was affirmed on appeal.

* * *

On May 11, 1982, the Appellate Division of the Superior Court ruled that Robert Reldan had been denied a fair trial in Reldan II because of the Rule 55 other crimes evidence that Judge Huot allowed the jury to hear—namely, the testimony of Bernice Caplan and Blanche Mate. The court said that the prejudicial effect of that testimony far outweighed its probative value. Reldan's convictions were reversed, and the matter remanded for a new trial. The State appealed to the New Jersey Supreme Court, which declined to disturb the lower court's ruling.

There would be a Reldan III.

Chapter 25

As far as I am concerned, he's fired.

While the Reldan II verdict was under appeal, Robert Leaman was promoted to First Assistant Prosecutor, the number two position in the BCPO. By the time it became clear that a third murder trial would be necessary, Roger Breslin's five-year term as County Prosecutor had ended, and, soon thereafter, Leaman chose to leave the office to go into private practice. Assistant Prosecutor Dennis Calo, head of the homicide squad, became the fourth prosecutor to take on the Reldan case. Some months later, the governor would appoint Larry McClure, a law partner of former Prosecutor Joseph Woodcock, as the next Bergen County Prosecutor.

Calo, whom McClure would name as his First Assistant Prosecutor, was by reputation one of the best trial prosecutors in the state; his selection to try the case (and bring closure to the longest ongoing BCPO prosecution anyone could remember) was universally hailed. AP Calo immersed himself in the Reldan files, preparing for what would be his most significant trial to date, but before he got his chance, circumstances forced still more changes.

The new Bergen County Prosecutor, Larry McClure, had been an assistant prosecutor under Joe Woodcock when the Heynes and Reeve murders and Reldan's indictment occurred. When Woodcock left to run for governor, McClure followed. After Woodcock's withdrawal from the governor's race, the two men formed a Hackensack law firm. While in private practice, McClure acquired two clients who figured prominently in the Reldan case—Clifford and Allison Williams. In fact, McClure had advised them while they were cooperating with the BCPO as witnesses against Reldan. That connection led Public Defendant Frank Wagner, who was still representing Reldan at the time, to file a motion to have the Bergen County Prosecutor's Office, headed by McClure, disqualified from further involvement in the Reldan case, on the grounds that it presented a conflict of interest.

In April, 1983, that motion came before Criminal Assignment Judge Fred Galda, who wasn't about to chance a Reldan IV by handing the defendant an appealable issue before Reldan III even got started. Galda didn't want to have to rule on the motion. He relied, instead, on his considerable powers of persuasion. He brought the parties together, trying to get the BCPO voluntarily to turn the case over to the Attorney General's office—specifically the Division of Criminal Justice. On May 17, 1983, AP

Dennis Calo (representing the BCPO), Deputy Attorney General Charles Buckley (representing the Division), and Public Defender Frank Wagner (representing the defendant, who was also present in court) finalized the deal.

"Here we are talking about the third trial of a matter that's been pending since January of 1977," Galda said. "And if this court could assist in any way to make certain we could eliminate any possibility of future issues in the event there were any appeals, maybe we ought to consider that in view of the tremendous expense on all sides and the length of time. And, it was because of that feeling, as I understand it, that the Attorney General has been asked to take over, and that is why we are here today. Do I substantially state the position?"

Both Calo and Buckley confirmed Judge Galda's understanding: The Attorney General had superseded the Bergen County Prosecutor's Office, and DAG Buckley would try the case.

With that decided, the parties moved to the next most pressing order of business—setting a new trial date. Judge Frederick Kuechenmeister had been selected as the judge for Reldan III, and any prospective trial date would have to be coordinated with his chambers. Galda asked Buckley when he could be ready. Any time in October, said the Deputy Attorney General.

While Judge Galda's law clerk was obtaining available October trial dates from Kuechenmeister (October 21, 1983, would be chosen), Galda used the time to engage in a bit of repartee with the defendant. The judge asked defense counsel, "Did you tell Mr. Reldan I am retiring June 1?"

"I follow your case in the newspapers," Robert Reldan replied. "I get *The Record*."

"We go back a lot of years," Galda said to Reldan.

"'67," Reldan replied.

"First conviction that you had," said Fred Galda, who had been the trial prosecutor who obtained Reldan's 1967 conviction for raping Bernice Caplan.

"They had to bring you in to get it after two hung juries," Reldan said, complimenting the judge.

"They said I was a pretty good prosecutor," Galda said.

"You were loud," Reldan affirmed. "I don't know about good."

* * *

In the Bergen County legal community, Judge Frederick Kuechenmeister was known as a no-nonsense, prosecution-minded judge. When they drew him as trial judge, defense attorneys and their clients reconsidered their options for plea bargains. Wagner and Reldan could not have been pleased that a reputed "hanging judge" would preside over their case.

BCPO staff affectionately called the judge the "Keek." He was a crusty, old bachelor and something of a health nut who had earlier lost a lung to disease. In those days, smoking was permitted in public, including the Bergen County courthouse—anywhere except in the Keek's courtroom or chambers. The judge's lunchtime walks around Hackensack in any kind of weather—rain, sleet, snow, or sunshine—were legendary. So, too, was the judge's second love (after the law): his vacation trips to exotic corners of the world.

Before the October trial date rolled around, the attorney general tapped DAG Buckley to take command of the Hudson County Prosecutor's Office. Hudson County's prosecutor had been indicted for bribery and the leaderless office went into a tailspin. (Ultimately, the prosecutor would return to head the office after he was found not guilty at trial.) But, until the matter was resolved, the attorney general had to send a replacement, as he had statutory authority over all 21 county prosecutors. He chose his workhorse, Charles Buckley, who would fill in as top law enforcement officer in five different New Jersey counties before his career was over. Because of the high priority of his new assignment, Buckley had to turn over the Reldan case to another deputy attorney general, William Lundsten. (In still another twist, Buckley would come back to handle the Reldan III trial, two years later.)

After taking over, Lundsten's first action was to file a motion to overturn Judge Madden's suppression of the hair evidence in Reldan I. In the years after Madden made that ruling in 1979, laws had changed and prosecutors felt that there was a good chance of reversing it. (Assistant Prosecutor Dennis Calo, in fact, had suggested the tactical move after relinquishing the case to the Attorney General's office.) The hair evidence could be a powerful addition to the State's case, especially since the prosecution could not use Bernice Caplan's and Blanche Mate's testimony.

The new suppression hearing involved several days of testimony. At the conclusion, Judge Kuechenmeister played it safe, finding, as Madden did, that the evidence seized from Reldan's Opel wagon on November 1, 1975, went beyond the scope of the search warrant, which was issued, ostensibly, for the two burglaries Reldan had committed. DAG Lundsten was granted leave to take an interlocutory appeal from that decision, meaning that the trial would wait for an appellate court to review it. The process consumed almost two years, as the matter wound its way through the courts. The Appellate Division sided with the State and reversed Kuechenmeister (and Madden), and then Wagner appealed to the New Jersey Supreme Court. On July 24, 1985, the Supreme Court held that the hair evidence would be admissible. The key piece of evidence, providing a strong link between the two murdered women and Reldan's Opel Kadett wagon, would be part of Reldan III.

Wagner did some maneuvering, as well. He tried to bar Raymond Lozier's testimony on the grounds that the hypnosis procedures that the State had used to help Lozier's recollection didn't conform to established guidelines. The gambit failed. Lozier would be permitted to testify.

Another crucial ruling went the State's way. The prosecutor would be permitted to use Reldan's escape at the end of the second trial to show "consciousness of guilt." Jurors in Reldan III would hear all about the escape. Further, Judge Kuechenmeister would charge that the jury could consider the defendant's escape as proof of his guilt.

Those motions and appeals consumed time. By the completion of the process, Lundsten had left the Division of Criminal Justice for private practice. To replace Lundsten, the Attorney General again designated Charles Buckley to take on the Reldan trial, since Buckley had completed his service as acting Hudson County Prosecutor. Buckley set up shop in the BCPO's spaces in July, 1985, and began reviewing the massive case file. Though he had been promoted in the interim, Lieutenant Al Cirello—the investigator who had assisted Leaman—would act as Buckley's trial investigator. This was a big help, considering the man's familiarity with the files and witnesses.

Judge Kuechenmeister, anxious to get the case moving again, held a pre-trial conference with Wagner and Buckley in chambers on November 22, 1985. During that conference, the judge set January 13, 1986, as Reldan's new trial date.

"There will be no more delays," Kuechenmeister warned. Despite the admonition, Reldan tried in late December to substitute noted Bergen County lawyer Brian Neary as his new counsel. This was possibly an indication that Aunt Lillian was back with her financial support.

Neary, a former assistant prosecutor who once headed the Bergen office's sex crimes unit, argued his substitution motion on January 8, five days before the scheduled trial date. He advised Kuechenmeister he would require an adjournment to prepare Reldan's defense.

Reldan's decision to replace Frank Wagner with a privately retained attorney must have come as a blow to Wagner. Although public defenders are often disparaged—unfairly—as inferior attorneys, Wagner had performed brilliantly for Reldan, especially given what he had to work with. In fact, near the end of the first murder trial, Reldan wrote a letter to *The Record* in praise of his attorney's efforts. "Win, lose, or draw, I want it known that no one will ever be able to knock the Public Defender's Office to me again," Reldan told the newspaper. "Let me say now that I have had private, paid attorneys in the past . . . . The paid attorneys talked about money . . . Mr. Wagner talked about justice."

Indeed, Wagner engineered a hung jury in Reldan I (although Reldan's "juror appeal," especially as it related to female jurors, played a role in that result.) Wagner's persistence in the second trial paid off, with a reversal of the conviction on appeal. He had represented Reldan faithfully and, as it turned out, effectively for more than seven years.

Easily recognizing the defendant's familiar delay tactic, Buckley objected to Reldan's last-minute attempt to change attorneys. The move was untimely, Buckley said, and would inconvenience witnesses' schedules, especially those traveling great distances. Jonathan Heynes, for example, had returned to England after his wife's death and traveled back to the States for each trial. Other witnesses had made arrangements to travel from California, Arizona, Georgia, and Washington DC.

"These people can't be played like yo-yos on a string," Buckley argued. He also raised the issue of Neary's status as a senior BCPO assistant prosecutor—who had been consulted by First Assistant Dennis Calo on issues pertaining to the case—during previous Reldan trials. Calo submitted an affidavit to that effect. Neary's "changing sides" in a criminal matter gave the appearance of impropriety, Buckley said, and it was a conflict of interest. Later, Buckley told the court that he would accept Neary as defense counsel, so long as the change caused no delay in the start of the trial. Neary, however, said that he would not take the case without adequate time to prepare. He was talking about an adjournment of weeks if not months—certainly not days.

Judge Kuechenmeister denied Reldan's application to substitute Brian Neary for Frank Wagner, and Neary hurriedly filed an appeal. When the Appellate Division ruled against him, Neary went a step further, to the New Jersey Supreme Court. Again, he got the same answer. The case was finally ready to proceed to trial and the first order of business was jury selection, but Robert Reldan had yet another surprise in store for the court, and everyone concerned.

Reldan III would open with almost as much dramatic effect as the close of Reldan II.

* * *

While attorney Brian Neary pursued his appeal of Judge Kuechenmeister's decision barring him from becoming Robert Reldan's fifth lawyer in the case,* the firm trial date of January 13, 1986, went the way of so many prior "firm" dates for Reldan trials. On January 16, with the Supreme Court yet to act on Neary's appeal, Judge Kuechenmeister held another in-chambers conference to review "a few items," as the judge put it, so he could "hit the ground running" when the case was finally ready for trial. The Appellate Division had already upheld the Keek's decision, and he fully expected the Supreme Court to do the same. Still technically representing Reldan, Frank Wagner was present, as was DAG Buckley. But Reldan was not in attendance.

The judge set two tentative dates for commencement of trial— January 21, if the Supreme Court ruled by then, or a fallback date of January 27, if they needed more time. It didn't take long for Frank Wagner to raise his voice and interrupt both the judge and Buckley. Nor did it take long for Judge Kuechenmeister to assert his control, in a peculiarly effective way.

"[If] you guys start yelling at each other [in front of the jury], I'm just going to sit back and watch and not say a word until you're finished. They all depend on the judge jumping in and stopping it. But it's a little sadistic, just watching you fellows. I may do that if you keep it up."

The conference continued without further outbursts from Wagner. Buckley, as usual, remained calm. He rarely raised his voice in the heat of a courtroom battle, although his even-tempered demeanor would be tested later on. Kuechenmeister settled on what his comments to the jury panel would be during the selection process, and he informed the attorneys that he would not be sequestering the jury. Judge Huot had to impose that drastic remedy to preserve jury integrity at the end of Reldan II, but Kuechenmeister hoped to avoid it for the new trial, unless something arose to warrant it. Wagner pushed for sequestration, but Kuechenmeister said he "couldn't get approval for it." Sequestering a jury for four weeks was expensive, and no judge could order such a step without the chief assignment judge's approval, which Kuechenmeister was not able to get, even given the experience in the previous trial.

---

*With his family's financial support renewed, Reldan went shopping for a lawyer. His first choice was Frank Lucianna, the attorney who had negotiated several favorable plea bargains and successfully defended him in the Fort Lee burglary and sexual assault case in 1963. Lucianna turned him down.

By the time everyone reassembled in court on January 27, 1986, the Supreme Court had spoken. Kuechenmeister's ruling was upheld. Frank Wagner would remain as Reldan's legal counsel for the trial. But, prior to beginning jury selection, as the judge reviewed procedures with the attorneys, Frank Wagner made a startling announcement. "Mr. Reldan vehemently objects to my representing him in this trial, and he wants to be heard," Wagner said. "I've just come out of the holding cell with him to try to determine whether or not his opinion was still thus, and he told me it was. He doesn't want me to represent him."

"What does he want to do?" Judge Kuechenmeister asked.

"You'll have to ask him, Judge," Wagner replied. "I can't speak for him."

"Bring him up here [to side bar]," Judge Kuechenmeister said.

"Good morning," Reldan said. "I am not prepared to go to trial with Mr. Wagner. I have dismissed him. I have made him aware of this for over a couple of weeks now. I have not been able to inform the court. I am also able to obtain private counsel and I wish to do so. It's been my intention since the beginning of this case to obtain private counsel and I'm not prepared to go to trial with Mr. Wagner. As far as I am concerned, he's fired."

"Are you aware of the Supreme Court decision?" Judge Kuechenmeister asked.

"Which one is that, Sir?" Reldan replied.

"Mr. Reldan," the judge said, "you know very well the Supreme Court has upheld my decision not allowing another attorney and requiring Mr. Wagner to represent you."

"You see, I wasn't made aware of the full hearing," Reldan claimed. "In that case—"

"Mr. Reldan, that's the way it is and that's the way it is going to be," stated Judge Kuechenmeister.

"Well, then, you're forcing me to defend myself and I will choose to do so," Reldan said. "Mr. Wagner—our strategies are opposed. I'm bound by his strategy if I accept him as an attorney, and I'm not willing to do that."

"He's going to be your attorney, period, and I'm not going to postpone the trial," Judge Kuechenmeister said. "We are going to start it."

"I believe under *Faretta* [a US Supreme Court case permitting defendants to represent themselves under certain circumstances], I'm allowed to defend myself," Reldan argued.

"You may do so," Judge Kuechenmeister said. "And I instruct Mr. Wagner to remain at your side for any aid that you find you'll require from him."

Kuechenmeister had no choice but to grant Reldan's request, but ordering Wagner to continue as Reldan's "legal advisor" was a shrewd countermove in keeping with case law. Having Wagner there for consultation would prevent Reldan from later arguing that the judge erred in allowing him—a lay person not trained in the law—to act as his own lawyer. But Wagner would not go quietly.

"If he won't listen to me, how can I be his counsel?" Wagner asked.

"Mr. Wagner, you will stay here and you will be at his side during this case," the judge instructed.

"I don't think that is fair to me or the defendant, Judge," Wagner protested.

"Mr. Wagner, this thing went up to the Supreme Court," the judge said. "This is what the Supreme Court decided. We are not going to adjourn this case. He is not going to get another attorney at this time. If he wishes to represent himself, fine, but you are going to stay at his side throughout this entire trial to aid him if he so desires that aid. That is my ruling and there will be no change to it."

Wagner and Reldan continued to bicker with the judge over the unfairness of the situation, according to their perception, but Kuechenmeister was adamant: no adjournment, even if it meant that Reldan had to represent himself. Frank Wagner and the full resources of the Public Defender's Office were to be at Reldan's disposal, should he wish to utilize them, for the duration of the trial.

The jury selection process would take seven days, during which Wagner complained bitterly on multiple occasions about being bound to Reldan, who could afford private counsel through his family's financial support. At one point, Wagner said his superiors in the State Public Defender's Office were refusing to pay for Reldan's defense. Kuechenmeister would hear none of it, even going so far as to threaten having Wagner's boss in Trenton hauled in to explain his refusal to comply with a court order. When Wagner continued to argue, the Keek exploded.

"When the court talks, you shut up," the judge said. "I'm a little bit tired of you trying to talk over me all the time."

In the end, Wagner's superiors capitulated. Wagner would sit beside Reldan during the trial. If Reldan refused to consult Wagner or to use Wagner's office for investigative help or witness procurement, well, that was Reldan's bed to lie in.

For his part, Kuechenmeister tried repeatedly to dissuade Reldan from representing himself and urged him to allow Wagner, who had full knowledge of the file and who had done a competent job on Reldan's behalf for more than seven years, to conduct the defense. "This court has a responsibility to ensure that your choice [to represent yourself] is knowingly and intelligently made," Kuechenmeister told Reldan. "You're waiving a right which is so important that the Constitution of the United States and New Jersey demand that you have a right to counsel and a right to have counsel appointed if you can't afford one.

"It has been settled that you will not get a substituted counsel or a postponement," the judge continued. "The question is whether you choose to proceed on your own or as represented by Mr. Wagner, the counsel of record. This trial will be conducted in accordance with the Rules of Evidence and Procedure. It is a grave danger and a considerable disadvantage for you not to be familiar with those rules. You may not be able to introduce evidence, which is beneficial to you in the proper manner. If that occurs, the information may not come into evidence.

"Also, you may not know how or when to object to evidence which is detrimental to you and which could be excluded. Similarly, there could be trial tactics, which you are unfamiliar with, and that, too, could be dangerous to your presentation of your case. Your lack of knowledge of the law could be detrimental. You should know it is often unwise to represent one's self, even if one is an attorney. The charges you face are serious. You have the ability to be represented by a very competent counsel. In light of all I have said and knowing the dangers and disadvantages of self-representation," the judge asked, "do you still wish to make this perilous choice?"

Judge Kuechenmeister, by this detailed exposition, was also carefully tending to the trial record, making sure any appellate court knew the lengths to which he had gone to get Robert Reldan to accept competent representation, instead of taking what had to be an ego-driven road of self-representation. But Reldan remained committed to representing himself for Reldan III.

On the first day of jury selection on January 27—after it was settled that Reldan would conduct his own defense—with the reluctant Wagner at his side, Reldan asked that the name of an additional witness be added to the list of witnesses that would be read to prospective jurors. At the start of every jury selection, it was standard practice for the judge to read the names of expected witnesses in the upcoming case, so that jurors who had a close connection to a witness could be excused from serving in that particular trial. For Reldan III, the names of almost 200 potential witnesses had been assembled—everyone who had any possible involvement, whether likely to be called upon to testify or not. If the prosecutor needed a last-minute witness to close a hole in his case, he did not want to be barred from calling that witness because the name wasn't on the list read to jurors; consequently, prosecutors normally included on their prospective witness list every name that appeared in every investigative report in the case.

Still, one name was conspicuously absent from Buckley's list, and Reldan wanted that name added—to *his* list. The witness? Eileen Dalton, whose first name Reldan incorrectly remembered as "Ellen."

"At the original trial, there was a Miss Ellen Dalton listed by the State," Reldan said. "And she's not listed on their list now and I have requested Mr. Wagner to add this [name] on my list. I notice you didn't name her."

"Ellen Dalton of where?" Judge Kuechenmeister asked.

"I have no idea," Reldan said. "I don't know where she is now."

Judge Kuechenmeister turned to Wagner. "You have any idea where she was?" he asked.

"Palisades Park," Wagner said. "But I object to this, Judge. You know, this is contrary to my advice. And I can't see the utility in the use of this witness."

This exchange indicates some of the differing strategies between Reldan and Wagner. Eileen Dalton was the bridge toll collector who observed a "light green" vehicle going through her booth, with a screaming woman locked in its trunk, on the night of October 14, 1975. The State had never used the witness, and, having read all the police reports in discovery, Reldan knew why. Investigators were never able to link Reldan to a light green vehicle, and the description that Dalton had given of the driver of that vehicle—5'7" to 5'9" tall, 170 pounds—was not close to Reldan's physical stature, as he was six-feet tall and 180 to190 pounds, even back in 1975. Dalton's evidence did not fit into the State's theory of the case, and Leaman and Buckley had chosen not to use it, surmising that, if they couldn't explain the disparities, the testimony would only serve to confuse the jury as a potential red herring.

A red herring is exactly what Reldan wanted. If he could show the possibility of another perpetrator of the October 14 abduction of Susan Reeve, he might very well be able to create reasonable doubt or, at the very least, another hung jury. While a hung jury wouldn't free him, there was a limit to how many times the State would bring the case to trial. A hung jury could get him another sweet plea bargain.

But Reldan would never get an opportunity to call Eileen Dalton to the witness stand in the third murder trial. His public defender investigators could not locate her and the court blocked his attempt to force Dalton's brother to reveal her new address. The court's action in this would be upheld on appeal.

At the beginning of the jury selection process, Judge Kuechenmeister collectively addressed the panel of prospective jurors, disseminating general information about the case—names of possible witnesses and such. Then, in the judge's chambers, with the attorneys and

Reldan present, each person in the panel was interviewed individually. Many had to be excused because the expected length of the trial would cause them financial hardship.* Others said that, for whatever personal reason, they could not be impartial in a case involving rape or murder. Each prospective juror's answers gave lawyers ammunition to make challenges "for cause," that is, for a legitimate reason that might affect that person's impartiality. Both the defense and the prosecution also had what are called "peremptory" challenges, which gives them the opportunity to excuse a juror without having to state a reason. Perhaps the juror presented body language that the lawyers perceived as contrary to their side's interests, or maybe someone had a "gut feeling" about a potential juror's leanings either way. In a criminal trial involving murder, the defense had 20 peremptory challenges, the State, 12. Reldan used almost all of his before the jury selection process was over; Buckley used just a few.

During the seven days it took to pick a panel of 16 jurors—a jury of 12 plus four alternates, as before—Reldan continually complained of lack of access to things he needed to conduct his defense; his two chief grievances were that he needed a typewriter and a private office in the courthouse, so he didn't have to lug files back and forth from the jail. He wasn't prepared, he said, and didn't have all the files he needed. And he objected strenuously to the extra security precautions the Sheriff's office was taking—understandably so, this time around.

Reldan was shackled with leg and arm constraints wherever he went, even while he was confined to a holding cell. He was even handcuffed going to and from the shower, he lamented on one occasion. Reldan seemingly had a short memory. After all, in October, 1979, he laid low one Sheriff's officer with tear gas and jumped out of a third story courthouse window. The BCSO was not about to allow a repeat of those events. Kuechenmeister did, finally, order that Reldan be given access to a typewriter and that his files be locked up in the courthouse during recesses in the trial. It was clear that the judge was not acting out of the goodness of his heart. He did not want to give Reldan any appealable issues beyond what would normally be available to him. That same consideration may have motivated Reldan's complaints, as he was likely building a record for the appellate courts.

Frank Wagner remained petulant throughout, smarting at having been dumped as counsel but forced to continue as "legal advisor." He volunteered little assistance to Reldan during the trial. On those few occasions when Reldan consulted him, Wagner responded appropriately,

---

*Jurors in New Jersey are paid the princely sum of $5.00 per day, an amount that hasn't changed in 40 years.

as his ethical obligation required. At one point, when the judge suggested to Reldan that he allow Wagner to do some legal research for him, the public defender let loose a torrent of invective, outside the presence of the jury.

"May I get one thing straight," Wagner said. "I am *not* Mr. Reldan's research clerk. I am advising him. I feel like a left thumb here. First off, I haven't been asked for advice and any advice I have seen fit to give, Mr. Reldan has rejected. I'm not here to furnish him with supplies or pencils or paper or anything of that nature. My understanding of my function is I'm merely here to give him advice when he requests it, to offer advice if I see him going astray, and that's it. He's his own counsel. He's appearing in the matter *pro se*. I'm not counsel for him."

Judge Kuechenmeister showed his own annoyance with Reldan at times, especially with the defendant's tendency not only to argue every ruling but also to seek legal advice from the bench. After Reldan asked still another legal question, the Keek reacted with his own rant.

"Why don't you ask Mr. Wagner some of those questions," the judge said. "He's there to advise you, not the court. You've got a legal advisor sitting there right next to you . . . . I'm not going to be your lawyer. I'm going to tell you that right now, Mr. Reldan. I'm going to tell you, you'd better rethink your whole position as to representation . . . . To start being your own lawyer when you know almost nothing about the law is, I think, ridiculous for you to do so."

The judge's speech fell on deaf ears. Reldan persisted in his desire to conduct his own defense. Near the end of jury selection, the judge found it necessary to again lay down the law to Wagner, this time in a formal order, leaving no doubt as to the public defender's obligations, even though Reldan was resisting his advice.

"Mr. Wagner, you are hereby ordered to diligently represent Mr. Reldan in accordance with the Rules of Professional Conduct," the judge began. "If you disagree with his strategy, you may state that for the record; however, you are not to do so in the presence of the jury. The jury should not be aware of any dispute between Mr. Reldan and yourself. You are to provide Mr. Reldan with all the resources customarily available through your office, including investigative services, the production of witnesses and evidence, legal resources, and other physical material which he reasonably needs to prepare. You are also to advise him when to object, how to cross-examine or ask direct questions. I realize you cannot provide Mr. Reldan with a legal education; however, you are to give him as much information and resources as you can. Of course, the advice you give Mr. Reldan must be sound and, if that requires some research on your part, so be it. If papers are to be filed, you must help him as much as possible. You are to retain an active and zealous interest in this case."

Wagner was polite to the court in his response, but, ever the feisty adversary, he was careful to put on the record the practical difficulties in implementing the court's order.

"Well, you can order me, Judge, but whether that order can be carried out effectively by me under these circumstances is very doubtful," Wagner said. "Not because of reluctance on my part, but because of an inability for me to communicate with Mr. Reldan or him to communicate with me. So, I don't say that I am refusing [your order], but I am saying it's impossible because of the relationship. I'm not his confidant, his advisor, his trusted aide in his mind, so how can he have any confidence in me and how can I attempt to influence him, in any decisions that he may make contrary to a legal opinion I might give?"

Wagner ended with a question, which Kuechenmeister ignored. "Anything else?" the judge asked. Wagner continued to ramble, in the same vein, but the judge had made his point. The trial continued without postponement, and Reldan was permitted to act as his own attorney, though he had to rely on a *diligent* Frank Wagner for advice and help—assistance he was free to accept or decline.

After two decades of firsthand experience with the criminal justice system, Reldan had become the quintessential jailhouse lawyer. He actually did a creditable job as his own counsel, with a few gaping exceptions. He crafted his legal arguments well, although he would not win many battles with Buckley. But Reldan's role as lawyer cost him an important edge. He lost his surface charm and the dignity he was able to project in previous trials. He was no longer the well-groomed, personable defendant who sat quietly at counsel table, looking confident despite the accusations being hurled against him. Instead, he was a combatant, and some of Reldan's conniving, too-clever-by-half side showed through, although he avoided the bickering that characterized Wagner's and Leaman's interactions. In an apparent attempt to win favor with the jury, Reldan embraced the underdog role. He was *David* fighting the State of New Jersey *Goliath*, but there were not many smooth stones—facts to refute DAG Charles Buckley's masterful array of circumstantial evidence—for this David's sling.

Chapter 26

Taped to the inside of one of those files were two razor blades.

DAG Charles Buckley dominated the courtroom in Reldan III. His thorough preparation was evident, if only in the streamlined case he presented. Instead of the 60-plus witnesses that the State presented in each previous trial, Buckley called just 41. It was the KISS strategy in a legal setting: "Keep it Simple, Stupid." Jurors are not stupid; they bring to the process the common sense and clear thinking necessary for the system to function as well as it does. But jurors are not permitted to take notes during a trial—a questionable prohibition, peculiar to New Jersey—and, in a complicated murder case like Reldan's, it was important to simplify what they had to absorb.

Both opening statements were uneventful. Buckley went first and satisfied his main goal of alerting jurors to the circumstantial nature of his case and to their need to hear all the evidence before they would be able to draw the conclusion of Reldan's guilt beyond a reasonable doubt. For a non-lawyer, Reldan also did a good job, holding to every defendant's strongest argument—presumption of innocence. He crossed the line a few times, but Buckley objected and was sustained on each occasion, setting a tone of professional control that would last the whole trial.

Buckley, like Leaman, started his case in chief with the testimony of Jonathan Heynes, a particularly strong witness. Heynes had important facts to relate to the jury, the most significant being his observations at the empty home he returned to on October 6, 1975, and information about the distinctive engagement ring his wife Susan always wore. But, whether victims' family members have relevant information to impart or not, prosecutors *always* call them as witnesses in murder cases, if only to remind jurors of the life that was snuffed out by the cold-blooded killer seated before them. Sympathy and emotions are not supposed to play a part in criminal trials, but they obviously do. The secret is to do it subtly.

Reldan cross-examined Jonathan Heynes as effectively as he could, with his main point being the incorrect description that Heynes had given to police of his wife's engagement ring. Heynes was able to explain his mistake, a reasonable error, given that he had been in a stressful and emotional state over his missing wife, shortly after her disappearance. (When he gave the ring description, her body had not yet been discovered.)

The engagement ring was the most crucial piece of evidence connecting Reldan to Susan Heynes. Reldan had already hinted to the jury—in his opening—what his argument would be on that point: He sold *another* ring to Macy's, one similar to the Heynes ring but *not* the Heynes ring. When he questioned any of the State's witnesses who were connected to the ring—Jonathan Heynes, John Truncali, and Melvin Norman—Reldan's thrust was always to insinuate doubt into the issue. But Reldan could not take the witness stand to explain more fully, because his prior convictions (especially the rape) would then be revealed to the jury. Other than what he could convey in his opening and closing statements and in questioning prosecution witnesses—discrepancies in their prior statements about the ring's description—the jury would never get Reldan's story of the Macy's ring transaction, no matter how falsely constructed that story might have been.

It was just as well. If Reldan had tried to take the witness stand and testify to an alternate version of the ring transaction, Buckley would have destroyed him. By only probing around the edges of the issue, without directly testifying, Reldan at least had a shot of convincing one or two gullible jurors of his premise, that he sold a different ring—not the Heynes ring—to Macy's. To accept that argument, given other indisputable facts about the ring, a juror would almost have to be a member in good standing of the Flat Earth Society, but it has been known to happen.

Soon after Susan Heynes's disappearance, Reldan showed a similar ring to John Truncali and Charles Wolthoff, before selling it to Macy's on October 21, 1975. He later told Truncali and Wolthoff that he sold the ring he'd shown them in New York City. On October 22, Investigator Ed Denning interviewed Reldan, who learned, for the first time, that he was a prime suspect in the Heynes (and Reeve) abductions. The next day, October 23, he went back to Macy's to retrieve the ring, creating a scene until the misplaced ring was located. His obsession with getting the ring back was clearly based on his guilty knowledge of what its discovery could do to him: tie him conclusively to the Heynes abduction and murder; he was the only one who knew that it was a murder at the time. Reldan never accounted for the ring thereafter, which meant just one thing: He got rid of it, in a way that couldn't be traced to him.

In trying to score points on this issue with Jonathan Heynes, Reldan blundered. While showing jewelers' brochures to Heynes, Reldan was pressuring him to admit that lots of rings similar to Susan's were for sale. Heynes would not concede it. He remained adamant about the uniqueness of the ring he'd bought at Harrod's in London. And, during this exchange, the Brit saw an opening to drive home the impact that his wife's death had on him.

"There are similar rings of fancy clusters [of diamonds] in these brochures," Heynes told Reldan. *"But there is not one ring that is the same as the ring that Susan was wearing on October the sixth in the morning when I said goodbye to her for the last time."* (Emphasis added.)

It is hard to imagine the pain and outrage that the spouse or parent of a murder victim must feel, sitting on the witness stand and being questioned not by an attorney for the defendant, but by the killer, himself. Jonathan Heynes maintained his composure, except for one poignant moment. Just as Reldan was beginning his cross-examination, Heynes lost it for a moment, silently but demonstrably to everyone in the courtroom. Judge Kuechenmeister asked if he would like a short recess, but Heynes said, "I wouldn't. I'll get on."

Reldan tried to capitalize on the moment with a not-so-subtle plea for sympathy toward himself. "I assure you, Mr. Heynes," Reldan said, "this is no easier for me."

In a disdainful, anger-laden voice, a departure from his usually calm demeanor, DAG Buckley *commanded* Reldan to "Just ask the questions."

More than 25 years later, the scene Charles Buckley best remembered about Reldan III occurred at the end of Jonathan Heynes's testimony. Before Heynes left the witness stand, he silently and pointedly made eye contact with each of the 16 jurors in the box—every last one of them. Holding his gaze until a juror responded and made eye contact with him, Jonathan Heynes then turned his head toward the next juror. It probably took two minutes or less, but seemed longer. Its powerful message was clear to every soul in the courtroom and Robert Reldan, as smart as he was, couldn't have missed it. But Reldan just sat there, not knowing what to do, probably, and afraid to open his mouth while the blatantly emotional appeal played out. Wagner, too, sat with his mouth shut, perhaps liking, just a little, the disquieting effect the incident was having on *"pro se"* Robert Reldan.

Right on the heels of Jonathan Heynes's memorable exit from the stand, Buckley called Barbara Reeve—Susan's mother—as his next witness. It was a one-two punch from which the accused murderer probably never recovered.

Mrs. Reeve was the only Reeve family member to testify. Arthur, her husband and Susan's father, was in the courtroom throughout the trial, providing support for his wife and holding a silent vigil for his daughter, just as he had been, every day, throughout the previous two trials.

It is impossible to overstate the grace and composure—and the courage—with which Barbara Reeve handled herself in the face of her daughter's killer. Her testimony was necessary to establish Susan's routine on the day she disappeared. Mrs. Reeve identified a sketch of the dress Susan was wearing that day, which she had drawn shortly after the disappearance. It matched almost perfectly one that Mary Fabrocini drew, independently, after having seen Susan walking toward home after she got off the commuter bus. It helped prove the time and place of the girl's abduction, beyond any doubt.

Barbara Reeve was also asked to identify a pair of earrings, which were removed from the dead girl's body by Dr. Zugibe during the autopsy. "Yes," Susan Reeve's mother said. "Those were the earrings she had on that day."

The rest of the first day's testimony was consumed by witnesses who verified the manufacturer's sketch of the Heynes engagement ring and retraced Susan Reeve's path of travel after she alighted from the bus and walked north on Anderson Avenue. To that point, no witness had specifically tied Reldan to either abduction or murder. That changed on Day Two.

* * *

Mary and Joseph Fabrocini both provided key testimony. Mary's went to identifying the young woman they saw walking from the County Road/Anderson Avenue intersection. Her keen eye enabled her to draw a sketch of Susan Reeve's dress, a near duplicate of what the girl's mother said she had been wearing that day. Joseph provided a link to Robert Reldan by recalling the small station wagon—loaded with junk in the back—that turned abruptly in front of them and headed in the direction of the young woman. Reldan spent a lot of time cross-examining Mary and Joseph Fabrocini, but couldn't shake the essence of what they testified to.

The court sat just half a day on February 11, sending the jurors home for a brief vacation—February 12 was Lincoln's birthday, which was a state holiday separate from Washington's birthday. Even with the jury gone, Judge Kuechenmeister had business to attend to, involving Robert Reldan's father, William, then in his mid-70s.

Before their departure, three jurors had passed a note to the judge concerning an incident at a local restaurant during lunch that day. An elderly man, who was a constant spectator during the trial came to their table and just stood there, glaring at them, without saying a word. Sufficiently shaken by the man's actions, they reported it. The jurors didn't know who the man was, but pointed him out to Sheriff's officers. In chambers, Kuechenmeister had William Reldan brought in for questioning—and a warning. The two lawyers and Robert Reldan were present, and the entire discussion was recorded. William Reldan said he was a law-abiding man who had no intention of intimidating anyone. In fact, he barely remembered the incident. Nevertheless, Judge Kuechenmeister came down hard on him, telling him to stay away from the jurors in the future or he would face severe consequences, including being jailed for the duration of the trial for contempt. That morning, the trial had lost one juror whose father had died the night before, and the judge wasn't about to risk losing more jury members because of the actions of William Reldan, or anyone else.

Robert Reldan, in fact, wanted the judge to call the three affected jurors into chambers for questioning, to make certain that they could still serve impartially; Kuechenmeister refused, not wanting to emphasize what was still a relatively minor matter that he had nipped in the bud.

On the next court date, February 13, Raymond Lozier became the star of the show, as he had in both previous trials. His testimony, mostly on cross-examination, lasted all morning and half of the afternoon. Lozier seemed relaxed in this court appearance, owing, perhaps, to his having endured the process on two prior occasions. And DAG Buckley had done a thorough job of preparation. So confident in Lozier placing Robert Reldan at the scene of the abduction of Susan Reeve, Buckley had decided not to call Stephen Prato as a witness in the trial—part of his KISS strategy.

Prato had placed a man who fit Robert Reldan's description in close proximity to Susan Reeve on Anderson Avenue. He was stalking her, in fact, from 20 feet behind. But Prato couldn't identify Reldan; he didn't get a good enough look at his face and couldn't pick him out of a photo lineup right after he reported his observations to police. Additionally, Prato placed Reldan and the girl on the *west* side of Anderson Avenue, opposite to where Raymond Lozier placed them when he made his observations farther north on that roadway. The difference in Prato's and Lozier's placement of the man in workman's clothing could have been explained; the two men saw the scene at different times, and Reldan could very well have crossed back over to the east side of Anderson, where he had parked his Opel wagon, with Susan Reeve somehow under his power. But, Buckley thought, why complicate things for the jury? He was content to go just with Raymond Lozier, who not only could describe the chilling scene across from Orchard Road, where Susan Reeve lived, but also could identify Reldan in court as the man he saw in control of the girl. He had already done so successfully in Reldan II, and there was no doubt he could do it again. He could also credibly claim to have identified Reldan's Opel wagon, when he saw it in the Closter Police impound garage six weeks later.

Buckley's direct examination of Lozier went smoothly. When he turned the witness over to Reldan for cross-examination, the jury already had a clear picture—the man about to question the witness was the man who had been standing alongside the victim on the evening she was kidnapped and the last time she was seen alive, on October 14, 1975.

Reldan did everything he could, hitting every imperfect and contradictory prior statement Raymond Lozier ever uttered. He went over what may have been an ill-advised attempt by the State to use hypnosis to enhance Lozier's recollection of events. He covered Lozier's multiple interviews with investigators, each peppered with factual discrepancies, including a vehicle color that went from dark brown to light-colored to, finally, red—the correct color. But Reldan was shoveling sand against the tide. Buckley's strategy had paid off, and Lozier left the stand with his testimony and credibility intact. Imperfect at times, but believable.

Later, Matthew Shaindlin and a Clarkstown police officer, the last witnesses of the day, testified about the discovery of Susan Heynes's body in woods near the Lake DeForest reservoir in Valley Cottage, New York. Their testimony went quickly, with little in dispute about the finding of the victim's remains. Reldan's cross-examination was short and perfunctory.

On February 14, 1986, Robert Conklin and Michael Bettmann testified to circumstances surrounding the discovery of Susan Reeve's body, establishing the fact that the body was placed in that location between October 20, 1975, when Bettmann had taken water samples and saw no body in the reeds, and October 28, 1975, when Conklin took the samples and saw the body. That scenario perfectly fit the State's theory of the case: A guilty Reldan, scrambling to cover himself after his interview with Ed Denning, had to retrieve the Heynes ring from Macy's and he had to move Susan Reeve's body, so that it would not be found at the same dumping site as Susan Heynes's body. Later, the Rockland County ME's testimony about inconsistent rigor mortis and lividity in Reeve's body, along with the willow leaves, would corroborate the evidence given by Conklin and Bettmann. The body had been moved, probably from the Valley Cottage site to the new site in Tallman Mountain State Park.

BCPO investigators could not locate Roberta Gimbel Davis, Reldan's former girlfriend, and Buckley had to use her testimony in Reldan II in order to put in her important information about Reldan taking her to the vicinity of the two spots where he had dumped the bodies. When a witness cannot be located after a diligent search, evidence rules allow that witness's testimony in a prior court proceeding to be read to the jury, who may consider it as evidence. This was so, provided both sides in the new court proceeding had the same interests in the prior court proceeding and, also, provided the witness had been subject to cross-examination. Since all of those conditions were met in this situation, the court reporter who originally recorded Gimbel Davis's testimony in Reldan II read it to jurors in Reldan III.

Live testimony in the case resumed on Tuesday, February 18, after a long weekend, as Monday was another holiday. Sheriff's officers Hendrik VanDerWerf and Floyd Dempsey were called to show Reldan's escape from their custody on October 15, 1979, near the end of Reldan II. Judge Kuechenmeister had ruled that the escape would be admissible to show Reldan's consciousness of guilt—a key prosecution victory. If they didn't already know whom they were dealing with, jurors soon learned, with VanDerWerf's description of Reldan's tear gas attack. Later, the jurors would get the actual tear gas canister in the jury room with them, as they deliberated. On cross-examination, Reldan tried to bring out a different motivation for his escape—not guilt, but concern over being treated unfairly. He attempted to get information in about the jury tampering incident—the five bribery letters—and the witnesses who testified about his prior crimes—Caplan and Mate—but his forays into those areas had to have been confusing to jurors, who likely saw nothing that justified Reldan's extreme act of escaping and harming others in the process.

The main witness that Tuesday was Clifford Williams. Buckley did not call Allison, but relied on Clifford's testimony, alone, to bring out Reldan's incriminating statements while he was in Rahway State Prison. But there was one problem: The State had to avoid letting jurors know that the conversations took place in prison. To reveal Reldan's incarceration would introduce a prejudicial factor into the case—namely, that Reldan was serving a sentence for other crimes that he had committed, and that the jury wasn't supposed to know about.

During Reldan II, the lawyers and Judge Huot had settled on a fiction: that the Williams brothers met Reldan "in a movie house in Rahway," where the conversations took place. But Buckley wasn't satisfied with that pretext; he didn't think it gave a reasonable basis for jurors to conclude that the discussions between Williams and Reldan took place in so ephemeral a setting. Reldan, perhaps thinking appealable issues, said he didn't care about any mention of prison. He said that the jury had already been prejudiced against him by hearing of the previous trials. However, he forgot that the record would show that he was the one who first mentioned them. The judge, however, wanted to keep Reldan's status as a prisoner out of the case. Finally, everyone settled on a compromise. The initial meeting would be characterized as taking place in a movie house, but later conversations would happen at a no-name restaurant, where Williams worked in the kitchen and Reldan worked nearby. The parties assumed that the sanitized setting would be close enough to be plausible, yet it would not color jurors' perceptions as the true situation would.

One other prohibition is worth noting. No mention would be made of the conspiracy to rob and murder Lillian Booth and Misha Dabich. Since those charges had resulted in Reldan's conviction, they could not be used in the murder trial; again, they were *other crimes* evidence, barred except for the limited Rule 55 purposes, which did not apply in his murder trial. The only comments that Clifford Williams would be allowed to mention relevant to the murder case were Reldan's statements about disposing of the two bodies in New York State to avoid Bergen County jurisdiction and Reldan's concern—though Williams remained vague about specifics—about a "ring."

Judge Kuechenmeister ruled against the defense using certain aspects of Williams's criminal past to attack his credibility—namely, the allegations that he had bumped off witnesses who were to testify against him and his brother. In the conspiracy trial, Judge Malech had allowed the defense attorneys free rein to "dirty up" both Williams brothers any way they saw fit, but that would not happen in Reldan III. Still, the prosecution would see little benefit from Kuechenmeister's ruling.

Since gaining his prison release in 1979, Clifford Williams had been a busy man. As he took the stand on February 18, 1986, he was under indictment in Burlington County, New Jersey, for four counts of murder, under separate indictment in the same county for distribution of controlled dangerous substances, and under still another indictment in Pennsylvania for drug distribution. Out of jail on $500,000 bail, he had posted a 10% cash bond. Williams, it seemed, had branched out, beyond the secondhand jewelry business.

Despite the handicaps to his credibility, Clifford Williams's testimony scored with the jury. They believed him and accepted that Robert Reldan, for whatever reason, had let slip the comments that Williams attributed to him. One might wonder how upstanding citizens could take the word of so unsavory a character as Williams, someone beyond the imaginings of the average person, but Buckley had already laid the groundwork for the jury to believe the worst about Robert Reldan. Jonathan Heynes, Barbara Reeve, Raymond Lozier, and Hendrik VanDerWerf had seen to that. Nude bodies of strangled young women dumped in woods and swamplands had seen to that. And, if they needed further convincing, Dr. Frederick Zugibe's testimony the next day would provide it.

* * *

Before the start of testimony on Wednesday, February 19, 1986, Reldan had a request of the court. Kuechenmeister had already alerted the parties that no testimony would be taken on Friday, February 21. He had other court matters to attend to, so jurors and everyone else, except him, would have a long, three-day weekend. Reldan wanted to use that break to go back to Trenton State Prison, where, he said, he would have access to a better law library than what was available in the Bergen County jail, his home since the start of the trial. He could also use the phone there to interview prospective witnesses, something he was having trouble doing in the jail. He had repeatedly complained about it.

"I have personal notes down there on this case," Reldan told the court. "I have personal letters down there that are going to be pertinent to this case, and, again, like I said, I would have access to the law library and I would have access to a phone and a couple other things I need."

Judge Kuechenmeister said he would take Reldan's request under advisement, but, later, he approved it. Prison guards would transport the defendant at the close of trial on Thursday to Trenton State, where his old cell and personal papers awaited, and bring him back to court by 9:00 AM the following Monday. That bit of business handled, the State called its first witness of the day, Dr. Frederick Zugibe, Chief Medical Examiner of Rockland County, New York.

Zugibe was a professional. He handled Reldan's amateurish attempts to challenge his medical conclusions smoothly and expertly. Buckley got all the main points he needed into evidence: the uncanny similarity in the way both women had been strangled; the strong inference that Susan Reeve's body had been moved, based on the ME's observations; and the contusion and abrasion on Reeve's vaginal wall, which provided evidence of forcible penetration within six to eight hours of her death. From that forcible penetration, the jury could reasonably find that Susan Reeve had been raped before she was killed, the key element to classify her murder as a first-degree crime.

Reldan could not get away from those three major conclusions that jurors would logically take from Zugibe's testimony. He spent hours cross-examining the doctor, but couldn't shake him. The same person killed both women. Jurors knew that, beyond a reasonable doubt. And if, indeed, Robert Reldan was the last person with whom Susan Reeve was seen alive, as Raymond Lozier pretty well proved, the link with Susan Heynes was established. If there had been any doubt about the Heynes engagement ring being in the possession of Robert Reldan, that doubt was out the window, as clearly as Robert Reldan went out the window on October 15, 1979.

* * *

Before the long weekend break, Buckley called four witnesses on Thursday, February 20, to further tie Reldan to Anderson Avenue on the date and at the approximate time when Susan Reeve was abducted. John Rudolph, Reldan's helper on October 14, 1975, described how Reldan had used a sandblaster that day to remove old paint from the exterior of the house they were re-painting. He told how the mask had been dropped and the faceplate broken. Mark Pittaluga told how he found the mask on Anderson Avenue that same evening, perhaps 50 yards from where Lozier had seen Reldan, in his work clothes, accosting Susan Reeve. Elliott Pickens, owner of Taylor Rent-All in Closter, told how, earlier that day, Reldan had rented the sandblasting equipment and then, the next day, Reldan returned everything but the mask. Reldan told Pickens that he lost the mask, or it was stolen, but all he had of the mask to give back to the store owner was a broken face plate. Finally an FBI fingerprint expert explained to the jury why fingerprints would not take hold on the rough surface of the mask.

People always wonder about fingerprints, given their exposure in television and motion picture crime portrayals, where everything falls into place with nice, tidy explanations and proofs. If Buckley hadn't provided the explanation about why no fingerprints were found on the mask, one or more jurors might have wondered about that during deliberations, potentially causing enough doubt to result in a hung jury.

* * *

Reldan's sojourn at Trenton State Prison may have had another purpose. When he was returned to the Bergen County jail on Monday, February 24, Sheriff's officers searched him as well as all of the belongings he brought back with him—files that he said he needed for his defense. Taped to the inside of one of those files were two razor blades.

Reldan would offer a weak explanation. Razor blades were common at Trenton State, he said, and no one thought they posed a security threat. That may have been so; it was never verified. But Reldan could not explain *why* he brought them back to the Bergen County jail, where they were not allowed, and why he took pains to hide them from the guards by taping them to the inside of one of his files. Kuechenmeister was furious with this breach. He let Reldan know that his movements would be further constrained in the future.

"You've been told many of the requests during this trial were denied for security reasons," Kuechenmeister said. "It is obvious the concerns for security are real. You should not plan on returning to State Prison during the course of this trial for preparation of any kind."

Prosecution witnesses that Monday and early Tuesday were primarily concerned with housekeeping matters, including the chain of evidence. Every piece of physical evidence that the State intended to introduce had to be accounted for, from the time it was originally collected to the time it landed on the prosecutor's table at trial. Much of this preparation led to the testimony of FBI Special Agent James Hilverda, who, in late 1975, was attached to the FBI laboratory in Washington DC, where his duties included microscopic examination of hair evidence. He had examined hair specimens taken from Reldan's Opel wagon during the November 1, 1975, search, which the New Jersey Supreme Court had ruled to be admissible.

After qualifying Hilverda to be an expert in this type of examination, Buckley had his witness conduct a tutorial on hair analysis for the jury.

"Basically, what we're looking at when we do a hair comparison," Agent Hilverda began, "is for characteristics which we can observe microscopically. If I look across the members of the jury, I see a number of different types of hair. I also observe a number of different colors . . . . Most everybody would say a hair is a hair . . . but when we look at it microscopically, generally each hair is composed of a root, a shaft, and a tip, and varies in length . . . ." The agent went into detail, but used layman's terms to make the science more understandable. He explained that hairs do not present unique identifiers, like fingerprints. No expert could say a particular hair belonged to a particular individual. (Again, this was before DNA science turned that limitation aside, in many instances.) But Hilverda testified that, based on his experience, it was "unlikely to find hairs from two individuals that are so alike that you cannot separate them and tell them apart."

When asked to discuss his particular findings related to Susan Heynes and Susan Reeve, the agent said that he was asked to compare known hair samples taken from the two murdered women to hair specimens recovered from Reldan's vehicle during the November 1, 1975, search. He, himself, participated in that search and took the specimens by means of manual retrieval—spotting the hair and picking it up with tweezers—and vacuum sweepings. He preferred not to use only vacuum sweepings, because that method made identification more difficult.

"Were you able to make any comparisons?" Buckley asked.

"I did a number of comparisons of the hairs that were removed from the automobile," Hilverda answered. "And I compared them with the known samples, which I received from the two victims. I did do that, yes."

"Now, were you able to establish any positive similarities between anything you found in the car and the known samples from the two victims?" Buckley asked.

"Yes, I was," Hilverda said. "I found hairs located from the right front floor mat of the vehicle that were like those of Reeve and I found hairs from the debris from the rear seat that were also like Reeve's, and I also found hairs from underneath the rear seat that were also like her hair. Also in that sample, I found hairs that were like the victim Heynes's hairs."

Buckley asked him what he meant when he said, "like."

"They compared in all microscopic characteristics with those of the known samples," Hilverda explained.

In his cross-examination of Agent Hilverda, Reldan showed that he had done his homework on the science of microscopic hair examination, but his questions seemed designed more to show off his own knowledge than to challenge Hilverda's findings. In the end, all he did was solidify some very strong evidence against him. He reinforced the State's contention that both Susan Reeve and Susan Heynes had been transported—either dead or alive—in his own Opel wagon.

The court, again, had other matters to attend to Wednesday, February 26 and, when the trial resumed on Thursday, DAG Buckley was ready to put the finishing touches on the State's case. He put Melvin Norman on the stand, to establish the facts of Reldan's sale of a woman's engagement ring to Macy's on October 21, 1975. Norman identified the ring as Susan Heynes's ring, both through the Saunders Jewellery sketch and photographic enlargements of the ring on Susan's hand the day she was married to Jonathan. The BCPO had used the Saunders sketch to have a replica of the ring—a physical copy of what the ring actually looked like—made up for trial (starting with Reldan I). Norman said that the replica also looked like the ring he purchased from the defendant.

Buckley had Melvin Norman step down from the witness stand, briefly, while he called Ed Denning (who had risen in rank over the years to Captain of Investigators) to testify about his October 22, 1975, interview of Reldan regarding the Heynes and Reeve abductions. The DAG was careful not to go into details; he wanted only to establish the fact of the interview and the general subject matter, in order to draw the inference that, as a result of that interview, Reldan became aware of his suspect status. After Denning testified, Buckley called Joseph Cohen, another Macy's employee, who described the commotion that Reldan made when he returned to retrieve Heynes's ring on October 23, 1975. Then, Buckley called Melvin Norman again, in order to tie up the final act: Reldan retrieved the ring and returned the $100 that Macy's had paid him for it.

In cross-examination, Reldan did his best to cast aspersions on Melvin Norman, whom Macy's fired for shoddy recordkeeping. But that did not change the facts, nor did it significantly damage Norman's credibility. Norman held up well, more than 10 years later, and he did his duty as a citizen to testify truthfully about what clearly was an embarrassing moment for him, personally.

Charles Buckley rested the State's case, but the trial was not over. Robert Reldan would begin presenting his case the next day.

Chapter 27

Those are willow leaves embedded in the body.

The trial would last seven weeks—the longest of Reldan's three trials—despite Buckley's paring down of the State's case. Reldan, himself, would call 27 defense witnesses, in contrast to Wagner's decision not to call a single witness in previous trials. But, in presenting his own case, Robert Reldan faltered the most, in a manner that was, at times, simply wasteful and unimportant and, at other times, outright damaging to his cause. One juror would comment, 25 years later, that the thing she remembered most about the trial was how bored she and other jurors were by Reldan's rambling, often with no apparent purpose. In other words, instead of focusing on areas where he could build reasonable doubt (at least in the minds of the one or two jurors he needed to achieve a hung jury), Reldan had something to say about almost everything. That approach risked causing jurors to tune out when he needed them to be tuned in. Reldan's ego—his compulsion to prove himself skilled as his own lawyer—wouldn't allow him to shut up.

Dr. Peter DeForest, a professor at John Jay College of Criminal Justice in New York City, was Reldan's first witness. The defense had hired him to conduct an independent analysis of the hair evidence found in the Opel wagon and then to give an expert opinion as to his findings. The only problem, for the defense, was that Dr. DeForest was unable to challenge the testimony of FBI Special Agent Hilverda.

DeForest had been given access to the same evidence specimens that Hilverda had examined, along with use of lab equipment at the New Jersey State Police Laboratory, to make his own independent evaluation. The defense expert's conclusion? Well, his conclusion was that he reached no conclusion. On the witness stand, he testified that he did not have time to examine all of the hair specimens. In other words, his analysis was incomplete, with no explanation given as to why he didn't have time to do a thorough job. Despite the obviously deficient testimonial, Reldan called the man to the stand anyway, telegraphing to the jury the pointless course his defense would take. Buckley pummeled Reldan's direct examination of Dr. DeForest with objections, each one exposing the defendant's inept performance as his own counsel.

In his cross-examination, Buckley established that the defense expert had been given a fair opportunity to conduct his own independent tests and that the State had been cooperative at every turn. DeForest confirmed the methodology used by Hilverda.

"If Agent Hilverda were to use [microscopic comparison as a] way of drawing his conclusions," Buckley asked, "he would not be doing something, in your opinion, improper or unreasonable?"

"No," DeForest said. "The microscopic comparison is state of the art. It's been that way for about 80 years. There have been attempts to find something better, but we have not succeeded in finding a better approach to the problem."

DAG Buckley asked Dr. DeForest if he was familiar with Agent Hilverda's report and the conclusions the State's expert had drawn regarding the hair comparisons—namely, that Susan Reeve's hair matched hairs found in the Opel wagon on the front passenger-side floor mat, in the rear seat area, and in debris under the rear seat, and that Susan Heynes's hair also matched hairs found in debris under the rear seat. DeForest said that he was familiar with those conclusions.

"Is it your testimony as an expert that [Hilverda's] conclusions are wrong?" Buckley asked.

"No," DeForest stated.

In effect, Buckley had taken the defense's expert witness and turned him into a corroborating witness for the State's expert. Not only was Reldan's decision to call the witness a colossal waste of time, it also did irreparable harm to his case. Imagine Frank Wagner's private advice to Reldan *not* to use DeForest as a witness, and Reldan's complete disregard of that advice, to his detriment. DeForest's testimony came at the end of the day on Friday, February 28, 1986. The jury had all weekend to contemplate the fiasco.

Reldan didn't fare much better with his first witness the following Monday. On March 3, he called Haworth Patrolman Victor Pizza to the stand. Pizza had responded to Jonathan Heynes's call about his missing wife on October 6, 1975. His testimony amounted to nothing new—no information that conceivably helped the defense. Buckley didn't need to cross.

One defense witness that day might have helped, if he had been handled better and if Reldan, during his opening statement, had alerted the jury to the important testimony. Malcolm Topalian had observed an incident on Anderson Avenue that he duly reported to Demarest police on October 16, 1975, after Susan Reeve's disappearance became public knowledge. He had seen a young woman, a blonde, in Susan Reeve's age range, talking to the driver of a car, a Mercedes, Topalian thought. There was a male passenger in the vehicle, too. The car was stopped in the middle of the road, about 150 yards north of the intersection of County Road and Anderson Avenue. Topalian said that the driver "was well dressed, pale skin, cleanly shaven, and full-faced. He looked like what I thought was a refined Pete Rose, if people know who [the professional baseball player] Pete Rose is. I guess most people do." Topalian's descriptions obviously did not fit the Opel wagon or Robert Reldan, who was trying to show that, in the Reeve case, investigators had another possible suspect, whom they had ignored.

One problem with Topalian's recollection of the scene was the woman's clothing; it didn't match the clothing Susan Reeve's mother said that she was wearing on the day of her abduction. It also did not fit the account given by Mary Fabrocini. A more serious shortcoming was Topalian's uncertainty about the date of his observations. He didn't know whether it had happened on October 13 or 14. Buckley had not used Topalian during the State's case because of those discrepancies, but Reldan wasn't interested in consistency. His aim was to introduce into the mix another red herring—to point a finger at someone else. Buckley cleared up the matter with one question.

"Are you sure which day it was you made the observations?" Buckley asked.

"No," Topalian said. "I told them that."

Reldan spoke with Topalian for five minutes before the witness took the stand. If Reldan had spent more time with Topalian, or allowed the public defender's investigator to spend more time with the man, instead of insisting on doing all the witness interviews himself, he may have gotten from Topalian a better performance on the stand—one in which the witness's memory about the exact date of his observations had been properly *refreshed*.

Reldan also called Demarest police officer Thomas Prime, who had conducted a canvas of the neighborhood after Susan Reeve's disappearance. One of the houses he visited was the Fabrocini residence. At the time of his visit, neither Mary nor Joseph Fabrocini had anything to report. Only when more details came out in the newspaper did the witnesses recall their observations on the evening of October 14, 1975, and they came forward. Reldan attempted to counter the testimony that both Fabrocinis had given. If they had been the only witnesses against him, it may have been a worthwhile move, but the weight of the testimony regarding Susan Reeve's steps that evening, after she got off the bus, was too great for a minor issue like the Fabrocinis' delayed reaction to have much effect.

On Tuesday, March 4, Roberta Gimbel Davis appeared as a surprise witness for the defendant. She'd failed to respond to any of the prosecution's efforts to locate her. Her parents, sister and daughter had most likely communicated those inquiries to her, but she had no wish to appear as a witness for the State. Reldan's request for her to testify was different. Roberta Gimbel Davis and Susan Reldan had been school chums and, in addition to being a close friend of the Reldan family, Gimbel Davis was romantically involved with Reldan when he was married to Judy.

Reldan's sole purpose in calling Gimbel Davis was to counter Detective Ralph Cenicola's report of an incriminating statement that Reldan had allegedly made to Gimbel Davis. Cenicola said that Roberta Gimbel told him, in an interview, that Reldan asked her not to take investigators to Old Mill Road or Tallman Park "because it would look bad" for him. In her new appearance on behalf of the defense, Gimbel Davis said that she had never said that to Cenicola. On cross-examination, Buckley established the woman's close relationship with Reldan. Asked to weigh Gimbel Davis's likely bias in favor of Reldan versus Detective Cenicola's credibility, it would not have been hard for jurors to come down on the side of Cenicola.

Reldan spent all his court time on March 5 with FBI witnesses, trying to get Ed Denning's interview of Eileen Dalton, the bridge toll collector, into evidence. Contrary to Frank Wagner's advice, Reldan was obsessed with getting Dalton's observations on October 14, 1975, into the case. But DAG Buckley effectively blocked those attempts. Any recollection that the FBI agents had of the girl's interview would be hearsay, and Kuechenmeister wasn't about to allow that violation of evidence rules. Reldan would have to put Eileen Dalton, herself, on the witness stand—if he could find her. Later, he would call Dalton's brother to the stand to try to get him to reveal, outside the presence of the jury, his sister's whereabouts, but he refused and Kuechenmeister would not force the brother, a Fort Lee police officer at the time, to comply. Reldan would raise that refusal on appeal, but the appellate courts gave it short shrift.

In a last ditch attempt to somehow get the Dalton observations into the trial, without Dalton appearing, Reldan would also call Jim Lillis to the stand. Lillis manned the toll collection booth next to Dalton on the night of October 14. Lillis's memory of the 10-year-old incident was so spotty as to render his testimony useless to the jury.

On March 6, Reldan's first witness was his old standby, Irene Lippert, the corrections officer who managed the food services operation at Rahway State Prison. Before Reldan got far into his direct examination, Buckley objected to the witness's testimony on the ground that it had no relevancy to the murder case. Judge Kuechenmeister excused the jury and allowed Reldan to continue with his direct examination. In effect, he was giving Reldan a chance to show the relevancy of Lippert's testimony outside the presence of the jury. If Reldan succeeded, the jury would have been brought back into the courtroom and Reldan would have gone over the same ground in front of the jury. Unfortunately for Reldan, he had not discussed Lippert's testimony with her beforehand, as any competent attorney would have done, refreshing her recollection as required.

Reldan's purpose with Lippert was to cast aspersions on the character of Clifford and Allison Williams, in order to discredit Clifford's earlier testimony regarding Reldan's incriminating statements. But Lippert could scarcely recall *anything* about the Williams brothers, except that she didn't trust them—hardly a sound basis for her testimony. She was imprecise and unresponsive, so much so that Reldan, himself, had to withdraw her as a defense witness. She left the stand. Without seeing or hearing from her again, the jury was left with the inescapable conclusion that it was just one more screw up by Reldan, in his own defense.

Next, Reldan called three jurors from Reldan II—Sharron Suffern, Peter Carson, and Mary Lou Daub. With Suffern and Carson, Reldan's purpose was to bring out the bribery attempt, in order to explain or justify his escape during the trial. But, in his cross-examination, Buckley showed that Mrs. Suffern was removed from the jury with Reldan's knowledge, so she did not sit in judgment and, therefore, Reldan had no reason to be fearful of the bribery attempt tainting her deliberations. Buckley showed that Carson never got possession of the bribery letter addressed to him, which Reldan also knew. Again, there was no reason for Reldan to fear Carson remaining on the jury.

With both Ms. Daub and Carson, Reldan tried to raise the issue of Bernice Caplan's near-faint as she left the witness stand at the end of the second trial, still trying to justify his escape. Reldan couldn't bring out anything about Caplan's emotional testimony, or he would have shown himself to be a rapist. He could only show that a witness had almost fainted when she completed her testimony and that someone—perhaps her husband—had assisted her from the courtroom. It was hardly enough to convince jurors that Reldan had a bona fide reason to spray tear gas in the faces of VanDerWerf and Grimaldi while staging a wild escape from an ongoing trial.

Dr. Marvin Aronson, the Medical Examiner from the City of Philadelphia, was actually a good expert witness for the defense, and Reldan handled direct examination well. He called Aronson to refute Dr. Frederick Zugibe's conclusion that the strangulation method used on both murder victims pointed to the same killer.

"There's no way a forensic pathologist can conclude," Aronson said, "even if all the details were identical, that the two incidents were definitely made or performed by the same individual. There may be other evidence that indicates that, but it's not within the expertise of the forensic pathologist to say so."

Aronson also said that Zugibe's opinion about the contusion and abrasion on Susan Reeve's vaginal wall did not necessarily mean a forcible penetration had occurred. There could have been other explanations, he said, something that would *not* lead to a conclusion of rape.

On cross-examination, Buckley brought out that Aronson had read Zugibe's report but had not spoken to him; did not examine scientific evidence that the Rockland ME had gathered in the two autopsies; and had not viewed specific photos of the forcible penetration evidence. In the end, it was a matter of dueling experts, and Zugibe seemed to have the upper hand in that battle.

March 6 was a busy day for the defense. Reldan called another expert witness, on the subject of tides. His purpose was to show that Susan Reeve's body may have come to its final resting place in the marshes of Tallman Mountain State Park, right next to the Hudson River, through the natural action of the tides in that area. In other words, someone could have dumped the body into the Hudson River at another location, and the tides could have carried the body to the spot where Conklin first saw it.

Reldan's expert spouted technical terms that likely went over the jurors' heads, but his theory on how Susan Reeve's body may have found its way to the park location near where Reldan and Roberta Davis had picnicked—well, that was so far-fetched as to be just another obvious waste of the jurors' time.

Another defense expert, a botany professor at Rutgers University, never made it to the witness stand. Frank Wagner had engaged him to refute Dr. Zugibe's contention that the leaves he found embedded in Susan Reeve's body were willow leaves. That conclusion by Zugibe reinforced the State's position that the Reeve body had been moved, probably from a site in Valley Cottage near where Susan Heynes's body was found and where willow trees abounded, to the site in Tallman State Park, where no willow trees could be found.

Wagner didn't have time to interview the witness before he showed up for court, so he invited Buckley to join him when he met with the professor in the hallway. Attorneys have an obligation to share expert reports before the expert takes the stand, and Wagner was fulfilling that obligation in a collegial way with Buckley.

Wagner showed the tree expert an autopsy picture of Reeve's body, which depicted the embedded leaves.

"That's interesting," the expert said. "Those are willow leaves embedded in the body."

"Thank you, Sir," Wagner said, "I won't be needing your testimony." When testimony ended that Thursday, the jury and participants were treated to another three-day weekend. Things would pick up again on Monday morning, March 10, with a criminal trial rarity—the testimony of a sitting judge, called to the stand by the defendant.

* * *

One of the first questions Reldan asked of Judge Paul Huot about his presiding over Reldan II was, "Were there any unusual incidents relating to the jury that you can recall?" Huot properly responded that, indeed, there were.

Reldan was once again trying to explain to current jurors the reason for his escape. The prosecution would characterize that escape as the defendant's consciousness of guilt—and would get a jury instruction to that effect—and, to counter that, Reldan wanted to show that his motive was a good one (in his mind, anyway): namely that he felt he was being railroaded during the course of that trial, particularly on the basis of some jurors receiving bribery letters. One of those jurors, Lewis Blanda, had actually read the letter and had been in contact with a fellow juror, who was his roommate in the sequestration hotel. The fact that Blanda knew about the letter's contents was not discovered until later, after Blanda had a chance to infect his juror roommate.

Judge Huot had not reviewed the prior trial's transcripts before testifying, so his memory of the events six and a half years earlier was not sharp; however, he did refresh his recollection by looking at certain passages that Reldan had pointed out to him. In doing so, Huot reaffirmed the very point Buckley made when the actual jurors in Reldan II had been called to the stand days earlier. All jurors who were potentially tainted as a result of the bribery attempt—including Blanda's roommate—were removed from the jury and did not participate in deliberations. And Reldan knew that. Therefore, it would have been hard for Reldan III jurors to swallow the defendant's rationale that the attempted bribery letter gave him cause to escape.

Reldan's defense investigator finally located Stephen Prato in California, and the young man was subpoenaed to testify on the afternoon of March 10. Once again, Reldan's purpose was to insert a red herring into the case—a situation where someone else could have been in pursuit of Susan Reeve as she walked home that evening. Though Prato had not been able to identify Reldan, he gave a pretty good description of the man stalking the young woman, and the description fit Reldan well: 5' 10" to 6 feet tall, 170 to 190 pounds in weight, muscular and athletic-looking, with dark hair and wearing workman's clothing. On cross-examination, Prato said that he couldn't say it was Reldan and he couldn't say it was not Reldan.

Prato could easily have been recounting a valid part of Susan Reeve's experience that evening. The location of his observations was south of where Raymond Lozier had made his observations, but on the opposite side of Anderson Avenue. The difference was not necessarily an unexplainable conflict. Reldan could very well have taken control of Susan Reeve, shortly after Prato saw him stalking her, and led her across the street to where his Opel wagon was parked—the spot where Lozier made his observations.

Reldan ended the day's testimony by calling his sister, Susan Reldan, to the stand. He tried to establish that investigators asked her if anyone in their family had access to a green car, an obvious reference, again, to the Eileen Dalton matter. She answered no, but it is hard to believe that the jury could make heads or tails out of this sequence without Dalton as a witness. Reldan also tried to establish that his sister knew him to be a regular buyer and seller of jewelry in New York City, as if that would explain his sale and repurchase of Heynes's engagement ring. Susan Reldan's testimony boiled down to a loving sister's attempt to help her brother's case.

With the trial nearing its end, Reldan had one final witness on Tuesday, March 11. He called Ralph Cenicola, the retired BCPO detective. Again, his purpose was to show the BCPO's futile search for a green car— the vehicle that Eileen Dalton had reported—that Reldan might have had access to. Again, the exercise was likely nothing but a blur for jurors, who still had no clear idea of the green car's significance.

Buckley had no need to cross-examine the former detective. When Cenicola left the witness stand, Reldan rested his case. Buckley called one more witness in rebuttal, an investigator with the Rockland County Bureau of Criminal Identification. The officer was familiar with tidal waters in the Hudson River, near where it converged with the swampland adjacent to Tallman Mountain State Park. He testified, from personal experience, that the tidal flow never reached levels that could transport a body to the location where Susan Reeve's body was found. The expert witness whom Reldan had put on the stand to float this preposterous theory had not visited the site and probably had little credence with the jury, but Buckley was not one to take a chance. He tied up that loose end with his rebuttal witness, putting the issue to rest.

With testimony completed, all that remained were summations by Reldan and Buckley, to be followed by the judge's charge to the jury. Reldan began his final argument shortly after the lunch break. He talked for two-and-one-half hours straight. Judge Kuechenmeister sensed that the jury was getting tired and called Reldan and Buckley to side bar to see how much longer Reldan thought he would be. Reldan said a half hour to an hour and fifteen minutes more, and the judge decided to break for the day to allow Reldan to pick up where he left off in the morning. On Wednesday, Reldan did just that, telling the jury at the start, "I have some good news for you and some bad news. I'm not starting at the beginning. I've lost my voice, but it is still going to take me about an hour." In fact, Reldan spoke for another hour and a half.

Reldan's summation was excruciating in its detail—so much so that it lost effectiveness. He reviewed the testimony of just about every witness in the case, important or not, rambling at times and, at other times, misstating or misremembering the actual evidence presented. He was obsessed with exposing discrepancies, no matter how inconsequential they may have been. It is difficult to imagine how any juror could have maintained attentiveness through the ordeal.

In contrast, DAG Buckley took less than an hour and a half, crisply pulling the case together for the jury. He followed his KISS strategy through to the end.

Before charging the jury, the judge decided to question each of the jurors individually and in chambers to ensure that none of them harbored ill feelings toward the defendant because of William Reldan's staring incident earlier in the trial. Reldan had requested that the jurors be questioned on this, and, at first, the judge refused. But he had second thoughts and did not want to leave the issue out there for appeal. It took some time, but the judge was satisfied that none of the jurors attached any importance to the incident. Most didn't even recall or remember anything untoward happening; the few who did said that it would not influence their deliberations.

The judge then delivered his jury charge, ending with the set piece, "You may now take the case, members of the jury, and render such verdicts based on the instructions given to you in my charge, as your conscience, reason, and candid opinion deem to be just and proper."

From the 15 jurors who heard the entire case, three alternates were selected. They stood aside as the final 12 members retired at 2:50 PM on March 13, 1986, to begin deliberations. Shortly after 5:00 PM, the judge asked the parties if they wanted the jury to continue, or if they would prefer to adjourn until the following morning. They put the question to the jurors, who, at 6:10 PM, sent back a note: "We all concur to adjourn until 9:00 AM tomorrow."

The jurors resumed deliberations at 9:10 AM on March 13. At 11:05 AM, they requested that Closter jeweler John Truncali's testimony be read back to them. That process took 40 minutes, after which the jury again retired to resume deliberations. By 2:45 PM, they had reached a verdict. Robert Reldan and Frank Wagner were seated at the defense table and DAG Charles Buckley was seated at the prosecutor's table when the clerk of the court made the time-honored formal inquiry: "Foreman of the jury, please rise. Have you reached a verdict?"

"Yes, we have," said the jury foreman.

"As to Count One, Susan Heynes, murder in the second degree," the clerk said.

"Guilty," declared the foreman.

"Is your verdict unanimous?" the clerk asked.

"Yes."

"As to Count Two, Susan Reeve, murder in the first degree," the clerk asked.

"Guilty."

"Is your verdict unanimous?" asked the clerk.

"Yes."

Judge Kuechenmeister then asked the clerk to poll the jury, whereupon each juror was required to verify the verdict as to each count. Robert Reldan sat while affirmation of his guilt rang out, loud and clear, 12 times for Susan Heynes and 12 times for Susan Reeve.

The judge thanked the jurors for their service. When they were excused, he ordered a presentence report and set April 25, 1986, as the sentencing date. In the meantime, he remanded Reldan to Trenton State Prison to continue serving his other sentences.

On April 25, the parties reassembled in Judge Kuechenmeister's courtroom for sentencing. The judge asked Wagner if he wanted to say anything on behalf of the defendant, and the public defender obliged by making what amounted to a perfunctory statement, with little of the emotion he had displayed almost seven years earlier after Reldan II ended. The judge next turned to Reldan and asked if he had anything to say before the sentence was pronounced. Reldan used the opportunity to complain about the criminal justice system in Bergen County and to declare his innocence, blaming his indictment and conviction on a conspiring prosecutor's office.

Judge Kuechenmeister was not impressed.

"Two lovely young women," the judge began, "appeared to have futures destined for happiness and fulfillment, only to have that promise suddenly end in horror, degradation, and pain. Words are inadequate to describe the abject evil of these depraved acts. The pain and tragedy does not end with their deaths. There is the pain of the heart that the loved ones of these young women will carry to their graves.

"It has been said," the judge continued, "that the courts have awesome power, but that power cannot bring Susan Reeve and Susan Heynes one more second of life, nor can that power mitigate one second of the horror and pain of their final moments of life. But this court can act so that no other woman's life and virtue can be put in jeopardy by this defendant."

Judge Kuechenmeister then sentenced Robert Reldan to 30 years in prison for the second-degree murder of Susan Heynes, consecutive to all other sentences that he was then serving. He also imposed life imprisonment for the first-degree murder of Susan Reeve, consecutive to the Heynes sentence and consecutive to all other sentences that Reldan was then serving.

Ten and a half years after committing two of the most heinous crimes in Bergen County and New Jersey history, Robert Reldan was finally brought to justice. Appeals would consume additional years and more criminal justice resources, but this time the convictions stuck. The Appellate Division of the Superior Court denied Reldan's appeal on May 15, 1989, remanding the matter back to Kuechenmeister solely on the issue of a minimum term on the second-degree murder sentence. He had imposed the maximum term of 30 years, but had failed to impose a required minimum term. On remand, the Keek set 29 years, 364 days as Reldan's minimum term. The Public Defender's Office filed a petition for certification with the New Jersey Supreme Court on November 30, 1989. On January 17, 1990, the Court denied that petition.

The case was over, for good. Reldan had been put away, for good, just as every judge involved in his cases over the years had thought necessary for the protection of society. But, in time, Aunt Lillian would reenter the picture and make her Bobby a millionaire, the richest lifer in the New Jersey prison system. Robert R. Reldan would have at his disposal the finest lawyers money could buy and the best expert witnesses money could buy—the resources, in other words, to convince a parole board that this charming man, no longer young but still at his scheming best, deserved another chance at freedom.

The future looked promising for Robert Reldan, until octogenarian Arthur Reeve, Susan Reeve's father and, now and forever, her champion, brought the curtain crashing down on inmate #62212 using the most potent weapon at his disposal—due process of law.

Chapter 28

Money from a double-murderer . . . to educate young men and women.

Lillian Booth died of a stroke on November 22, 2007, leaving an estate valued at $220 million. Despite having donated millions during her lifetime to Columbia University (Ferris Booth's alma mater), hospitals and health clinics, churches, a home for aged and infirm actors, and other causes, she had more than quadrupled the inheritance left to her by Ferris Booth.

"An angel on earth—that's what she was," Misha Dabich, her 51-year companion was quoted as saying in *The Record*. "She did more for others than she did for herself. Every man should have a gal like her. She took care of her community. She took care of her family."

She also took care of Robert Reldan, although indirectly. Her will, which was executed on June 11, 1958, when Reldan was just 18 years old, was a legal tangle of trusts, terms, and conditions. The bulk of her estate went to five siblings, or to the children of those siblings if any of her brothers and sisters did not survive her. In fact, all of Lillian Booth's siblings, including Marie Reldan, predeceased her. In that way, nephew Robert Reldan became eligible for his share of his mother's share, along with his sister, Susan Reldan Peck.

The estate shares for all beneficiaries were to be held in a trust, with each beneficiary getting income from the trust, but not the principal. The principal was to be kept intact, with its final disbursement to be paid to descendants of the original heirs.

The will was a tangle that Booth's lawyers took 17 pages to set forth, but the result, after taxes and legal fees, was that Robert Reldan, himself, became the beneficiary of a trust worth $8.9 million. He was to get the annual income every year of his remaining life (the amount would depend on the rate of return on the trust's investments), but could not touch the principal. Upon Reldan's death, because he had no natural children of his own (Eddie was Judy Reldan's natural child, not his), income from his trust would revert to Susan Reldan Peck for her lifetime; then all that was left—principal and income—would go to her children.

Despite all Reldan's crimes—two murders, at least two rapes, more than a dozen assaults and robberies, countless burglaries, and a conspiracy to rob and kill Lillian and her companion, Misha Dabich—Aunt Lillian Booth never took steps to block nephew Bobby's potential inheritance. It would have been a simple thing to do, as simple as picking up a phone and telling her lawyer to draft a codicil. But she never did.

Because of Lillian Booth's wealth and celebrity, especially in the New York metropolitan area, her death and the circumstances surrounding the distribution of her estate—markedly, the sizeable share going to a convicted murderer—received wide publicity. Word got to Arthur and Barbara Reeve, then retired and living in Florida, that their daughter's killer was about to reap a windfall, and the thought of that person coming into such wealth incensed Arthur Reeve. There was little good the money would do Reldan in his prison environment, but it could surely finance his efforts to win release on parole—something Arthur Reeve could not stomach. Reeve resolved to do something about it. He retained the Hackensack law firm of Joseph Rem and Robert Zeller to investigate what legal steps he could take to deprive Robert Reldan of his inheritance.

Arthur Reeve had no intention of keeping the money for himself. His purpose was to make sure that Robert Reldan remained in prison, uncomforted and unaided by wealth that he didn't deserve. Soon after Susan's death, her father and mother set up a scholarship fund in her memory at Hollins University in Roanoke, Virginia, the school from which Susan had graduated just months before she died. Arthur Reeve was about to bring a lawsuit against Robert Reldan, and any proceeds from that action would go to that memorial fund.

Robert Zeller, the lead attorney working on Arthur Reeve's behalf, had his work cut out for him. The law, as it then existed, was on the side of the murderer, not the Reeve family. The so-called "Son of Sam" law, which prevents murderers from garnering book or movie deals and profiting from their crimes, did not apply. Reldan's newfound wealth wasn't derived from such sources. But two legal premises under New Jersey law might support the contemplated legal action: the "Wrongful Death Act" and the "Survivor's Act."

Prior to 2000, a two-year statute of limitations applied to both of those laws, imposing a requirement that the lawsuit be brought within two years of the "cause of action"—that is, the death-causing event. In 2000, the New Jersey legislature removed the two-year limitation in the case of Wrongful Death Act lawsuits, but failed to do so in the case of Survivor's Act lawsuits. That oversight drastically reduced the Reeve lawsuit's potential because damages under the Wrongful Death Act were limited to economic losses. Susan Reeve had been out of college a few short months and had not come close to her potential earning capacity; moreover, she was single and had no children. The economic loss suffered by her parents would be negligible, hardly causing a dent in Reldan's finances. The true measure of the Reeves' loss was the pain and suffering they would endure for the rest of their lives because of their daughter's murder—but pain and suffering were only compensable through the Survivor's Act, which still had the two-year statute of limitations.

Attorney Robert Zeller's approach to the problem was brilliant. His first step was to file a lawsuit in Bergen County under the Wrongful Death Act, which he followed up on December 9, 2008, by obtaining a pre-judgment "writ of attachment" precluding the estate of Lillian Booth, a party defendant in the suit, from making any distributions under the will. Zeller then set about trying to determine whether the legislative omission in 2000 was intentional or inadvertent. He approached the co-sponsors of that legislation, and they acknowledged that the omission of the Survivor's Act from their bill was inadvertent; they had meant to remove the two-year limitation from lawsuits filed under that act, too, but had left it out. Armed with affidavits from those legislators, Robert Zeller amended his original lawsuit to include a Survivor's Act claim against Reldan for the pain and suffering he had caused the Reeves.

Zeller then approached State Senator Gerald Cardinale and State Assemblyman David Russo and obtained their support in sponsoring a new bill that removed the two-year limitation from Survivor's Act lawsuits arising from homicides. The bill passed both houses of the New Jersey legislature and was signed into law on January 17, 2010, by Governor Jon Corzine, shortly before he left office.

Three days after amending the lawsuit, Zeller moved for summary judgment on the issue of liability. His argument was that Reldan's conviction for the murder of Susan Reeve under the criminal law standard of "beyond a reasonable doubt" had effectively decided that issue, since the civil law standard is lower. Superior Court Judge John Langan agreed. In April, 2010, the judge granted summary judgment to the Reeves, ending the lawsuit, except for the amount of damages to be awarded. At that point, Reldan, through his attorneys, offered to settle the case for $1,000,000. Arthur and Barbara Reeve rejected the offer, which would have left substantial resources at Reldan's disposal, even after paying out the settlement.

Preparations for trial on the issue of damages went forward. That included the right of the plaintiffs—the Reeves, through their attorneys— to depose the defendant, Robert Reldan. On June 8, 2010, Robert Zeller and Michelle Sweet, an attorney in the Rem Zeller Law Group, journeyed to Trenton State Prison to take the defendant's video deposition. It would be the first time Robert Reldan would be required, under oath, to answer questions about his murder of Susan Reeve.

Reldan had already admitted that he caused the death of Susan Reeve. That admission came not in any trial or other legal proceeding, but in Reldan's February 2009 hearings before the New Jersey Parole Board. He met with the Board twice that month. Reldan hired Raymond M. Brown, a criminal defense attorney with a national reputation, to champion his parole application and shepherd it through the process. Reldan knew from experience that a prerequisite to a successful parole bid was the inmate's acceptance of responsibility for his criminal behavior, so, he told the state parole board he was responsible for the deaths of both women. But he did so in *Reldan* fashion. That is, he admitted his responsibility in a way that lessened, to the extent possible, his culpability for the crimes.

Reldan followed the same tack in his June 2010 deposition, but attorney Robert Zeller's aggressive questioning exposed Reldan's invented scenario for Susan Reeve's death for what it was—a pack of lies. It was also clear that Reldan's memory had deteriorated,* a problem for liars because they can't keep their stories straight. Reldan had a goal that he wanted to achieve with his not-so-carefully crafted story of the death. He wanted it to appear almost as an accident. He had meant only to rob Susan Reeve, not kill her. And the way Reldan told the story . . . well, among the bizarre details Reldan had contrived, the most grotesque was surely Reldan's assertion that Susan Reeve actually had a hand in causing her own death.

Zeller asked Reldan how he first came to view Susan Reeve that day, October 14, 1975. Reldan said that he was heading home from the house-painting job in Closter between 5:30 and 6:00, just before sundown. He was driving south on Anderson Avenue when he saw a "handful" of people get off a commuter bus and walk toward Anderson, among them the woman he later learned was Susan Reeve. We can immediately see inconsistencies between Reldan's version of events and the known facts. Driver John O'Hanlon had said that he made an unexpected stop to let a young woman off his bus on County Road, about 75 to 100 feet past its intersection with Anderson Avenue, and that the woman—who had to have been Susan Reeve—was the only person who got off. Reldan could not have seen her get off the bus from the vantage point of someone driving south on Anderson, well before it ran into County Road. And there was no handful of commuters who got off with her—she was alone.

Reldan also said that he saw her walking north on Anderson, on the west side of that roadway, as he was driving south. He said he thought he recognized her from a chance encounter he had with the same woman a week or two beforehand, at a Friendly's restaurant. Supposedly, he was leaving Friendly's (he didn't remember where the restaurant was) as a young woman wearing expensive jewelry was entering. On October 14, as he was driving south on Anderson, Reldan said, he thought the woman

---

*At one point, Zeller asked Reldan when he married Judy Rosenberg. Reldan responded, "November 7, 1971." He was off by almost four years. His marriage certificate shows June 17, 1975, as the date.

he saw walking was the same woman he vaguely remembered from the Friendly's encounter. And, on the spur of the moment, he decided to rob her of the jewelry she was probably wearing; that robbery would take place right there on the well traveled thoroughfare of Anderson Avenue.

The pure fantasy of this story is apparent. Reldan had never, in his 20-year criminal career, committed a daylight robbery—out in the open—as he was describing. Also, one must keep in mind that Reldan was not financially strapped at the time. He would tell BCPO Investigator Ed Denning in an interview eight days later that he had about $14,000 in the bank. Out on parole for less than six months, Reldan would not likely have risked his freedom on the possibility that a woman he glimpsed as he drove by was the same woman he'd seen wearing expensive jewelry a week or two before as they walked past each other in a restaurant. It's mind-boggling that Reldan, an intelligent man if nothing else, found this story plausible. But, then again, he had also crafted the "hoax" explanation for plotting the robbery and murder of his aunt, so maybe he wasn't as smart as people allowed.

Keep in mind that Reldan did not form this part of his story—the motivation behind his initial encounter with Susan Reeve—on the spur of the moment. It was meant to be a version that he could use to win parole, and he had plenty of time to think that through. He could *not* deny responsibility for Reeve's death; the parole board would not countenance that. But Reldan could only accept responsibility in a way that would not portray him as a sexual predator. If the board viewed him as such, there was a risk that he would go after women again, despite his age, and they would surely deny him. But if the board accepted that he was motivated by money—the profit he would get from stolen jewelry—well, then, in his mind, he would have a better chance. As the beneficiary of an $8.9 million trust fund, he would never again have a need to rob and steal.

In response to Zeller's asking what he did after noticing the young woman walking north on Anderson Avenue as he was driving south, Reldan said he drove down to the T-intersection with County Road and made a U-turn, to head north again on Anderson in the direction the woman was walking. He had made the decision he was going to rob her. He drove past her once again, and then, some distance north of her, he made another U-turn and went back in her direction, stopping along side the roadway, still north of her on Anderson. He had parked on the west side of Anderson, facing south. He watched as the girl walked toward him.

Reldan's story has Susan Reeve on the west side of Anderson Avenue, exclusively, from the time she got off the bus until the time he encountered her, but we know from the testimony of Mary and Joseph Fabrocini that Susan Reeve crossed Anderson in front of them and started

THECHARMER

walking north on the east side of Anderson, where there was a sidewalk. We also know from Joseph Fabrocini that Reldan made his turn onto Anderson to follow the young woman coming *from* County Road and not by a U-turn on Anderson at the intersection.

As the woman he later learned was Susan Reeve approached his parked Opel wagon, Reldan said he got out when she was three or four car lengths away and went to the rear of his vehicle to wait for her. Once again, it was still light out—near dusk, but not dark—and there was traffic on Anderson, according to Reldan, passing from both directions.

"Now, describe for us what happened next," Zeller said.

"Once she came abreast of me," Reldan said, "that's when I said, 'This is a robbery. Give me all your jewelry.'"

After clarifying which direction Reldan was facing at the time, Zeller asked him to repeat what he said to Susan Reeve. Reldan replied, "Something to the effect of, 'This is a robbery. Give me all your jewelry and your cash.'"

In the ensuing exchange between Robert Zeller and Reldan, the convicted double murderer's story becomes more incredible.

"What happened next?" Zeller asked.

"We just stood there looking at each other for a couple of seconds," Reldan said. "And then she said, 'What?'"

"Okay," Zeller said. "And then what did you say or do?"

"I repeated what I had said," Reldan said. "I said, 'This is a robbery. Give me your jewelry and cash.'"

Zeller asked, "And what happened next?"

"She was still looking at me and she said, 'Don't I know you?'" Reldan said. "And I said, 'No. Just give me the jewelry and cash.'"

Zeller continued. "And what happened next?"

"And she kept repeating, 'Don't I know you? I think I know you,'" Reldan said. "And I said to myself, 'Oh, crap.'"

"Why are you thinking that?" Zeller asked.

"Because if she does know me, I'm screwed," Reldan said. "It won't go down as a random robbery. She'll be able to pick me out."

Manipulating his description of the scene, Reldan suggested that Susan Reeve remembered him from the alleged, brief encounter a week or two before at some Friendly's restaurant and, because of that prior meeting, which may have lasted a second or two as he walked into the restaurant and she was leaving, she would be able to identify him as her attempted robber. Never mind that, if his story were true up to this point, she would have been in his presence far longer during the robbery attempt than during the restaurant pass-by. The stretching of credulity would increase tenfold as Reldan's story progressed.

"And what happened next?" Zeller asked.

"I said, 'The hell with this,' to myself and started to go back," Reldan said.

"You started to go back?"

"Around my car," Reldan said.

"So for what purpose did you start to go back?" Zeller asked.

"I was going to get in the car and leave," Reldan said.

"And what happened next?"

"As I am walking away," Reldan said, "*she's following behind me saying, 'I know you, I know you.'*" (Emphasis added.) Amazingly, Reldan was suggesting that Susan Reeve, after he had just tried to rob her, became the aggressor and followed him as he was trying to abandon his robbery attempt and leave her alone.

"And you kept walking?" Zeller asked.

"Right."

"And where did you walk to?" Zeller asked.

"The back of my car," said Reldan.

"And what was she doing as you continued to walk to the back of your car?" Zeller asked.

"Following behind me," Reldan claimed.

"How far behind you was she?" Zeller asked.

"Couple of steps."

"And what was the tone of her voice?" Zeller asked.

"Just she was talking loud," Reldan said. "'I know you. I know you.'" Reldan added that he turned back toward the woman and said, "Listen, just forget it."

"What was going through your mind as you were walking toward the back of your car and she was speaking to you?" Zeller asked.

"I got to get out of here," he claimed.

"So you get to the back of your car and you said you turned and you faced her and you said, 'Just forget it.' Is that correct?" Zeller asked.

"Words to that effect."

"And what happened next?"

"I noticed some cars on both sides of the road coming down and coming up," Reldan said.

"So there were cars that would be passing you in both directions," Zeller said. "Is that what you are saying?"

"Well, either passing or about to pass," Reldan said.

"And so, what did you do when you noticed the cars passing or about to pass?" Zeller asked.

"When I tried to go back around the car out into the street, she came behind me," Reldan said.

"So you were walking behind your car trying to get around to the driver's side?" Zeller asked.

"Right."

"So you were behind your car and she continued to follow you," Zeller said.

"Right."

"And what were you saying to her and what, if anything, was she saying to you?" Zeller asked.

Now, we come to the part when Reldan explains how he caused the death of Susan Reeve, how he accepted responsibility for that.

"Well, at that point in time," Reldan said, "it looked like she wasn't going to stop following me, so I turned back and I reached out and I grabbed her around the neck." Reldan went on to explain that he thought that cars were still passing them on Anderson Avenue while this scenario was playing out, but he wasn't paying attention to the cars, he was concentrating on the woman, who wouldn't stop following him. Zeller asked him how he knew that Susan Reeve was still following him when he was trying to walk away from her. Presumably, his back was toward her. He said, "I could hear her footsteps."

Zeller asked what happened after Reldan grabbed Susan Reeve by the neck. "And what happened next?" he asked.

"When I stepped back," he said, "I reached out and grabbed her and I said, 'Listen, stop following me.' And I guess she attempted to struggle and I felt something snap." In saying that he "felt something snap," Reldan tried to make his story fit the fact that Susan Reeve's hyoid bone was broken, as determined by the autopsy.

Zeller asked whether Susan said anything in response to his demand that she stop following him.

"She didn't have time to," Reldan said.

"So you said you grabbed the front of her throat?" Zeller asked.

"Right."

"And you squeezed," Zeller said.

"Yes."

"And you felt something snap?" Zeller asked.

"Right," Said Reldan, who went on to say that she "looked shocked" and "had a startled expression" on her face. He said he heard a "snap" and could feel "a vibration. A pop." He said, "I didn't realize I was squeezing. I just—I wanted to control her. I wanted her to stop following me."

"And what happened the moment you felt something snap?" Zeller asked.

"Her legs gave way and she collapsed," Reldan said, adding that she fell to the road. He was going to leave but he saw that she was partially in the roadway and he didn't want her to get run over by any cars, so he went back to move her to the side of the road. "When it looked like she wasn't breathing," Reldan said, "I took her carotid pulse, in her neck pulse." He felt no pulse, then felt for a heartbeat. There was none. That's when he knew that she was dead.

Reldan estimated that, from the time he felt something in Susan Reeve's neck snap to the time he determined, at the side of the road, that she was dead, approximately 35 to 45 seconds had elapsed. All the while, cars were passing the scene while it was still light enough to see clearly, for 35 to 45 seconds, and not one person stopped to investigate a situation in which a man had his hand on the throat of a woman, who struggled briefly and then fell to the ground and was dragged to the side of the road. By this point in Reldan's contrived story, it is hard to imagine how any sane person could give it an ounce of credibility. But the story gets even more bizarre, if that is possible.

After seeing that the woman was dead, Reldan said that he did not want to leave her body there at the side of the road, for fear that his crime would be discovered right away. So, he dragged her to the passenger side of his car, opened the door, and stuffed her body into the front passenger-side floor, thus accounting for the FBI lab finding Susan Reeve's hair on that floor mat. Again, while he was dragging the body (Zugibe's autopsy found no evidence of drag marks) and lifting it into his Opel wagon, cars were still whizzing by and no one stopped to investigate or render assistance. Reldan said that he drove to Route 9W and took that highway north to Tallman Mountain State Park, with which he was familiar because he had been there during the summer with Roberta Gimbel Davis. By the time he got to the park, it was dark.

In describing this trip, Reldan estimated that the park was 45 miles from the point where he got on route 9W and that it took him 20 minutes to get there. Obviously, those two numbers are mutually exclusive—he would have had to drive 135 m.p.h. to accomplish that feat. The park was actually about 10 miles away. The mistake is illustrative of Reldan making up things as he went along with this story. Any relation to reality was a side benefit, but not required.

Reldan said that he did not recall having or using a flashlight to see his way. He said he had not decided how to dispose of the body. He thought about digging a hole in the park with his hands (he didn't have a shovel), and then he saw "some weeds by the water that looked fairly thick." He decided to dump the body there, but first removed all the girl's clothing and jewelry to prevent her from being identified. As he took off her pantyhose, an idea struck him.

"I said, let me try to confuse the investigation a little more," Reldan told Zeller. "So I wrapped them [the pantyhose]—since I knew I had strangled her by hand, I said, let me try to make it look like something different."

Reldan had to account for the pantyhose ligature around Susan Reeve's neck, so he came up with the absurd explanation that he was a trying to confound investigators. It served only to highlight his scheming nature, both in the lawsuit and in his parole application. It would fool no one.

At this point in the deposition, Zeller backtracked, asking Reldan how long his hand was on Susan Reeve's neck before he felt something snap. He replied, "Maybe 15 seconds." Again, the response indicates Reldan's disconnect from the implausibility of his story. If he was trying to push Susan Reeve away to prevent her from following him and, in the process, accidentally strangled her and fractured her hyoid bone, 15 seconds is an inordinate amount of time for that *accident* to play out. Instead, it shows a conscious desire to kill—not to defend.

After picking up the body and carrying it about 10 feet to the water, Reldan said that he dropped it, got back in his car, and drove away. On the way home, he stopped and buried Susan Reeve's clothing and jewelry in a wooded area, digging the hole with his hands. He arrived back home in Tenafly about eight o'clock. Judy and her son Eddie were there. He said that he and Judy had a discussion when he got home—understandable, considering the state he must have been in—but he couldn't recall what they said.

Reldan claimed that he never touched Susan Reeve sexually, another departure from the autopsy evidence.

In a civil action deposition, an attorney is allowed to pursue a wide range of subjects—anything that might lead to discovery of relevant information. With that in mind, Zeller probed into Susan Heynes's case.

"Do you know who Susan Heynes is?" Zeller asked.

"Yes," Reldan said.

"Who is Susan Heynes?" Zeller asked.

"One of my claimed victims," Reldan said.

"What do you mean, 'claimed victims'?" asked Zeller.

"One of the victims I was charged with," Reldan said.

"Did you cause the death of Susan Heynes?" Zeller asked.

"It's part of the public record," Reldan said. "I was convicted."

"I'm asking you of your personal knowledge, did you cause the death of Susan Heynes?" Zeller asked.

"I was convicted of it," Reldan said again. He would not answer Zeller's direct question, although he would say that he came into contact with Susan Heynes at her home in Haworth in October, 1975. With that, the deposition ended. But it did, in fact, have a positive outcome for the Reeve lawsuit. The lawyers on both sides began settlement discussions while at the deposition, and those discussions eventually led to a resolution of the case.

On September 15, 2010, Judge Langan issued a 19-page consent judgment against Robert Reldan and in favor of the Reeves for $10 million. The judgment was to be secured by a writ of attachment against Reldan's $8.9 million trust. The interest the trust had already earned amounted to just over $1 million, which was being held in escrow (because Zeller blocked its distribution at the outset). Of that amount, the consent judgment decreed that $131,000 would be paid to Reldan's attorneys, $200,000 go to Reldan, himself, and $705,000 would go to the Reeves. From future annual income earned by the trust, Reldan would get $2,080 each year deposited in his prison account, and the Reeves would get the balance, which could amount to hundreds of thousands, depending on the rates of return on the trust's various investments. The Reeves would be responsible for their own attorneys' fees out of their share of the settlement. If Reldan were to gain his parole at any time in the future, his annual stipend from the trust would increase to $50,000.

The distribution plan under the consent judgment would continue until the Reeves had received the full $10 million awarded to them or until Robert Reldan died, whichever occurred first. Upon Reldan's death, under the terms of Lillian Booth's will, his trust fund would revert to his sister or to her children, if she were not living.

When the consent judgment was entered, Robert Reldan was 70 years old. He would have to live into his nineties for the Reeves to receive the full amount of the settlement, but for Arthur and Barbara Reeve it mattered not how long he lived. Their motivation in filing suit was not monetary, and they had achieved their goal simply by depriving their daughter's killer of the unjust enrichment. The funds they were to receive from the consent judgment, after attorneys' fees, would go to the scholarship fund they had set up at Hollins University in Susan's memory.

"I think it is a wonderful resolution," Arthur Reeve would later say, "that this money that came from a double-murderer is going to go to the education of young men and women."

* * *

Within weeks of the September 15, 2010, consent judgment in the Reeves' lawsuit, noted Bergen County attorney Thomas Herten filed a similar lawsuit against Robert Reldan on behalf of Jonathan Heynes. That case was settled, too, before the end of 2010. Though the terms of the settlement remain confidential, it is safe to speculate that little, if any, part of Aunt Lillian's bequest will ever inure to the benefit of her Bobby.

Epilogue

You have an established record of manipulating people and the system.

In late summer, 2008, Robert Reldan became eligible for parole.

He had been sentenced to life in prison plus 30 years for the murders of Susan Reeve and Susan Heynes, respectively. But, at the time, a life sentence did not mean life without the possibility of parole, as it can mean now. His murder sentences were to run consecutively to other sentences he had received—notably, 20-to-25 years for the conspiracy to rob and kill Lillian Booth and Misha Dabich, 15 years for his escape from the Bergen County courthouse during Reldan II, and 15 years for his attempted escape from Trenton State Prison using Sherry Ann Stevens as an accomplice. Reldan had accumulated life plus 80 years. But, in the complicated way of determining parole eligibility, his number came up after serving about 30 of those years.

When he first became eligible, Reldan was already a beneficiary of Lillian Booth's estate. (She had died in November 2007.) The Reeve lawsuit had not yet been filed and Reldan was financially able to hire Raymond M. Brown, Esq., to represent him during his parole application process. Brown's 61-page Curriculum Vitae attested to his international reputation.

Reldan laid out an ambitious plan to win his release. He'd already taken up poetry and had won writing awards. He also continued paralegal activities, turning his efforts from personal goals to helping other prisoners, several of whom owed their releases to his help. He worked on a lawsuit that succeeded in making prison life more bearable for the mentally ill. He was active in prison ministries, working with visiting clericals. And, using part of his inheritance, Reldan set up a charitable foundation in memory of his deceased mother, Marie Vulgaris Reldan.

On February 6 and 20, 2009, Reldan went before a two-person panel of the New Jersey State Parole Board and was given an opportunity to make his case for release. He argued that the main sources of stress in his life—his father, mother, and wife, Judy—were now all deceased and would no longer impact him negatively. Because of his sizeable inheritance, Reldan said, he also had no further financial problems, which would preclude any need to rob people.

After weighing mitigating factors, including letters of support from friends and family, the two-member panel denied Reldan's parole application on April 1, 2009. In arriving at their conclusion, the board members cited nine aggravating circumstances among 27 regulations governing their decision, the most significant of which were Reldan's extensive criminal record, the nature of his most recent crimes, prior parole failures, and "insufficient problem resolution," exemplified by his lack of insight, denial, and continuing attempts to minimize his culpability. While in prison, Reldan had committed rule infractions (some 28 in all) and, more seriously, had instigated the Booth murder conspiracy and attempted the Trenton escape.

"You have an established record of manipulating people and the system," the panel told him. They concluded that, if released, Reldan would likely commit other crimes. All that remained was for the two-person panel to fix a future parole eligibility date.

For the crime of murder, the NJ Administrative Code set a 27-month incarceration period as the presumptive time before a denied inmate is eligible for a new parole hearing, with the panel having leeway to quicken or delay that time frame by nine months. In other words, the new parole eligibility date could be as early as 18 months after denial, or as late as 36 months. If a two-person panel believed the prescribed 27-month (plus or minus nine months) schedule was not sufficient, it had the right to refer the matter to a three-person panel, one empowered to set a longer parole ineligibility period. On October 8, 2010, the three-person panel issued its report.

"The panel finds that any expressions of remorse are superficial, at best," the report said. "Moreover, your current recitation of events is at stark variance with the official record and testimony offered in your trials. The panel finds that such inconsistencies, combined with a willingness to admit or deny or prevaricate based on whatever benefits you at the time, constitute an ongoing criminal thinking. It is this criminal thinking that helps to establish the likelihood of further *conscienceless* criminal behavior.

"Your preoccupation with alleged defects in the prosecution's case is alarmingly misplaced when viewed against the horror of your admitted crimes. The panel finds that the ongoing self-centered nature of your current thinking bespeaks a remorseless, selfish, dangerous, criminal mindset."

The three-person panel set 240 months, or 20 years, as Reldan's enhanced term of parole ineligibility. The Charmer had charmed his last victim.

The panel's decision is under appeal. It if holds up, Robert Reldan will be 89 years old before he gets another chance to gain his freedom. Arthur Reeve, now 84, and Barbara Reeve, now 83, will not be around, but they have made financial arrangements with the Rem Zeller Law Group to oppose any future Reldan parole application. For Susan.

Richard Muti has more than 70 publishing credits—mostly op-ed pieces on history, law, politics and government—in *The New York Times*, *The Record* of Bergen County, *New Jersey Lawyer*, and other publications, in addition to two prior books. He spent 19 years as a successful trial prosecutor and has taught writing, American government and politics, criminal justice, and history at three New Jersey universities. He is a former Navy pilot and former mayor of Ramsey, NJ, his hometown.

Before his retirement, Charles Buckley spent 25 years as a prosecutor. For most of that time, he acted as a modern-day legal Paladin—"have briefcase, will travel"—crisscrossing New Jersey as a deputy attorney general who tried the most difficult cases on behalf of the State. He also served as the acting prosecutor—the chief law enforcement officer—in five New Jersey counties.

Acknowledgments

Charles Buckley's goal of writing about the most interesting case he had ever prosecuted took form in his mind even before the jury in Robert Reldan's third murder trial rendered its guilty verdicts in March 1986. Buckley saved all of his trial documents for that specific purpose, but never got around to writing the book. In 1995, while serving as acting Bergen County (NJ) Prosecutor, that county's chief law enforcement officer, Buckley needed an office manager, someone he could trust to run the business side of the office—budgets, purchasing, personnel, labor negotiations, and such. His first assistant prosecutor, Frank Puccio, had just the person to recommend—a former assistant prosecutor who knew the office well, but who was also a Harvard Business School graduate with experience in business. And, so, Buckley and his co-author, Richard Muti, met and began their friendship, but it wasn't until years later, when both men had left the prosecutor's office (Buckley for retirement and Muti for a new career in politics, teaching, and writing), that Buckley approached Muti with the idea of co-authoring a book about the Robert Reldan case.

At the time, Muti was finishing his second book—*Good Lawyer, Dead Lawyer*, a crime novel—and expressed scant interest in taking on the Reldan project, but Buckley persisted and finally convinced his friend to delve into the saved files—thousands of pages of trial transcripts, police reports, witness statements, newspaper clippings, and such—to see if that aroused Muti's interest. It did, and the result was *The Charmer*, a joint effort that took three years to complete.

The co-authors wish to acknowledge the many people whose help and encouragement were key, including, at the top of that list, our agent, Jill Marsal of Marsal Lyon Literary Agency. Jill's advice was indispensable, and she succeeded in finding a publisher who was a perfect fit for our book.

Bergen County Prosecutor John Molinelli was gracious in opening his office's files to the authors. Prosecutor Molinelli had been a law clerk in the chambers of Superior Court Judge Frederick Kuechenmeister, who presided at Reldan's third murder trial, and maintained a keen interest in that case throughout his law enforcement career. The prosecutor also gave permission for photos and illustrations from the case to be used in this book.

Former Deputy Chief of Investigators Ed Denning had the longest and, perhaps, most important ongoing role in the prosecution of Robert Reldan, and the co-authors are deeply grateful for Mr. Denning's cooperation. The advice and guidance of former Chief of Investigators Alan Grieco, who served in the Bergen County Prosecutor's Office when Buckley and Muti did, was another strong boost to the completion of this book. The co-authors also acknowledge the help of other former colleagues in the Bergen County Prosecutor's Office, including First Assistant Prosecutor Dennis Calo and Richard Galler, the assistant prosecutor who handled Reldan's murder conspiracy trial, another aspect of this legal saga. Former Appellate Section Chief John Scaliti provided research materials that were invaluable to the authors.

Retired Superior Court Judge Paul Huot is the last survivor among the judges who presided at the various Reldan trials, and the authors greatly appreciate his cooperation, especially in providing firsthand recollections of the dramatic events during the second murder trial. The authors thank Mrs. Loretta Malvasi, who served as a juror in the third murder trial, for her impressions of Robert Reldan's performance as his own attorney.

Robert Zeller and Joseph Rem of the Rem Zeller Law Group in Hackensack, New Jersey, were instrumental in introducing the co-authors to Arthur Reeve, father of victim Susan Reeve. Bob Zeller successfully represented Arthur and Barbara Reeve in their wrongful death lawsuit against Robert Reldan, after Reldan became heir to a trust valued at $8.9 million. With their client's permission, Zeller and Rem opened their files to the co-authors, allowing them access to much valuable information about the final measure of justice administered to Robert Reldan.

The co-authors cannot say too much about the kind and, yes, brave, cooperation of Arthur and Barbara Reeve, Susan's parents, who made themselves available for multiple interviews. Soon after Susan's murder, the Reeves set up a scholarship fund in their daughter's memory at her *alma mater*, Hollins University in Roanoke, Virginia. The proceeds they receive from their lawsuit against Reldan have also been directed to that scholarship fund. Readers who wish to make a donation in Susan's memory may send a check, payable to the "Susan Reeve Class of 1975 Scholarship Fund," care of External Relations, Hollins University, P.O. Box 9629, Roanoke, VA 24020-1629 (1-800-TINKER1).

Jonathan Heynes, husband of Reldan's other murder victim, Susan Heynes, was kind enough to provide information to the authors that was painful for him to relive. He now resides in England with his family. In 2010, Prosecutor John Molinelli, in England on other business, met with Jonathan Heynes and gave him a key piece of evidence in the trial—a replica of Susan's engagement ring. It was a moment of closure that Heynes appreciated.

Finally, the co-authors wish to acknowledge *The Record* of Bergen County, which provided the most complete contemporary coverage of the Reldan trials, and its publisher Stephen Borg for their permission to use photographs from the newspaper's files for this book.